Acknowledgments

A world of thanks to the people who inundated me with detailed information, helped separate fact from fiction, and shared countless insider tips for other retirees who dream of finding their ideal retirement destination.

Many thanks to:

Ann and Bob Berra

Selwyn Berg

George and Kernochan Bowen

Ken Bower

Betsy and John Braden

Norm Burgo

Dan Clarke

Jim Dodson

Bernadette Engelhardt-Hoegerle

Gerald Flavin

Don Green

Margot and Matt Halliday

Ed Healey

Howard Itzkowitz

Ed Jacob

Wendy James

Robert and Dian Jones

Erhard and Gundrun Kelz

Ann King

Deborah Knorr

Antoinette Larmore

Claire Larson

Judy Lawrence

Andrea Lorenzetti

Mike MacDonald

Lynne Marriott

Claire and John McGovern

William Oliver

Jan and Earl Palmeter

Done Price

Howard Rosenzweig

Rick Rule

Bill and Cathy Service

Pamela Skibinski

Bob and Sue Stapleton

Robert Starkey

Bob Story

Dorothy van Schooneveld

Gilbert Wells

David Willour

The Grown-Up's Guide to Retiring Abroad

ROSANNE KNORR

Ten Speed Press

BERKELEY / TORONTO

A Kirsty Melville Book

Ten Speed Press
Box 7123
Berkeley, California 94707
www.tenspeed.com

Distributed in Australia by Simon & Schuster Australia, in Canada by Ten Speed Press
Canada, in New Zealand by Southern Publishers Group, in South Africa by Real
Books, in Southeast Asia by Berkeley Books, and in the United Kingdom and Europe
by Airlift Book Company.

Cover design by Kathy Warinner
Cover illustration by Kathy Warinner
Interior design based on a design by Laura Lind Design
Interior map illustrations by John Knorr

Library of Congress Cataloging-in-Publication Data
Knorr, Rosanne.
   The grown-up's guide to retiring abroad / by Rosanne Knorr.
      p. cm.
   Includes index.
   ISBN 1-58008-353-6
1. Retirement, Places of—Foreign countries. I. Title.
HQ1063 .K647 2001
646.7'9—dc21
                              2001005093

Printed in Canada
First printing, 2001

1 2 3 4 5 6 7 8 9 10 — 05 04 03 02 01

Contents

Island Hopping

Exotic and Entrepreneurial

Note to Readers

This book is about dreams. But it's practical too. It provides information to guide you in creating an enriching new lifestyle that includes long-term adventure overseas.

Part I presents general factors to consider when planning a long stay abroad and choosing a destination. Part II profiles some of the world's most popular and intriguing countries with an overview of their ambiance and daily living conditions, and provides essential background information for the person who wants to stay longer than the typical two-week vacation. Each country is rich and fascinating in its own right. Obviously, everything can't be covered in a single chapter; that would take several books and still not cover the myriad aspects of day-to-day life in that country. But by flipping through this book, you will discover numerous retirement possibilities and be able to choose one or several countries that appeal to you. After you've narrowed down your search for the land of your dreams, concentrate on a specific region and city for further detailed research. This book will tell you how to do that as well, with tips and sources.

PRICING

Prices in this book are for general reference only. They're provided so you can compare the various countries on general affordability and determine which countries are feasible for you based on your budget. Quite often they also serve as reassurance that living overseas does not require a financial portfolio in the millions, but is something the average retiree can enjoy.

While the prices are as accurate as possible, they are only a quick snapshot of average costs. Naturally, costs vary widely within a country. Also you may choose the most basic item or the most luxurious. In any case, market factors can increase prices dramatically in a short time (gasoline being a prime example) or they can bring prices down, as is currently happening in several countries for telephone and Internet services. When you're ready for your adventure, investigate the current cost of living at the locale you've selected, especially for big-ticket items like housing, and set your budget based on those results.

EXCHANGE RATES

Sample prices in this book are provided in dollars rather than the local currency. However, exchange rates rise and fall, affecting living costs overseas. The dollar has been especially strong recently, but these amazing highs may or may not continue. For this reason, prices are based on a middle-of-the-road rate of exchange, not the current highs.

Below are the rates of exchange used in this book to convert foreign currency to the dollar. If the rate for a country is vastly different at the time you are reading this, adjust accordingly.

COUNTRY	EXCHANGE RATE
Australia	1 U.S. $ = 1.52 Australian Dollar
The Bahamas	1 U.S. $ = 1 Bahamas Dollar
Belize	1 U.S. $ = 2 Belize Dollars
Cayman Islands	1 U.S. $ = .80 C.I. Dollar
Canada	1 U.S. $ = 1.46 Canadian Dollar
Costa Rica	1 U.S. $ = 295 Colones
Czech Republic	1 U.S. $ = 35 Crowns
Euro*	1 U.S. $ = 1.12 Euros
France	1 U.S. $ = 6.4 French Francs
Germany	1 U.S. $ = 2.285 Marks
Great Britain	1 U.S. $ = .61 Pound
Greece	1 U.S. $ = 320 Drachmas
Honduras	1 U.S. $ = 14.5 Lempira
Ireland	1 U.S. $ = .76 Punt
Italy	1 U.S. $ = 1,874 Lire
Mexico	1 U.S. $ = 9.52 Pesos
New Zealand	1 U.S. $ = .44 NZ Dollars
Portugal	1 U.S. $ = 194 Escudos
Spain	1 U.S. $ = 161 Pesetas
Thailand	1 U.S. $ = 37.7 Baht
U.S. Virgin Islands	1 U.S. $ = 1 Dollar

Euro currency will replace the French franc, German mark, Greek drachma, Italian lira, Portuguese escudo, Republic of Ireland's punt, and Spanish peseta, among others, on January 1, 2002.

SEEK PROFESSIONAL ADVICE

I hope this book will provide the inspiration and the initial information you need to follow your dream overseas, but despite having lived overseas and traveled widely I'm not a professional accountant, customs agent, or legal lion tamer. When you've narrowed down your search to the destination that interests you, research your specific situation. Consult current sources in detail, and contact the experts who can provide professional advice, including financial advisors, tax consultants, relocation experts, real estate agents, and of course, the embassy or consulate of the country involved.

PART I

YOUR PRIMER FOR DREAMS

1

The Challenge and Joy
of Retiring Overseas

W e need a new word for "retirement." That term was created in an era that assumed retirees would be aged, decrepit, and too tired to do much but sit on the porch swing when the decades of work were done.

That's not true anymore.

Contemporary retirees are healthier, more active, better educated, and often retire earlier than the traditional age of sixty-five. The old concept of retirement doesn't work with the many years of active life we still have before us. What will we do with our free time now that we have so much of it? Many of us count the years ahead of us and discover that we won't be content with repeating the daily round of eighteen holes until we reach that final hole in the ground.

We're revitalizing and reinventing ourselves with a second life overseas. You can too.

An empty nest and the freedom from a nine-to-five grind provide the ideal opportunity to live in another country, immerse yourself in a new culture, meet fascinating people, and travel from an overseas base.

Retiring overseas takes you into new territory filled with life-enhancing experiences. You learn firsthand about the world by living in it. You meet new friends and neighbors and learn about their lifestyles.

Most of all, living in a different culture encourages you to keep learning, to see things with fresh eyes, and to stay youthful in spirit.

DREAMS ARE MADE FOR DOING

People who retire overseas are like you and me. Many of us never imagined that we'd enjoy living abroad, but the idea evolved. My husband and I laugh when we think back to the retirement plans we made years ago during a job transfer to Atlanta. We specifically chose a home in a golf course community, with a practical ground-level master bedroom. How ideal, we thought, for those golden retirement years when we'd have time for rounds and rounds of golf but wouldn't want to climb stairs. This would be our last house.

Then we chose to retire early and realized that we had a lot of years left to explore, but already knew the back nine by heart. We decided to live overseas for five months to travel and investigate different cultures, which we had never had time to do when working.

Five months is now five years and counting. Our home in France serves as a base for immersion in French life and travel near and far. We can reach Spain, Italy, Switzerland, the Netherlands, Belgium, and Germany by car within six hours. A slightly longer drive takes us to Portugal, eastern and northern Europe, or across the channel to England or Ireland by ferry. Each foray whets our appetite for more. Each trip leads to another country we'd like to know better and to new friends in other regions who invite us to share their world. On and on we go, creating memories more thrilling than any we dreamed of when we bought that so-called retirement house.

> Our travels are characterized by the fact we only buy one-way tickets, as we never know where we are going next. . . . We never reminisce about the "good old days" because these are the good old days.
>
> Selwyn Berg, France

WE'RE FAR FROM ALONE

Our experience is mirrored by other American retirees in countries around the globe. More than 3.3 million Americans live abroad. The big mystery is how many more there are. No one counts Americans living abroad. The U.S. census doesn't cover Americans living overseas, and the U.S. State Department admits they have no idea how many Americans live in foreign countries—especially retirees.

We do know that almost four hundred thousand Social Security checks are sent overseas, but even that is just the tip of the croissant. This figure counts only those checks that are directly mailed outside the United States. The fact is that the vast majority of American retirees have their checks automatically deposited in their U.S. bank accounts. The same is true of pensions and interest from investments. In addition, most American retirees overseas have ties to the States in the form of family and friends. They may return to the States regularly for visits or split their time between the United States and overseas.

Simply put, American retirees overseas are hard to pin down. They're free spirits. Unfettered by a job, they're free to pick up and go as the whim strikes, and it's hard to count a moving target.

WHY DO RETIREES VENTURE OVERSEAS?

The reasons people give for spending time abroad are varied, but most of them can be boiled down to familiar refrains. First, many retirees move overseas to fulfill a lifetime desire to travel. After all those years of being hemmed in with a set number of vacation weeks, the retiree can make their vacation last year-round, and their destination becomes the world.

Many people choose to retire in countries where the cost of living is less than in the United States, thus improving their standard of living. Some people are financially well-off, but appreciate living in a less materialistic society, where art and culture are valued more than the nameplate on a car.

Tranquility and a slower pace of life draw many people overseas. Lower crime levels are part of that tranquility. The most popular countries outside the United States—and we're not counting Baltic war zones—are gun shy. With fewer loose cannons floating about, some retirees feel more content. Others choose countries

> We rented out our house [in the States], and our friends thought that was nuts since it had taken us eight years to build, but at some point you have to enjoy life.
>
> Earl Palmeter,
> St. Raphael, France

based on their heritage or, if they worked abroad, they retire to an area they enjoyed at that time.

Most of all, people who retire overseas are not just leaving their life in the States, they're driven by a desire to explore the world and do more with their life while they have the opportunity. They want to investigate a culture thoroughly, rather than just as part of a tourist pack.

HOW LONG WILL YOU STAY?

More retirees than I can count began their adventure overseas by planning a relatively short stay of under six months. Like us, many of them are surprised that they enjoy the lifestyle so much, and their return date to the States somehow keeps getting extended. They go back to visit family and friends, but also discover that more often family and friends come to them.

Some retirees consider their overseas stay a sabbatical or long sojourn based on a specific time frame of several months or a year. Others live at their second home abroad in the same way that some people in the States live at a summer cottage or winter ski condo, staying for a specific season or several months on a regular basis.

Some people retire overseas fully intending to live in their chosen destination for the rest of their lives. Many of these people either worked or lived abroad when younger and knew they always wanted to return there. They relish the adventure or the lifestyle and the concept of being "old" eludes them. "Perhaps I'll go back [to the States] when I'm old," said seventy-six-year-old Mary. To most people, that's always much later.

THE POSSIBLE DREAM

Dreaming of a destination for retirement overseas creates the joy of anticipation. The world opens up to you. Explore the possibilities and, hopefully, you'll fulfill a dream by selecting one—or more—places that you would enjoy exploring in person.

In this book you'll discover twenty countries worthy of consideration. Each offers a different reason for retiring there, whether it's low costs or lush landscapes, charming villages or hospitable people. They won't all be your cup of tea. If you don't like overcast skies, don't move to Great Britain. If you can't stand the heat, don't plan on Greece in August.

The decision is entirely subjective, which is good or we might all end up on the same end of the planet. The possibilities, however, are as varied as the world. Chances are, you'll find more than one intriguing haven that fits your idea of paradise, whether it comes complete with palm trees, ski slopes, or big-city lights. You may even want to try more than one location in a country, or several different countries. It's not unknown for retirees to try out different locales, renting for a month, six months, a year, or as long as the spirit moves them.

This book is your primer for dreaming. Use it to imagine the lifestyle you might enjoy in a far-off destination. Each chapter in Part II provides an overview of the ambiance and the vital facts of daily life that retirees are most interested in, including that country's culture, climate, access to health care, costs, and housing. Once you've narrowed your choices, it's time to broaden your knowledge. Start reading more extensively on your destination. (Some reading recommendations are listed at the back of each chapter and in the Sources-at-a-Glance section in Chapter 25.) Talk to friends and acquaintances who have lived or traveled extensively in your chosen country. If possible, visit the location and talk to people who live there before you pack everything for the long term.

Mostly, don't worry. Just remember to plan well, keep your options open, and take the plunge. If worse comes to worst, you can always turn around and come back. However, you probably won't want to. You may, like many of us, discover that a worldwide retirement is a rejuvenating experience that puts more vigor into your after-work life.

It definitely beats sitting home with a gold watch.

2

Where in the World Will You Go?

A funny thing happened as I was researching destinations for living overseas: I wanted to live in *all* of them. The more I learned about a country, the more fascinating it seemed. Each time I concentrated on one country, *that's* where I wanted to live. Each new culture was exciting in its own way. Each destination offered some intriguing reason to participate in it more fully. Of course, reality set in and my husband and I chose one country, France, as our base, and we make side trips to all the enticing destinations we can manage. What's down the road is anyone's guess.

Where in the world will *your* dream take you?

You may already have a dream location in mind. It could be a place you've felt drawn to for years based on its hospitable people, charming stone villages, or sun-dappled beaches. Perhaps it's a place you visited on a vacation, where the thought crossed your mind, "Wow, wouldn't it be great to live here!" If you've already chosen your destination, you have a head start. Go ahead and review that locale as a possible retirement spot. Chances are you'll find that it's easier than you thought to make the dream of living there come true.

Bear in mind, however, that attributes that charm you during a one-week vacation may not meet your needs for a long-term stay or retirement. The beach area with nothing more than palm trees and tourist cottages may seem a welcome respite from the work-a-day grind for a short visit, but would you be happy living there if it required an hour's drive to a movie theater or a good doctor? When selecting a specific location for retirement, consider the various factors that make that spot practical for daily living. If you still love it, go for it.

DESTINATION CHECK-LIST

Each person has different goals in selecting a dream destination overseas. What's essential for you may be irrelevant to someone else. Reflect on the aspects of life abroad that are most important to you, and then review potential destinations while keeping these factors in mind. The most essential factors in making your decision include:

ambiance	cost of living
climate	financial regulations
culture	health care
language	transportation
leisure activities	study/work availability

AMBIANCE

The ideal amenities for a footloose and fancy-free vacation spot can make the same place a nightmare for the retiree. Resort areas are built for the temporary visitor, replete with beaches or ski slopes, hotels, and restaurants. But does the area also have a good infrastructure for residents? If you don't want your shopping limited to plastic palm trees, then be sure that there are good shopping facilities for food and the various necessities that a household requires at a reasonable distance.

> We're not just traveling. We make each new place our home.
>
> Jan Palmeter,
> San Raphael, France

More important, will you have access to a social life? Resort communities are by nature transitory. Do you want your only friends to be people who come and go with the tides? Or will you choose an area where there is a base of long-term residents that provides a social life that extends throughout the year and not just during the high season.

Will the crowds create unbearable traffic and noise during the tourist season, then leave you looking at deserted streets and shuttered stores and restaurants the rest of the year?

CLIMATE

Consider how much of the year and what seasons of the year you intend to live at your chosen site. The tropical pleasures that were ideal for a beach vacation in winter may be uncomfortably hot in summer. Or the pleasant summer days may turn frosty or depressingly cloudy all winter. Before you move, check out the climate in all four seasons.

Don't just look up average temperature charts or ask other people about the weather; one person's idea of comfortable is not the same as another's. For example, even if you think that summer in the south of France would be ideal, try it before making a full-time commitment. You may discover that access to a pool or the sea would make the hot summer months more bearable.

CULTURE

Are you comfortable with the basic values of your new society? Will you be able to adapt to the different cultural habits of the people or the practical details of living there? Can you accommodate shops that shut for three hours at lunch? Will you enjoy the natural exuberance of a culture where the inhabitants don't dine until 10:00 P.M. and party hearty until 4:00 A.M. on Saturday nights? The culture in a foreign country is different, and enjoying and adapting to it are important parts of the experience you're seeking. Give yourself the opportunity to become accustomed to your new environs, but if you discover that there is something about a country's lifestyle that you absolutely, positively cannot abide, you would be better off looking elsewhere.

LANGUAGE

Learning a new language is part of the overseas adventure for some retirees. (It's even said to be excellent exercise for our brain cells as we age.) If you're not willing to make the effort, however, select a country where English is the main language or at least the second one. This is becoming easier as English expands in use throughout the world thanks to international commerce and the growth of the Internet. That said, learning the local language would be helpful and would make daily life and social interaction more pleasurable.

LEISURE ACTIVITIES

Does the country, region, and specific area you've chosen provide you with access to the sports and entertainment you enjoy? If you're an avid tennis player or golfer, will you have access to good courts or courses and partners to share them with? Is there a community center nearby to meet new people or to enjoy hobbies, be they bridge or painting or genealogy? What cultural activities are available in the way of theaters and concerts?

COST OF LIVING

Two major factors affect your basic cost of living overseas: the actual cost of living in the region you choose and the exchange rate.

Some countries offer the American retiree a better value for the dollar or are downright cheap. If you opt for an area that's very inexpensive based on the dollar, consider whether the discrepancy in income will affect your social life and conscience. You may choose a location for its low cost, but if you're living like royalty while everyone else in the village lives like your servant, you won't have a lot of social life and you may feel uncomfortable.

On the other side of the coin, if you want to stretch your dollar don't choose a prime spot in Switzerland or Monaco. Beautiful as these countries might be, their high costs make them off limits for all but the extremely well-heeled, which is the reason neither country is profiled here.

In between these two extremes are countless countries where you can have your fun and cut costs simply by downsizing with a smaller home, using public transportation, and buying fresh local produce. Keep in mind that living in expatriate areas tends to raise costs since you'll be living with American business and government personnel who are still working and spending on the dollar, rather than on the local currency. Likewise, living in the countryside or in small towns is generally less expensive than life in the big cities or major tourist resorts. Remember, too, that you'll pay top dollar for furnished accommodations designed for the short-term visitor. Compare the cost differential. If you'll be staying at your new home six months or more at a time, consider finding an unfurnished place and managing with used furniture and basic supplies.

In recent years, the exchange rate of the dollar versus many foreign currencies has been strong, enabling retirees to live at a higher standard overseas than at home. The thing to remember, however, is that exchange rates are in constant flux. Usually they change in minuscule amounts day by day, but they can trend upward or downward. This affects how you will live in your new location. It's always safer to be relatively conservative in your plans when living overseas in case the foreign currency strengthens. Maintain a lifestyle that's easily affordable. That way you won't find yourself in a tight spot if the exchange rate changes for the worse or inflation increases your costs.

FINANCIAL REGULATIONS

Income taxes and inheritance taxes can have a significant impact on your financial well-being, especially if you have substantial assets. Some of these regulations are quite surprising. For example, inheritance regulations in countries such as France, which are based on the Napoleonic legal code, require leaving a set percentage of assets to children, rather than the spouse. A will cannot supercede the code.

Do not assume that your U.S. will takes precedence if you live overseas. If you become a legal resident of another country, that country's regulations will take precedence. While having your adventure, you may want to assure that your residence remains legally the United States or otherwise take steps to assure that your assets remain protected or are distributed as you wish. Consult experts, such as tax attorneys, and make sure that the people you choose are knowledgeable in dealing with these complicated international issues.

PURCHASING POWER

Just for fun, here are a few statistics comparing purchasing power in several major cities around the world, excluding housing and taxes. Using New York City as the baseline of 100, or $100,000, here's how the cities compare.

CITY	VALUE
New York City, USA	$100,000
Tokyo, Japan	$91,975
Paris, France	$88,504
London, England	$86,768
Dublin, Ireland	$74,621
Canberra, Australia	$59,003
Chiang Mai, Thailand	$46,277
San Jose, Costa Rica	$38,178

HEALTH CARE

"What if I get sick?" people ask when they consider living overseas. This remains a primary concern, as well it should. However, good doctors and hospitals do exist outside U.S. borders. Fact is, sometimes the access to care is better in other countries. The World Health Organization's recent list of best countries for overall health services rated France as number one and Italy as number two in the world. Even Greece, still struggling compared to many other countries economically, was rated number fourteen. The United States was rated thirty-second.

However, the specific location you pick in a country will determine your access to excellent care. If you choose a deserted island in the Pacific, all bets are off. If you pick a town near a teaching hospital in France, you're in great shape.

Note that Medicare does not cover people outside the United States. You may need to purchase expatriate health coverage. In some cases, you can buy into a state-sponsored program. In Mexico, for example, $300 a year will get you medical coverage, which can be used throughout the country, including at American-financed hospitals in some of the more popular expatriate communities.

TRANSPORTATION

Living in a central hub, whether it be Rome or Paris or London, ensures easy access by train and plane to the world. You may want a more tranquil (or affordable!) lifestyle, but check to be sure that the small country village you select is not so far off the beaten track that you can't hit the road occasionally. That road works both ways. Convenient access also encourages visits by family and friends.

If you don't want to drive everywhere, check into public transportation in the city or town you're investigating. Walking counts as transportation. If you want to be out and about daily, find out whether the location you choose provides pleasant walking conditions.

STUDY, VOLUNTEER, AND WORK AVAILABILITY

You're retired, what do you want to work for? Surprisingly enough many early retirees discover that they actually want something organized to keep them busy. The availability of a community with adult education classes or access to volunteer or paid work gives their life structure. If you think this description fits you, then keep an eye out for your site's educational and work potential.

You may even want to finance your overseas adventure through a work program. This could be a volunteer program such as the Peace Corps or a paid job. Jobs teaching English, consulting, or providing marketing services are often the easiest positions to find overseas, but other opportunities may present themselves depending on your skills and persistence.

When we came to Portugal, it was difficult to find volunteer work because it is not part of the Portuguese culture. We now work one day a week pouring medicines at the local Salvation Army nursing home. The leadership is mostly northern European, and they understand and use volunteers.

Gilbert Wells, Portugal

WHERE HAVE ALL THE AMERICANS GONE?

You'll find Americans around the globe. Below are some of the numbers of Americans who reported to consulates overseas. Note that these figures (obtained from the U.S. State Department) are far lower than actual numbers of Americans living abroad. People who didn't report to a consulate, who don't have their Social Security check sent overseas (because they were deposited automatically in a stateside bank), or who traveled from one place to another were not counted.

COUNTRY	AMERICANS
Argentina	900
Australia	63,800
Bahamas	7,600
Belgium	31,614
Bermuda	4,250
Canada	626,585
Costa Rica	19,000
France	86,037
Greece	82,500
Ireland	36,000
Italy	146,100
Japan	66,316
Mexico	619,147
Portugal	9,045
Spain	62,698
Switzerland	32,600
United Kingdom (England, Ireland, Scotland)	216,000
Venezuela	23,425

3

Staying Part-Time, Full-Time, or Forever

"How can you live overseas? Don't you miss your family?" That's the phrase most retirees abroad hear from acquaintances at home. The answers vary; the people who retire overseas are as different in their family situations and flexibility as are their calendars.

Many people begin with plans for a relatively short stay abroad and are surprised at how much they enjoy the lifestyle and the adventure; the time goes so quickly that they haven't seen or done all they'd planned. They keep extending their stay, not yet ready to come back to the States. Others came over fully intending to live in their chosen destination for the rest of their lives. In between are people who live abroad for a specific season or several months on a regular basis.

What you will do depends on your goals, personality, family, desire to travel, and budget. How do you decide whether you seriously want to live overseas and what arrangement would suit you best? Let's look at some options you may not have considered that make such an adventure more feasible.

START SMALL

Even people who move lock, stock, and barrel overseas started with regular visits before planning a full-time move. You know you're interested in living somewhere if your vacation plans target it for years on end.

You don't have to literally move to enjoy a long sojourn abroad. That's what John and Claire did when they rented another American's summer home overseas for five months. They have seven, yes seven, children and twenty-one grandchildren and didn't want to stay away from the States forever, but as Claire says, "This trip was different. It was the first time we only had ourselves to consider and no baby-sitting!"

THE PART-TIME OPTION

If you intend to live overseas for a few months, choose rented accommodations that leave you free to come and go without the commitment of purchasing a home. You can try new locations when the spirit moves you, and commit to a favorite spot later if you decide it's for you.

> We do have a few other Americans who have moved into the area. They come and then one day, they sell up and move out again. It's not for everyone.
>
> Mike MacDonald, France

Check with real estate agents who also handle rentals. Look in local papers. Often, you'll find another American who already has a place that they don't use regularly and will rent. It's easier to arrange with a compatriot because you're both speaking the same language—literally and culturally—and using the same dollars. Check the grapevine, universities, and the Internet.

HOME EXCHANGES

A home exchange, in which you trade houses with another person for a specific period of time, can be a wonderful, cost-cutting solution to trying out different locations. You get to travel overseas and live like a native in a home setting, and the other person stays in your home in the States. Both of you live rent-free. Sometimes cars and bicycles come with the deal. Finding a home exchange can be as simple as a referral from a friend. However, you may need to widen the field with more formal arrangements.

Intervac International is a major player in the home exchange business. They publish five directories a year with about 12,500 listings. You can list your home and receive their directory for $93 a year. A Web-only membership costs $50. For information call (800) 756-4663.

Vacation Homes Unlimited has helpful information on their site with suggested terms for an exchange agreement. They have Internet and directory memberships for $65 and $30 respectively. For information call (800) 848-7927 or check www.vacation-homes.com.

HomeLink International has twenty-six offices around the world and publishes five directories each year. You can view listings before you join, but to get the names and addresses of the exchangees you have to be a member. Membership costs $98, or Web-only membership costs $50. For information call (800) 638-3841 or see www.us.homelink.org.

An Internet-only source is Home Exchange.com, which charges $30 to list a property, but nonmembers can view listings and contact the owners free through email. For information call (805) 898-9660 or see them online at www.homeexchange.com.

If you've set your sights on Europe, a British agency called Home Base Holidays provides three directories and online memberships for $105 a year. Web-only memberships are $57. For information you'd need to call Great Britain at (44) (20) 8886-8752, but check it out on the Internet first at www.homebase-hols.com.

Seniors Home Exchange is specifically geared to retirees with an online database that you can browse for free. You'll have to pay the fee for contact information. It costs $50 for a three-year membership. Check before paying your fee, though, because many of this service's properties are in Florida, not overseas.

THE FULL-TIME DECISION

Even if you've decided to live overseas, take your time before setting down roots and making a major property purchase. You may change your mind based on the weather or the location's ambiance. Or you may decide that renting's preferable. In many countries, even the locals rent since home ownership in some areas of the world is not a high priority.

It's best to live in an area for at least a year, to experience all its seasons and to note the distinctions in housing and prices, before jumping in with a purchase. Buying a home overseas can be as simple as in the States or fraught with unknown complications. Study the local laws, including inheritance regulations, before you buy.

ROAMING RETIREES

Don't want to limit yourself to just one retirement destination? Choose several in sequence. One couple I know came up with a novel idea. They bought a VW bus and stocked it with collapsible furniture right down to a folding bookcase for travel books and plastic storage boxes that transform into nightstands with colorful scarves covering them. With their belongings, they're able to rent less expensive, unfurnished accommodations while enjoying the feeling of being "at home."

They rented in San Miguel de Allende for three months. Then they were off to Europe, van and all. We met them in central France. Next came the apartment in the south of France, a block and a half from the Mediterranean. They sublet that to spend several months in Copenhagen. Still on the agenda? "Greece, Italy, who knows? This is too much fun," says Jan. "Every time we move, it's a new chapter."

That's the whole point, isn't it?

4

How to Get the Inside Scoop

Let's say you've chosen a dream location but need more facts before you make the move. Is it better to buy furniture or rent furnished accommodations? If you enjoy sports, are facilities, such as tennis courts, available? Is there a good doctor, dentist, and hospital nearby? Researching a destination for daily life is far different from researching a travel destination. Tourist guidebooks don't help. They're designed to highlight hotels and museums, not daily marketing and taking the dog to the kennel.

You can uncover the facts you need. It just takes some digging. Begin by getting an overall view of the landscape to discover the best potential residential areas for you, then narrow your choices down gradually until the nitty-gritty details fall into place.

GUIDEBOOKS, TRAVEL MAGAZINES, AND TOUR VIDEOS

Guidebooks, travel magazines, and tour videos fall under the category of general information. The good news is these resources are easy to find at any library, bookstore, or shopping mall. They are good sources of general facts about a destination's cultural highlights. These materials are created for tourists, providing sightseeing tips and listing hotels and restaurants—all of which are designed to whet your appetite, but don't provide a clue as to what it's like to actually live somewhere. Read enough of them, however, and you will pick up some basic knowledge. Learn to read between the lines. If the guidebook for the city you're interested in living in mentions that a hotel is a good value but in a "seedy neighborhood" near the central train station, then you've already learned something about various sections of that city.

SPECIALTY BOOKS AND MAGAZINES

Specialty books and magazines (such as this one) that are specifically targeted to people moving overseas provide information from the point of view you need. These publications will concentrate on factors affecting the lifestyle rather than on tourism. Some of these additional reading materials are listed in this book at the end of each chapter in Part II. For more titles, have your local librarian or bookstore do a search for you emphasizing moving or living in your chosen destination. Search book sites online also.

LOCAL NEWSPAPERS

Local newspapers with classified sections are a gold mine of detailed information. Page through them for real estate, rental, and retail ads. Look for prices and product availability. Read between the lines to determine the availability of rentals and the price discrepancy between furnished and unfurnished rentals. Note whether furnished properties are available at reasonable prices. Or is the destination a resort location with accommodations designed for the pocketbooks of the two-week vacation splurge rather than the long-term inhabitant?

How do you get a local paper? It's easy if you happen to have a friend living there already or one who's planning to tour there. Pick up some papers yourself if you make an exploratory trip. Don't forget to stop by real estate offices when you're there. Many of them have free listings of current offerings. Or use your home computer. Many newspapers, even overseas, now provide their issues, including classified ads, online.

EMBASSIES AND CONSULATES

Embassies and consulates provide published information and will answer questions on specific situations. They are the place to find the most accurate and up-to-date regulations on current visa or pet importation requirements.

TOURIST OFFICES

Tourist offices are targeted toward short-term visitors, but they can often provide helpful information for finding furnished long-term accommodations or recommend other local sources. Remember that the people staffing the counter live in the area themselves so they can answer questions personally. Just avoid a time when a tour bus has inundated them, make friends, and ask away.

NETWORKING

Networking includes talking to people who have visited the destinations you are interested in and especially those who have lived or currently reside there. If your current neighborhood has restaurants or specialty stores featuring your destination—for example, an Irish country store, a French bistro, or a Portuguese pottery outlet—visit them. The owners or managers can probably answer questions about that country and may even have contacts living in that country. Most people are more than willing to put you in touch with someone who can provide you with valuable and interesting insights. Once you find one source, ask that person if they know anyone else who would be willing to talk to you . . . and so the network spreads.

MOVING COMPANIES

Moving companies that provide international services have packets of information on the details of moving overseas, and often they have specific information on various destinations. Some companies offer cultural training to ease your transition. This service is mainly for corporate clients, but even if you're moving overseas independently ask if you can join a class in progress.

THE INTERNET

The Internet is a real boon for getting the nitty-gritty details. You can use it to investigate many of the above sources in one fell swoop. Travel guides are online, with links that lead you to other sites. You can check weather and city data and connect to tourist agencies, embassies, and consulates. For practical help, you can find real estate agencies for rentals or purchases. Housing exchanges may help you find a person to trade homes with for several months.

Various search engines will help you find the information you're seeking. I head for www.google.com, www.askjeeves.com, and www.yahoo.com, but you may have your own favorites.

For networking, check message boards for people who are living at your chosen destination. Numerous sites target expatriate Americans directly. To name just a few, check out American Citizens Abroad, Escape Artist, Expat Exchange, and Expat World. (See their Web addresses and other sources under Sources-at-a-Glance in Chapter 25.) These contacts offer additional guidance and insider tips that will help you feel comfortable about your move.

PART II

DREAM DESTINATIONS

Some people collect stamps or seashells, teacups or miniature trains. Others collect countries, gathering the flavor of each new place and discovering its character and personality. I'll admit to being among the latter group, so writing this book was a bit like putting my collection out there for others to share. My goal is to help those dreamers among you who go on to experience more of the world.

My biggest regret is that there are so many wonderful places to go, so much to see and do, and so little time to explore it all. Because nothing beats firsthand experience, not even the glossiest color photographs. I've shot thousands of them in our travels and no matter how beautifully an image comes out, it's still two-dimensional. That photograph of Mont Blanc can't possibly re-create the sheer awe of ascending the mountain in that swaying cable car, pure snow fields glistening in every direction, and the murmurs of amazement among fellow passengers as we catch our first glimpse of a glacial river cascading in all its frozen glory.

Each experience is a personal one. Only you can appreciate what's important to you. But to provide a jumping-off point for your dreams, the next chapters are devoted to an overview of favorite countries for long-term and in-depth exploration. Of course, the options are truly as wide as the world, but the countries included here capture the hearts of many Americans. They are especially beautiful, affordable, or practical for daily living, with a few exotic destinations thrown in for anyone who prefers to travel off the beaten path.

You won't find tourist sites listed, except as they relate to your daily enjoyment of a location. Instead, the facts provided about each country pertain to basic living conditions and your ability to adapt there and enjoy a long-term stay or retirement.

To help your review, I've arranged the countries in five categories based on the primary advantage they offer the potential retiree. The categories are English Spoken Here, Stretching Your Budget, Cultural High Points, Island Hopping, and, for the experienced traveler looking for adventure or a postretirement career, Exotic and Entrepreneurial.

Please don't assume that just because a country is in one category, it doesn't also offer many benefits of another classification. Mexico, for example, draws American retirees by the droves due primarily to its low cost so it's an obvious choice for Stretching Your Budget. But Mexico also has a fascinating Spanish and Mayan culture to explore and enjoy. Another example is the U.S. Virgin Islands, which attracts retirees with the islands' warmth, azure sea, and sand. Since the islands are a U.S. territory, English is a rather obvious benefit, but the island lifestyle speaks louder as its primary draw so it's listed under Island Hopping rather than English Spoken Here.

I hope you enjoy discovering life abroad. If you're dreaming about moving, but nervous at the prospect, that's natural. Learn all you can about your destination, then gather up the gumption and do it. Try living overseas, if only for a few months. There's more to understanding the world in which we live than simply visiting the Eiffel Tower or the Colosseum. Exploring a new culture on a daily basis provides deeper insights and unique joy.

ENGLISH SPOKEN HERE

Learning a second language is a welcome challenge for some people. Others are tongue-tied, feel intimidated, or just plain don't want to bother. If you're the second type, you don't have to remain homebound. You can still have a long-term stay overseas. Many countries use English as their primary language. English is commonly used as a second language also. Even in areas where English is rare, I've known many brave souls who muddle through just fine by relishing the adventure, practicing patience, having a good sense of humor, and learning on the fly.

If you're not quite that ambitious, you can retire in a country where the natives speak a language you already know, or a close approximation. The accent might be different, but you'll catch the drift of things.

5

Australia

Australia's personality is as bouncy and boundless as its indigenous kangaroo. The country is one of the largest in the world, but it hasn't lost its youthful vim and vigor. Perhaps it has something to do with all those wide-open spaces to play in. Australians love the outdoor life, though it goes without saying that they don't all wrestle crocodiles for entertainment. The cities are some of the most cosmopolitan and cultural in the world, and the standard of living is high, offering a comfortable, thoroughly modern way of life.

Highlights

- High quality of life
- Pristine environment
- Relaxed outdoor lifestyle
- Hospitable people
- Wide-open spaces

THE BASICS

The Commonwealth of Australia, as it's officially named, was originally a British colony and still maintains certain ceremonial links to Great Britain. The country is independently governed from the capital of Canberra. The government is stable and democratic, and every adult Australian citizen can vote.

Australia's primary settlers were British and Irish. Later, when the country faced low population growth, the Australian government encouraged immigration from other areas, particularly from Asia. Australia now prides itself on having a multicultural society. However, Caucasians still make up about 95 percent of Australia's population, with Asians 4 percent, and Aborigines 1 percent. The Aborigines are the native Australians. Relations with the early white settlers were harsh to say the least, with attacks and prejudice running high. The situation is greatly improved in modern-day Australia, though many Aborigines still live in substandard conditions.

Some consider Australia the "America" of the twenty-first century since this huge land mass is still being explored and settled. The country is sparsely populated compared to its size, which makes it seem even more spacious—all of which is reflected in the way of life, the sense of freedom, and even the spaciousness of homes. Despite the enormous amount of land available, most people tend to group themselves with others and live along the more populated east and southeast coasts. It's not just for sociability. Much of the interior and western areas are relatively inhospitable, being largely desert—a frontierlike region the Australians call the "Outback."

Climate

The biggest switch for North Americans moving to Australia is the reversal of seasons. Winter occurs in June, July, and August. And Santa Claus has a bit of an adjustment when swinging down from the North Pole in his woolies in the heat of Australian summer.

Australia is a huge country, and the temperatures vary greatly. The most populous areas in the southern part of the country have a temperate climate with cool winters and hot summers; spring and fall are pleasant. Sydney, for example, has an average high of 78°F in January and 60°F in July.

Tropical temperatures are usual in the far north. Australia is the world's driest continent. The interior is arid or semiarid, though rainfall can be heavy in some parts north of the Tropic of Capricorn.

MATILDA WALTZES ON

Australia's national anthem is "Advance Australia Fair" but "Waltzing Matilda" could be considered its unoffical competition. Though this popular bush ballad relates more to the Outback than to the country's capital, it's far more recognized outside Australia than the official anthem.

YOUR NEW LIFESTYLE

The Australian lifestyle is relaxed and comfortable. How will you fill your days? Here's an overview of activities and interests that are part of daily life in Australia.

Food and Drink

Barbecues are popular events, especially with meat and potato lovers. But Australian palates are more varied than that would indicate. Due to its location in the Pacific, seafood and Asian cuisines are hugely popular. And in large cities, you'll find a full range of choices from French and Italian to Malaysian cooking.

Aussies have long enjoyed their beer, though excellent vineyards produce wines that are increasingly popular, including cabernet sauvignons, chardonnays, pinot noirs, and others.

Arts and Entertainment

The city centers, particularly Melbourne and Sydney, are sophisticated and charming with lovely Victorian architecture and extensive parks. Melbourne has a Chinatown and one of the largest markets in the world. Art galleries, museums, and professional performing arts thrive in both cities. After all, Sydney didn't build that world-class opera house to host sing-alongs.

Outdoor Life and Sports

Naturally, sports are popular in this country that loves the outdoors. The Summer Olympics in 2000 were a source of special pride, proving that those Aussies could really throw a party. For more daily sports, Australians love football, which combines rugby and basketball; cricket; horseracing; biking; and jogging. Tennis is big here. The Australian Open, one of the four major Grand Slam tournaments, is played in Melbourne. Most towns have public facilities for tennis, swimming, and other sports. The coastline is good for sunbathing and swimming except in certain areas known for dangerous surf and sharks.

Natural wonders can keep outdoor lovers happy for years with sites such as the impressive red Ayers Rock that rises more than 1,100 feet and the Great Barrier Reef. Thousands of national parks are home to exotic animals, birds, and plants.

> You can get just about anything you want here, though you have to search for it. You do not have the choices that you have in the States—fifteen varieties of vinegar and such. I can get Mexican products but I have to go across the city to get it.
>
> Jerry Flavin, New South Wales

Shopping

You'll find a wide range of products in the well-stocked stores. For the most part, products are comparable to those you'd find in the United States.

Social Life

Easing your transition to Australia is the fact that Australians tend to be casual, friendly, and welcoming to newcomers. They enjoy spending their free time at get-togethers such as outdoor barbecues, or "barbies" as they say, and playing sports.

Speaking English (even if not exactly Australian English) helps you befriend Aussies. Social clubs of all types, including those specifically for expatriates, exist in all major cities.

RIGHT YOU ARE, MATE.

Yes, they speak English in Australia so you won't have any trouble understanding the locals...or will you? British terms are the order of the day (boot for the car trunk, for example). But you'll soon pick up the lingo.

WHERE TO LIVE IN AUSTRALIA

Most of Australia's population lives in cities; almost 40 percent live in Melbourne and Sydney alone. The main living areas are along the east and southeast coasts. A few major spots are noted below.

Adelaide

The capital of South Australia, Adelaide is called the "Boston of Australia" due to its charming parks and pedestrian malls, superb restaurants, and attractive residential neighborhoods. Adelaide is an important arts center, holding the Adelaide Arts Festival, the best arts festival in the country.

Several nearby areas that are popular with expatriates include Burnside, Dulwich, and Hawthorn. The latter overlooks the ocean but is just half an hour drive from the city center. Belair also has beautiful ocean views and is about the same distance from the city.

Brisbane

Brisbane combines a subtropical climate and lush landscapes of flowers and gardens with contemporary skyscrapers and freeways. This modern city, the capital of Queensland, is located on the Brisbane River. Beaches here are superb—and just beyond them is the Great Barrier

Reef, making Brisbane a major tourist attraction. This is good or bad depending on your enjoyment of visitors and activity.

A variety of residential areas provide options for living within Brisbane or in the suburbs just outside. Ascot, Clayfield, and Hamilton are ten minutes away from the city center. Good train and bus services link them to the city. Housing tends to be individual homes with gardens, and most include swimming pools. Very few rental houses are available, though there are some apartments and townhouses. The area includes shopping and medical facilities.

Melbourne

Melbourne, in the southeastern corner of the country, is the capital city of the state of Victoria and the second largest city in Australia. Modern and elegant, Melbourne's a major port city and center for business. But it's not all business. Melbourne has been voted the "World's Most Livable City." It has lovely parks and tree-lined streets, charming Victorian houses, excellent shopping, and wonderful entertainment. Of course, with its amazing growth, traffic has become part of the scene.

Most areas of the city and its suburbs have shopping and medical facilities nearby. Albert Park, Carlton, East Melbourne, and St. Kilda are within a three-mile radius of the city center. Rentals are available in apartment buildings and individual one- and two-story houses, including period homes over a hundred years old that have been well renovated. The beach is nearby and within walking distance of some neighborhoods. St. Kilda is set along the water with a popular beach.

Sydney

The largest city in Australia, Sydney is a major financial and trading center. Sydney also prides itself on its wonderful lifestyle. Its downtown features one of the world's most beautiful harbors with the dramatic Sydney Harbour Bridge and the renowned opera house. Homes are tucked in the hills overlooking the bays, and the climate is pleasant year-round, encouraging a casual outdoor lifestyle.

Sydney's Summer Olympic Games in 2000 generated a facelift throughout the city. The airport is renovated and easy to reach by train or highway. Restaurants, entertainment spots, galleries, and shopping centers have mushroomed. The Royal Botanic Gardens feature a walking trail along the harbor side. Add the beaches and the vast national park area, and there's no lack of places to picnic or swim.

Sydney is the most expensive city in Australia, but a variety of apartments and houses are available in different price ranges. For less expensive housing, skip the central city and check out the suburbs. The Upper North Shore, which includes Killara, Lindfield, and St. Ives, offers individual housing with gardens and some low-rise apartments. Medical facilities and shopping are in the area, which is located about forty-five minutes by car or twenty to thirty-five minutes by train from downtown Sydney.

SETTING UP HOUSE

Australia's vast expanses encourage most Australians to own individual homes. Even apartments tend to be low-rise rather than space-saving high-rises.

Finding a Rental

Furnished and unfurnished accommodations are available, but you'll have an easier time finding an unfurnished one. You can expect basic kitchen appliances, but in some cases you'll need to purchase them. You may be pleasantly surprised, however, with a property that's "fully furnished," including even linens and dishes. If you need a place to stay while searching for long-term accommodations, look for temporary furnished apartments known as "serviced apartments" found in all major cities.

To give you a rough idea of rents, on the outskirts of Sydney in New South Wales an unfurnished two-bedroom apartment with laundry area and balcony rents for about $500 a month. A three-bedroom house with modern kitchen and spa bath was listed for about $700 a month while a four-level Victorian home with three bedrooms on a tree-lined street was for rent at $975 a month.

To rent an apartment or home, contact local real estate agents or read the classified ads in the local papers. Check especially the Wednesday and Saturday papers. If you use a real estate agent, be aware that it's rare to find a multiple-listing service. Different agents handle different properties so you'll need to contact several agents to review a large selection of units.

Rents are paid in advance, by the month, even though they are often quoted by the week—so make sure when you're talking prices that you know which ones you're dealing in! Plan to pay a security deposit, equal to about four weeks' rent for unfurnished and six weeks' for furnished properties. Leases are usually for twelve months though that's not a hard and fast rule; they can be for any length of time.

In renting a property you must receive a copy of the tenancy agreement, which includes a report of the property's condition. You also must receive a list of all expenses for which you will be responsible.

Buying a Home

Australian homes are usually made of brick or brick veneer, timber, or cement and board. Though individual homes are the norm, they may be smaller than in the United States, and room sizes may also be smaller, so you should beware of planning to take that king-size bed until you're sure it will fit.

Prices are downright reasonable. For example, in New South Wales a country-style house with three bedrooms, an eat-in kitchen, and a double garage was listed for $45,000. In Queensland, about twenty miles from Brisbane, a new two-bedroom townhouse with a luxurious kitchen, near the waterfront, was listed for under $60,000. Just seven miles from Brisbane, a four-bedroom home with views of Mt. Cootha and not just one, but two in-ground pools (one's saltwater!) was for sale for $197,000.

To look for a home in Australia, use the tried-and-true method of finding a good real estate agent. There are countless agents to choose from in Australia, but due to the immensity of the country they specialize in specific areas. Check the classified sections in the local papers. For an overview of the country and countless agents and homes, go online at www.realestate.com.au. For Sydney and its suburbs, you may contact Century 21 Australia, Level 12, 76–80 Clarence Street, Sydney NSW 2000; Phone: (61) (02) 8295-0600; Fax: (61) (02) 8295-0601; their Web address is www.century21.com.au.

Utilities and Infrastructure

Water: Tap water is safe to drink throughout the country.

Electricity: Electrical current is 220–240 volts so U.S. appliances (110 volts) will not work in Australia. You'll need to use converters or transformers, the latter for sensitive electronic equipment such as computers.

Communications: Australia is up-to-date with a full range of phone, Internet, and mail services.

Time Zone: Australia is just west of the International Date Line. The country ranges over three time zones. Eastern states (Queensland, New South Wales, Tasmania, and Victoria) are ten hours ahead of Greenwich Mean Time. Central areas are nine and a half hours ahead, and Western areas are eight hours ahead of GMT. Most Australian states follow daylight savings time from approximately the end of October to the end of March; however, the states have different regulations, and the exact timing varies.

Weights and Measures: The system of weights and measures is metric so you'll need to adjust measurements and recipes.

Moving Plans

Think carefully about whether or not to bring electrical items. Australia operates on 220 to 240 volts, 50 hertz power rather than North America's 110 volts, 60 hertz. You'll need plug adapters and converters or transformers for North American appliances. In addition, some electrical— and especially electronic—equipment won't work at all. This includes, but is not limited to, televisions, VCRs, and computer printers.

You must declare all drugs and medicines, even nonprescription ones such as herbal medicines and vitamins. Certain substances such as narcotics need an import permit. Of course, some items are forbidden outright. Among them are plants and seeds, weapons, and illegal drugs. If in doubt, check the Australian Embassy or Consulate for details.

PAPERWORK AND RESIDENCE RULES

Americans can stay in Australia for up to three months, but either a visa or an Electronic Travel Authority (ETA) is required to enter the country.

You must apply for, and receive, these before you enter Australia. There is no fee for the standard short-stay visa or an ETA.

You can stay in Australia beyond the three-month term, with a limit of six months per year. You'll need to apply and pay a fee for the privilege. To stay longer than six months, you are required to apply for immigrant status; however, the permission is notoriously difficult to obtain. Australia has rigorous criteria regarding health and character. The fee to apply is high and nonrefundable, even if you're refused.

Pets

Dogs and cats are permitted, but they must be quarantined so you may want to find your pet a good home in the States before you move. If you decide to bring your pet, you'll need an import permit that includes a health certificate and notes that the rabies inoculation and all vaccinations meet the schedule set out on the permit. Due to the complexity of the regulations, it's best to contact the Veterinary Counselor's Office of your nearest Australian Embassy for the most up-to-date regulations and applications.

GETTING THERE AND GETTING AROUND

With a country so vast, it's practical and popular to travel by air. Fortunately, domestic passenger service is excellent, and prices, though not cheap, are reasonable in Australia. The two major airlines are Qantas and Ansett, and there are several regional airlines.

Rail service links major cities, and sleeping accommodations on overnight trains make it easy to travel long distances. Major cities and suburbs have bus, tram, ferry, and rail services, and most major cities also have metered taxis.

Driving

Harking back to Great Britain, Australians drive on the left. Main roads are excellent, though if you plan to drive in rural areas of the Outback map your route carefully. It's bigger and drier than you might imagine so take precautions with water and other safety measures.

On a short visit to Australia you can drive with your current driver's license, but you must have an Australian driver's license within three months after you arrive. Australian third-party liability insurance is mandatory, and other liability and collision insurance is a good idea. Insurance costs depend on the place of registration and the size of your car.

Bringing a North American car to Australia is so difficult you might as well forget it. For starters, cars must meet Vehicle Safety Standards, and only right-hand drive vehicles can be licensed. Even if you had a right-hand-drive car, you'd have to meet an array of other regulations, plus pay freight, customs duty, and sales tax. It's easier and probably cheaper, even with the higher cost of cars in Australia, to buy or lease one there.

> Transport is good and cheap for me as a senior citizen. I can go anywhere all day for [the equivalent of] 50 cents. The Australian dollar is now so inexpensive, bringing in U.S. dollars is a bargain.
>
> Jerry Flavin, New South Wales

MANAGING YOUR MONEY

When is a dollar not a dollar? When it's Australian currency. Though the bills are called dollars and are divided into one hundred cents, just remember that the Australian dollar is not valued the same as the U.S. version. This is good for Americans since the Australian dollar is currently valued lower than the U.S. dollar so your cost of living will go down nicely. The Department of Immigration and Multicultural Affairs, taking into account that moving to a new country involves start-up costs, estimates that the average household of two who've been in Australia for less than two years spends about $500 a week. Depending, of course, on your spending habits, you could live moderately well on $25,000 to $30,000 a year.

The banking system is very much like that of North America. The Australian government regulates the banking system, which includes private banks as well as national and some state banks. Automatic teller machines are common. Checks are widely accepted, as are major credit cards.

Local and international banks serve the expatriate in all major Australian cities. You'll want a local checking account to pay daily bills, and you can open an account easily with just your passport and residency visa—if you do so within thirty days of arrival. After thirty days, the requirements are stricter.

Taxes

A Goods and Services Tax (GST) of 10 percent applies to most goods and services purchased; however, necessities such as food, education, health services, nursing home care, and certain other vital services are exempt.

You'll pay Australian income taxes only if you reside in the country continuously or intermittently for more than half of an income year. You can be taxed on income from all sources, in or outside Australia, unless you are a non-resident, in which case only the income earned in Australia is liable for Australian tax. Based on double tax agreements, income is not taxed in both the United States and Australia. You'll pay once, but where depends on the source of the money and your status as a resident or non-resident.

Capital gains and losses are based on your net gain, though there are specific exemptions, among them your principal residence, if you meet the requirements. Additional taxes include sales taxes, payroll taxes, stamp duty, and land taxes.

CONGRATULATIONS, YOU'RE LIVING IN A PENAL COLONY

Yes, Australia was originally used by England as a place to send its undesirables. Perhaps that's what has led to its rough and ready image. But don't worry, Alcatraz it's not.

STAYING HEALTHY AND SAFE

Australia is a modern country with good medical facilities, especially in all the major cities. Hospital facilities are modern and efficient, though crowded. You'll be pleasantly surprised with the cost of health care and prescription drugs, which are less expensive than in the United States. All residents contribute to a government-funded health care plan called Medicare. In return, residents get excellent health care, though it does not cover every service so private health insurance provides additional coverage.

If you have a temporary resident visa, you will *not* be covered by Australian Medicare so you'll need to find private health insurance. U.S. Medicare, despite the name being the same, has nothing to do with the Australian version and will not cover retirees in Australia. (See Chapter 25 for some expatriate insurance providers.)

All major cities have well-trained physicians, dentists, and other health care providers. Pharmacies are known as chemist shops, and they're convenient and readily available. In large cities, many chemist shops are open twenty-four hours a day. For a list of recommended doctors or dentists, ask at your embassy or consulate or request names from new neighbors and friends in Australia.

Security

Australia, in general, is a safe place to live. The street violence and guns found in the United States are not common Down Under. Of course, though crime is relatively low, you should take normal precautions late at night in major cities. Other than human beasties, Sydney has a particularly aggressive spider. Big and black, the funnel web spider's bite can kill. It's ugly enough that you hopefully won't go near one.

FOR MORE DETAILS

Below are some resources to help you further investigate a long-term stay in Australia.

Official Sources

Australian Consulate
19th Floor, Century Plaza Towers
2049 Century Park East
Los Angeles, CA 90067-3238
Phone: (310) 229-4800
Fax: (310) 277-5620
Email: dima-los.angeles@
    dfat.gov.au

Australian Embassy
1601 Massachusetts Avenue, NW
Washington, DC 20036-2273
Phone: (202) 797-3000 or
    (202) 797-3145 (immigration
    and visa inquiries)
Fax: (202) 797-3100
Email: dima-washington@
    dfat.gov.au

Chapter 5

**U.S. Consulate
in Melbourne**
553 St. Kilda Road
Melbourne, VIC 3004
Phone: (61) (03) 9526-5900

U.S. Embassy
Moonah Place
Yarralumla, Canberra, ACT 2600
Phone: (61) (02) 6214-5600

U.S. Consulate in Perth
16 St. George's Terrace, 13th Floor
Perth, WA 6000
Phone: (61) (08) 9231-940
Fax: (61) (08) 9231-9444

Internet Connections

Australian Customs
www.customs.gov.au

Real Estate Listings
www.property.com.au

Escape Artist Australia
www.escapeartist.net

U.S. Embassy in Australia
www.usis-australia.gov

Lonely Planet Guide
www.lonelyplanet.com/dest/aust/
 aus.htm

Background Reading

*Australia: True Stories
of Life Down Under*
edited by Larry Habegger and
 Amy G. Carlson
Travelers' Tales Inc., 2000

*Live and Work in Australia
and New Zealand*
by Fiona McGregor and Charlotte Denny
Vacation-Work, 1999
Note: This book is for British residents
 so note that sections related to visas
 and residency will not be applicable
 to citizens of other countries.

6

Canada

" I'm going to be an expatriate," said my friend Lynne, who was about to move to Canada. For a moment I was taken aback, thinking that the term *expatriate* certainly fit Americans living in Italy and France and Thailand. But Canada? Our good neighbor to the north is so close to ours in culture and proximity that most of us take it rather for granted as an extension of the United States. (One might add that we're wrong to do so and that Canadians abhor being considered just a northern adjunct.)

Highlights

- Comfortable, familiar lifestyle
- Cosmopolitan cities
- Invigorating outdoor activities
- Lower crime rate than the United States
- Relaxed atmosphere, friendly people
- Affordable with a good exchange rate

There are distinct differences between the two countries, and Canada offers advantages that are enticing more American retirees to settle there, especially during the summer months. Canada encompasses great natural beauty, with access to a superlative outdoor lifestyle and sports, along with cosmopolitan cities. Of particular importance to some retirees is the fact that they can easily assimilate into the Canadian lifestyle since it's comfortable and largely familiar to Americans. In addition, Canada has a significantly lower violent crime rate than the United States. And, currently, the healthy U.S. dollar buys American retirees more for their money in Canada.

THE BASICS

Canada stretches from the Pacific to the Atlantic Ocean and from the Arctic Ocean to the United States border, where Canada shares four of the five Great Lakes with the United States. Canada is the second largest country in the world after Russia.

Most of Canada consists of wide-open spaces. Mountain ranges encompass three sides of the heart of the country. The Appalachian mountains (called the Laurentians in Canada) extend from the U.S. chain.

The great majority of the people live along the U.S. border or in the major southern cities, which are all larger than the capital city of Ottawa. The country is multicultural, but much of the population immigrated from the British Isles and France; other European countries, the native Inuit, and a variety of cultures are also represented.

The major religion is Roman Catholic, though other faiths are practiced, especially in the major English-speaking cities of Calgary, Edmonton, Ottawa, Toronto, and Vancouver.

English is the most common language in Canada, but French is legally the second language. Both languages are required to be used in signage and product literature. This makes travel and fitting in that much easier for an English-speaking retiree from the States.

That said, if you decide to move to the province of Quebec, you'd be encouraged to learn some French. The separatist movement is alive and well; English is spoken, but French is strongly promoted.

ARCTIC
OCEAN

YUKON

HUDSON
BAY

BRITISH
COLUMBIA

QUEBEC

ONTARIO

1. VANCOUVER
2.

QUEBEC
MONTRÉAL

NOVA
SCOTIA

OTTAWA

TORONTO

1. VANCOUVER ISLAND
2. VICTORIA
3. NEW BRUNSWICK

Climate

Canada is massive in size, and the weather varies from mild to brrrrr depending on location. Temperatures are downright frigid in the upper north, but you'll more likely live in the more temperate southern areas along the U.S. border. The average maximum temperature in Toronto is 79°F in July; in January it's 30°F. Sunseekers may not relish the weather, but many retirees find areas to their liking. The coastal regions are warmed by ocean currents and feature mild summers and winters (albeit with high humidity). Vancouver's average high in July is 74°F; in January it's 41°F. Most American retirees spend summers in their Canadian homes but travel to warmer climes the rest of the year.

THINK CANADA'S NORTH OF THE UNITED STATES? THINK AGAIN.

The city of Windsor, Ontario, is connected by bridge over the Detroit River, just *south* of Detroit, Michigan.

YOUR NEW LIFESTYLE

This is a separate country, to be sure—but it's the closest in proximity and customs to the United States.

Food and Drink

Canadian taste buds run pretty much along the same lines as American ones. You won't find major differences from what you're accustomed to in the States, although Canadians are nuts for "chips"—french fries. Self-contained stands are common. You *will* find a wide choice of various ethnic cuisines, especially in the major cities.

Arts and Entertainment

Canada's major cities are cosmopolitan and offer an active cultural life. Music, theater, dance, and the visual arts all thrive. Toronto, Montréal, Quebec City, and smaller cities promote the arts through galleries, museums, and special shows. Movies are largely U.S. imports due to the strength of Hollywood. Finding English-language books and magazines is easy; even in francophone areas, English-language materials are readily available.

Outdoor Life and Sports

Canada has more lakes and inland water than any other country in the world. Fishing, canoeing, sailing, and swimming are all popular. The climate and geography provide scenic areas for hiking, mountain climbing, hunting, and bird-watching. Skiing is Canada's most popular outdoor activity, and British Columbia offers some of the most spectacular skiing in North America on sparkling, powder-covered slopes. Ice hockey is the national sport, with professional teams in all major cities. You can even follow the traditional American sport, baseball; Toronto and Montreal have major league teams.

Shopping

Products and stores are comparable to what you'd find in the United States, with varied styles, quality, and price ranges available. Canadian fashions tend to be more conservative and somewhat relaxed in the countryside, though those in cities such as Quebec and Toronto are cosmopolitan and often exhibit a European flair. Shopping areas range from major malls and large stores, such as Eatons, Simpson's, Holt Renfrew, and the Bay, to small boutiques, flea markets, and farmers' markets. Products of particularly good value in Canada include maple sugar, native Indian and Inuit art, and woolen blankets and clothing.

Social Life

Canada offers the same basic lifestyle and social activities as are found in the United States. If there's any complaint the Canadians may have, it's that Americans tend to identify them *too* closely with the United States. To make friends and influence people, just don't assume they're American clones! Otherwise, you'll find that Canadians are friendly and open. You should have no trouble making new friends if you become involved in local activities.

WHERE TO LIVE IN CANADA

Canada offers cosmopolitan living in its major cities as well as ski villages and coastal retreats. We'll look at just a few of these options, going from the largest city to more bucolic options.

Montréal (Quebec Province)

Want a French flavor without leaving North America? Montréal is a cosmopolitan city that is equally at home with French and English. Residential areas tend to be French-speaking or English-speaking based on the schools in the area. In general, areas in the northern and southwestern sections of the city tend to be francophone. Westmount, only a few minutes from downtown, features parks and some of the nicer residential communities—and some of the more expensive. However, a range of housing is available.

Old Montréal, in the center of town, showcases outdoor cafés, taverns, restaurants, and boutiques. Housing includes apartments and individual homes and tends to have a more multicultural mix of people. Housing prices vary depending on the area. For example, a 1,600-square-foot, two-bedroom apartment downtown was advertised for $1,700 a month, but homes in the suburbs go for less. You can rent a three-bedroom home for as little as $800 a month or a duplex for under $500 a month. In offers to sell, an updated European-style home with four bedrooms, two baths, a solarium, and hardwood floors in the close-in area of Mont-Royal was advertised for $157,000.

Toronto (Ontario)

Toronto is cosmopolitan and sophisticated yet extremely livable with good residential neighborhoods as well as a wide range of ethnic restaurants and entertainment. Yonge Street is the main north-south road and is central for many of the city's fine restaurants, boutiques, and entertainment.

The most expensive area for housing is in the city's center, where wealthy expatriates and senior-level executives often live in expensive high-rise apartments or condominiums. Many houses are semide-tached units sharing one or more exterior walls. A two-story semide-tached home with three bedrooms, two baths, and a finished walkout basement in central Toronto was advertised through an online real-tor for $175,000. If you want an elegant inde-pendent house, Victorian and Tudor-style mansions can cost $600,000 and up. Rentals are difficult to find here.

> It was pretty easy to slide into Canadian life. People are friendly in that sort of under-stated, Midwestern way. Think Garrison Keillor's Minnesota sensibility and take it down another notch.
>
> Lynne Marriott, Ontario

Several quieter areas with a lower cost of liv-ing are within range of Toronto and offer retirees access to the city for easy day or week-end visits. The city of York is forty minutes from downtown Toronto, and its housing ranges from rental apartments to luxury homes. Brampton, west of the city, is more low-end, also with a wide range of housing. Two hours from Toronto, Collingwood on Georgian Bay offers excellent access to out-door activities, lovely clear air, and reasonable prices. Niagara-on-the-Lake, just across from New York State, is a charming area known for its Shakespearean festivals and vineyards. Mississauga along Lake Ontario is a beautiful area and more upscale.

Vancouver and Environs (British Columbia)

Vancouver Island is an idyllic retreat for retirees who want a gorgeous view, tranquility, and a temperate climate. It's especially valued by those who love the outdoors. Golf and sailing are among British Columbia's most popular sports.

Victoria is Vancouver Island's principal city and the capital of British Columbia. A lovely city, filled with flower gardens, Victoria's moderate climate has attracted more than its share of retirees. Compared to most other areas on the West Coast, Victoria gets more sun and its temperatures range from an average of 40°F in January to nearly 74°F in July.

A new retirement haven is the Okanagan Valley, with towns including Penticton, Kamloops, and Kelowana. The area is reasonably close to Vancouver and is becoming more cosmopolitan, yet it's still fairly affordable and offers opportunities to participate in a host of outdoor activities.

South of Vancouver Island, the Gulf Islands have sunnier summers and mild winters. Salt Spring Island is the largest of these islands, known for its laid-back lifestyle. Housing on the Gulf Islands ranges from affordable cottages to elegant waterfront estates.

The city of Vancouver is not on Vancouver Island, but on the mainland. Though it offers all the benefits of a cosmopolitan city, its residents enjoy easy access to a pristine outdoor life. The city is surrounded by snowcapped mountains, and superb skiing is a short drive away. Oddly enough, the area enjoys moderate seasons. Winters are relatively warm with temperatures ranging from 32°F to 43°F, while summer days range from 54°F to 74°F. However, the rain here is about double that of Victoria on Vancouver Island.

Naturally, rural areas in British Columbia are less expensive than popular Vancouver. A typical single-family home in Vancouver East with three bedrooms sells in the $200,000s and up. In western Vancouver prices are even higher.

The metropolitan Vancouver area is spreading out toward smaller towns, such as Richmond and White Rock, where housing is less expensive.

SETTING UP HOUSE

Arranging for housing in Canada will be similar to what you're accustomed to in the United States. However, due to the strict immigration regulations, you'll most likely be looking for a short-term retirement abode for summer or ski visits rather than a full-time residence.

Finding a Rental

Rents are reasonable in Canada, especially outside the major city centers. Generally, you'll pay most for Toronto, Montréal, or Vancouver; suburban areas are less costly and the countryside is still less. Prices average about $700 and up per month for a one-bedroom apartment and $800 and up for a two-bedroom unit.

To find a rental, check the local classified ads or contact a real estate agent who handles rentals as well as sales. Check online sites as well.

Buying a Home

Americans can purchase property or buy a home in Canada. You can work with a real estate agent or find your home through an individual owner; however, be sure to have a Canadian lawyer review any purchase contract before you sign it.

Mortgages are available, but you must pay a minimum of 25 percent of the purchase price as the down payment or take out mortgage loan insurance that enables you to lower the down payment to 10 percent. Mortgage interest is not deductible in Canada so if you're paying income taxes there, take that under consideration when deciding whether to pay cash or take a mortgage.

If you're interested in real estate in Canada, you can start your search on the Internet. Two places make the search especially easy: International Real Estate Digest provides access to lists of agents in all areas of the country and thousands of homes via www.ired.com/int/canada/; MLS Online is the Canadian Real Estate Association site at www.MLS.ca.

For specific information, contact a real estate agent or the real estate association in the province where you wish to live.

Utilities and Infrastructure

Water: Tap water is safe to drink throughout Canada.

Electricity: Electrical current is 110 volts, with the same type of wall outlets as in the United States so appliances or electronic equipment from the States will work in your new home in Canada.

Communications: Phone, Internet, and postal services are modern and efficient and offer a full range of services.

Time Zone: Canada covers six time zones: Newfoundland, Atlantic, Eastern, Central, Mountain, and Pacific Standard. Daylight savings time is followed in some, but not all areas, from the first Sunday in April through the last Sunday in October.

Weights and Measures: Canada uses the metric system. It will take some time to adjust to buying groceries measured in kilograms and liters and ordering wallpaper in meters.

MOVING PLANS

If you are approved for residency in Canada, you can move most of your household goods and personal belongings. They will be free of tariffs and taxes providing that you used them prior to moving and that you keep them for at least twelve months after arriving. You can also import your personal cars or trucks, owned and used before arriving in Canada, if they meet Canadian safety regulations.

Canadian customs restricts other categories of goods, including weapons. Handguns can only be imported for use at an approved shooting competition; they must be registered. If you have any questions, contact the Canada Customs Office.

PAPERWORK AND RESIDENCE RULES

Americans can live in Canada for up to six months a year by simply showing that they have sufficient funds for support and private medical insurance. Part-time retirement works for many Americans who have second homes here for a cooler summer or for winter skiing.

Beyond the six months, Canadian immigration laws are extremely strict. Only those with a close relative living in Canada can be sponsored for full-time residence. Officials will ask for birth or baptismal certificates, separation or divorce papers, educational transcripts, technical or professional certificates, and letters of reference to go along with your application for residency. As a retiree, you must also show bank statements, Social Security, or pension records to prove you have enough income to support yourself.

Canada provides its residents with a form of health care, so you must also pass a medical examination; if you have a preexisting condition, be aware that this may count against you. For current regulations, contact the Canadian Embassy or Consulate nearest you in the United States.

Pets

If you have a pet, bring a health certificate—issued by a veterinarian 7 days before entry into Canada—that certifies that your dog or cat is healthy and has had all routine vaccinations. Include the original rabies certificate proving that the vaccination was administered more than 30 days but fewer than 180 days prior to your pet's arrival. No quarantine is required. For information and up-to-the-minute regulations, contact the nearest Canadian Embassy.

GETTING THERE AND GETTING AROUND

When you consider a country as being "abroad," you don't usually think of driving there. With Canada, however, it's easy to get there and back in your own vehicle. If you prefer to fly, flights are regularly scheduled from the United States to major Canadian cities. Carriers include Air Canada and U.S.-based airlines. Regional airlines serve smaller cities.

Within Canada, train service is superb, thanks to VIA Rail and BC Rail. Public transportation is available in larger cities. Montréal and Toronto have excellent subway systems called the Métro, plus bus service. Vancouver has very good bus service through BC Transit. Senior fares apply to people over sixty-two for travel in some provinces so ask when you purchase tickets.

Driving

You can drive using your U.S. driver's license in Canada. The rules of the road are very similar to those in the States, except for the right-turn on red rule, which does not apply in Quebec.

The metric system rules here so you'll note kilometers, not miles, on the signage. You'll buy gas and oil by the liter, not by the gallon.

You must have proof of car ownership and insurance with you when driving. You must also carry a minimum of $200,000 coverage in liability insurance, except in Quebec, which requires $50,000. If you are not a Canadian resident and your car will remain with your U.S. insurer, ask the insurer for a Non-Resident Interprovincial Motor Vehicle Liability Insurance Card.

HOW LOONIE DOES IT GET?

Canadian dollar coins have pictures of a bird, the loon, on them. They're nicknamed "loonies." So what's a two-dollar coin? A toonie, of course!

MANAGING YOUR MONEY

The Canadian unit of currency is called a dollar, which is divided into one hundred cents. Don't get confused when someone tells you a price. Remember that the Canadian dollar's value is different from the U.S. dollar's. Currently this is to the American's benefit since the exchange rate is extremely favorable to the U.S. dollar. An individual or couple can live moderately well on $30,000 to $40,000 annually.

The Canadian banking system is similar to that in the United States. If you're drawing U.S. Social Security, you can have your Social Security check deposited directly into your Canadian bank account. If you want, you can even open a Canadian bank account using U.S. dollars.

Opening a checking account with a Canadian bank is a simple matter. You'll need a local address, an identification card, your passport, and funds. Most banks charge a fee for writing checks. Automatic teller machines are common. If you don't want to keep your funds in Canada, maintain your U.S. bank account and simply draw from it using your automatic teller card in Canada.

Taxes

If you reside full-time in Canada, you will be required to file Canadian income tax. This can be steep, depending on your income level; the minimum tax is 34 percent on income exceeding $38,125 per year. You receive a basic tax deduction of $2,064. Another $715 applies if you receive U.S. Social Security. Additional taxes are added by the various provinces, and the rate varies. In British Columbia, combined federal and provincial taxes are 50.46 percent. Nova Scotia residents pay a total tax of 51.85 percent. You must still file a U.S. tax return based on your worldwide income though tax treaties between Canada and the United States protect you from double taxation.

You'll pay a 7 percent Goods and Services Tax (GST) on most goods and services. If you retire part-time (as opposed to being a full-time resident) in Canada, you may be able to apply for a rebate on the GST. Individual provinces also tack on a PST, Provincial Sales Tax, ranging from nothing (Alberta) to 8 percent or as much as 12 percent.

STAYING HEALTHY AND SAFE

Health, dental, and vision care standards in Canada are comparable to those in the United States, with fees about the same. Some prescriptions may cost more, but many are less costly in Canada than in the United States.

Medicare is not accepted in Canada, and your U.S. health insurance may or may not be valid there. Be sure to check. If you're not covered through the U.S. insurer, find a Canadian insurer. Programs such as Blue Cross offer services in Canada, and you may be able to simply transfer your coverage. (For additional expatriate options, see Chapter 25.)

The provincial governments manage a Canadian national health plan, but you can't join it unless and until you establish residency—and then there's usually a three-month waiting period. Each province's plan is slightly different, with different premiums and services. Note that your provincial health-care program doesn't provide full coverage when you travel, whether outside the country or just outside your home province. You'll need supplementary insurance.

Due to the socialized medical plan in Canada, provincial insurance plans normally pay for doctors' services. If you do not have coverage, you'll have to arrange payment yourself or through a private plan.

Physicians' organizations in Canada's major cities offer referral services or you can contact your consulate or embassy for recommended physicians.

DASHING MOUNTIES IN DRAB BROWN

Those romantic symbols of Canadian peacekeeping are the Royal Canadian Mounted Police, or Mounties, for short. We all recognize their scarlet tunics, but it may surprise you to learn that those are only used at ceremonies and tourist sites. Their daily uniform is standard brown serge.

Security

Canada is proud of its reputation as a safe country, and it's generally free of crime, especially violent crimes. When these do occur, they are more likely to happen in urban areas than in the small towns and rural areas. Handguns, pepper spray, and mace are not permitted in Canada. Hunting guns must be declared at the border. Though the country is much safer on the whole than the United States, you should still follow basic precautions, especially in major cities.

FOR MORE DETAILS

Below are some resources to help you further investigate a long-term stay in Canada.

Official Sources

Canadian Tourism Commission
Phone: (800) 577-2266

Chapter 6

Embassy of Canada
501 Pennsylvania Avenue, NW
Washington, DC 20001
Phone: (202) 682-1740
Fax: (202) 682-7726

U.S. Embassy in Canada
490 Sussex Drive
Ottawa, Ontario K1N 1G6
Canada
Phone: (613) 238-5335

Internet Connections

**British Columbia
Travel and Tourism**
http://travel.bc.ca

**Greater Vancouver Convention
and Visitors Bureau**
www.tourism-vancouver.org

Canada Online
www.canadaonline.about.com

Nanaimo on Vancouver Island
http://tourism.nanaimo.bc.ca

**The Canadian Real
Estate Association**
www.mls.ca

Official New Brunswick Tourism
www.gov.nb.ca/tourism

Canadian Tourism Commission
www.travelcanada.ca

**Vancouver Island and
the Gulf Islands**
www.islands.bc.ca

Government of Canada
www.canada.gc.ca

Greater Halifax Visitor's Guide
www.halifaxinfo.com

Background Reading

*Living and Working in Canada:
A Survival Handbook*
by Janet MacDonald and
David Hampshire
Survival Books, 1999

The Canadians
by Andrew H. Malcom
St. Martins Press, 1992

7

Great Britain

British retirees remove themselves from England's notoriously damp weather whenever they can, taking in sunnier climes for at least part of the year. Their places are often filled by American retirees who are charmed by the English lifestyle, rambling countryside, and friendly people. After years of short visits they have the time to "retire" in jolly old England for longer periods. And, for those who dream of living in Europe but don't want to tackle a foreign language, Great Britain is just a short plane hop, ferry ride, or Chunnel trip by train or car to the continent for "vacations" from their new retirement abode.

Highlights

- Tranquil country villages
- Cosmopolitan London
- Historic sites and scenery
- Close to continental Europe
- Gardening, hiking, and teatime!

THE BASICS

Great Britain includes England, Wales, Scotland, and Northern Ireland (though we'll limit the discussion to the island that includes the first

three) and lies close to France with its nearest point just thirty-five kilometers away. England is linked by a tunnel under the English Channel,
nicknamed the "Chunnel."

The English monarch heads the Church of England, members of
which are called Anglicans. Though this is the established church, the
society is secular and allows freedom of religion. Other religious
groups represented in Great Britain include Roman Catholics,
Muslims, Presbyterians and Methodists, Sikhs, Hindi, and Jews.

Great Britain is highly populated, with ten times the number of
people per square mile than in the United States. However, most of
the population lives in the major urban areas. Outside its large cities,
Great Britain tends to be rural, with pastoral land that stretches from
flat to rolling plains in the east and southeast and a few rugged hills
and low mountains.

SPEAKING ENGLISH, NOT AMERICAN

We call our spoken language English, but what the British speak is a mite different. You'll be in for some interesting moments until you learn to ask for the "loo" or "WC" when requiring the facilities in a pub. You'll need to put oil under the car's "bonnet" and baggage in the "boot."

Climate

Great Britain has a temperate climate, meaning there are no dramatic changes throughout the year. That's not to say it's warm and sunny. You'll find a lot of damp days, with more than half the days overcast. The Lake District is especially wet, while the sunniest regions are situated along the southern coast. Temperatures vary with the sun, but London's average temperatures range from 40°F in January to 64°F in July. Snow is rare in England, though it occasionally occurs over hills.

YOUR NEW LIFESTYLE

How will you fill your days? Here's an overview of activities and interests that are part of daily life in Great Britain.

Food and Drink

Britain was long known as the home of the worst food in Western Europe. Fortunately, you can now find good meals, even excellent ones, especially in London, where the cuisine (and often the prices) compete with the finest anywhere. You'll also find a range of excellent Indian restaurants, reflecting Britain's colonial past.

Pubs are popular for the beer that Brits love as well as for simple but hearty home-cooking, such as bangers and mash—bangers being sausage and mash being mashed potatoes. For fast food, fish and chip shops (chips are french fries) are ubiquitous. In good weather, you're likely to have yours served in newspaper for carryout to a nearby bench. Recent concerns over cattle with mad cow disease make some people think twice before choosing beef, but it doesn't seem to stop the Brits who love their roast and Yorkshire pudding—not to be confused with pudding, which is the British name for any dessert. If you love cheese, don't forget the wonderful Cheddar and Stilton.

MAD COWS AND ENGLISHMEN

Livestock problems are hounding Great Britain and ruining its tourist industry. But that doesn't have to ruin your plans for a stay there. Yes, mad cow disease can cause Creutzfeldt-Jakob disease in the human brain. But the danger, if any, applies only to beef and beef products. Most Brits claim that now their beef is regulated better than in other countries! But if you're concerned, just don't eat those foods. That leaves chicken, turkey, lamb, pork, duck, fish, shellfish—and pizza. You won't starve.

Arts and Entertainment

For English-language theater you can't beat London. Best of all, tickets to the top shows can be a fraction of the prices in New York. As a retiree with free time, take advantage of matinee performances, which are often less expensive. Even better, buy your tickets in Leicester Square the day of the performance for drastic discounts.

Visit Stratford-upon-Avon for Shakespeare. See movies (in English, of course) whenever you want, even current American exports. Finding English-language books is as easy as entering any of the multitude of bookstores.

Outdoor Life and Sports

Rugby, cricket, soccer, tennis, and golf are popular sports in Great Britain. You can join clubs to participate or attend matches and cheer avidly. Wimbledon, just outside London, is the home court for one of the tennis world's Grand Slams, which is played on the traditional grass.

Anything to do with horses is popular in England, including horseback riding, horse shows, and horse racing. The most famous races are the Grand National steeplechase, the Derby at Epsom Downs, and the Royal Ascot Race Meeting at Windsor.

Hiking, walking, and jogging are especially enjoyable in the countryside. Many town parks have walking and jogging trails that are excellent, including in downtown London.

Shopping

Department stores and specialty shops carry fashions and home furnishings in wide variety, though most items are more expensive than in the United States. Clothing and shoes use British or Continental sizes; look for a conversion chart to U.S. sizes or ask a salesperson.

Britons, like Europeans, tend to shop daily at their local specialty shops for meat, fish, and fresh produce. You'll also find supermarkets, including many chain stores. International stores in London carry many U.S. products.

Social Life

Most Brits are polite and many are tranquil souls who enjoy tending their gardens and having quiet chats over tea. As a result, your neighbors may seem a bit introverted at first. To meet people, join a local club, church, or civic organization. Groups such as the Anglo-American Institution and the American Society are helpful. Check the U.S. Embassy for a list of expatriate clubs.

WHERE TO LIVE IN GREAT BRITAIN

London attracts visitors, including retirees, for its vibrant culture, restaurants, shopping, and entertainment. Like big cities everywhere, London is extremely costly. Most retirees find life more affordable, as well as more peaceful, in smaller towns and country areas, of which there are countless charming choices. We can't cover every single corner but a sampling follows.

London

Though a big city, London is also a city of neighborhoods, each of which has its own personality. Be warned, however, that you would do well to have a hefty pension and inheritances to live here. London has always been expensive, and recently prices have been rising at a rapid clip. Even simple accommodations are pricey. A one-bedroom apartment in the more fashionable areas of downtown London easily sell for $250,000 and up. To rent a fully furnished two-bedroom flat in a top area of South Kensington near popular Brompton Road costs over $4,000 a month. Other popular residential areas are Belgravia, Chelsea, Hampstead, Hyde Park, and Mayfair. You'll find better long-term values if you select something farther from the center of town.

Areas along the Thames River are being renovated to include more housing and amenities. Though Chelsea offers picturesque homes and apartments, areas such as Fulham, farther out, can offer a better value and more green space.

I have always been an enthusiastic Anglophile. After retiring we explored the Vale of Evesham and neighboring Cotswolds and I simply fell in love with the place—enormous beauty, lots to do, peace and quiet when wanted, and the most terrific gardens I had ever seen. We bought our cottage, began spending three months a year here, and now I spend upwards of eight months a year here and have never been so happy and contented.

David Willour, the Cotswolds

Cornwall

If you're intrigued by anything to do with the sea and sailing, check out the county of Cornwall. On the far southwestern tip of England, Cornwall's small villages line a beautiful coastline where the sea breeze is brisk but relatively warm compared to other spots in Great Britain.

In the city of Falmouth you'll discover the third largest natural harbor in the world and an incredible sailing environment. Truro is known for its hundreds of beaches and a beautiful cathedral. Countless other towns and villages provide a tranquil, seaside lifestyle.

The Cotswolds

The names of villages in the Cotswold hills are as picturesque as the villages themselves: Chipping Camden, Bourton-on-the-Water, Stow-in-the-Wold, Upper and Lower Slaughter. Though just an hour and a half northwest of London, the Cotswolds is reminiscent of fairy tales, with quiet winding lanes and thatched cottages laced with roses and honeysuckle.

There are dozens of towns and innumerable villages in this region. Chipping Camden, for example, is listed as one of the most attractive small towns in England. Bourton-on-the-Water is known as the Venice of the Cotswolds. The area is popular, and prices can be higher than in other, less well-known areas of the English countryside. (Prince Charles lives at Highgrove in the Cotswolds so that should tell you something.) New houses are being offered in some areas starting at about $150,000, but don't expect the full country charm in a subdivision.

Scotland

More and more popular with tourists, Scotland is another option for living in Great Britain. Besides its attractions, Scotland tends to be less expensive than England. Even the main cities of Edinburgh and Glasgow are still affordable, with fully furnished and unfurnished apartments available starting at less than $500 for a one-bedroom, one-bath, and $700 for a two-bedroom, one-bath in nice residential areas. Outside the main cities, prices are even lower.

SETTING UP HOUSE

Since the language is the same, looking for lodgings may seem less intimidating in Great Britain than in some foreign countries, but the infrastructure is different. Plan to take your time when comparing the housing options before you sign on the dotted line.

Finding a Rental

An estate agent can help you find rental accommodations, but try to work with several of them since multilisting is not common; each agent will have different deals in their stable. Real estate agents are paid by the landlord though the tenant also pays a small amount, usually about $35. Landlords usually require six weeks' rent in advance plus a security deposit of between one and several months' rent. Leases usually run for six months or more and are renewed with the owner informally.

To find accommodations on your own, check the classified listings in local newspapers such as the *Evening Standard* and the *Hampstead and Highgate Express*. In the English countryside try Rural Retreats at (44) (1) 386 701 177. Several Internet sites cover Great

Britain, among them UK Property Gold (www.ukpg.co.uk) and Smart Estates (www.SmartEstates.com).

Buying a Home

Multilisting, in which real estate agents share listings, does not exist in Great Britain so to review a wide variety of homes you'll need to work with several different estate agents who will list different properties. Each agent specializes in specific areas. If an agent finds you something, you'll pay a small commission of about 3 percent of the purchase price. It's worth the help, but if you want to seek out other properties, check the local papers and notices on bulletin boards, and make your wishes known to people in the neighborhood where you'd like to live.

Make a purchase offer much as you would in the States. At that time you'll make an initial deposit. Be sure to have a lawyer (called a solicitor) review any offers and contracts before you sign. The solicitor will charge about 1 percent of the purchase price.

Mortgages at rates under 7 percent are currently available through building societies, which will survey the property and charge you for the service. If the surveyors find a fault in the house, you can withdraw from the contract (make sure the contract states this) and collect your deposit and down payment. Otherwise, your solicitor should make sure the property has a clear title and, if all goes well, the seller's solicitor will prepare a transfer document. The buyer and seller both sign this document to finalize the sale. You'll pay a 2 percent stamp duty if the property costs more than $64,000. If the property has not been previously registered, you'll have to pay a registration fee also. All told, transaction costs are reasonable in Great Britain, tending to be just 2 to 3 percent of the total cost of the house.

Note that in some areas homes are sold on a "leasehold," which allows the buyer to buy the house but not the property on which it stands; technically the property's leased for 999 years.

Scotland and Wales have slightly different systems. When you become serious about purchasing property there, research the topic with local estate agents and find a good solicitor.

Utilities and Infrastructure

Great Britain offers all the modern conveniences so you should be able to set yourself up comfortably. Of course, you may want to seek out central heating rather than the old-style radiators!

Water: Tap water is safe though you may prefer bottled.

Electricity: The current in Great Britain is 240 volts, 50 hertz. Wall plugs are a different shape as well. You'll need transformers or converters and adapter plugs for electrical appliances from the States.

Communications: British Telecom offers modern services, but phone calls are billed by the minute. Remember this when you log onto the Internet! If you're addicted, then you might save money by finding an Internet provider that offers a service plan that includes a certain number of hours online for one monthly fee.

Time Zone: Great Britain is on Greenwich Mean Time, which is five hours ahead of Eastern Daylight Time in the United States. Daylight savings time is observed from the end of March to the end of October.

Weights and Measures: The British use the metric system for weights and measurements though distances are shown in miles as well as kilometers.

MOVING PLANS

Speaking English doesn't mean that Great Britain speaks your language when it comes to electric current. When packing up, remember that U.S. appliances will need adapters and transformers. Many electronic items, such as TVs and VCRs, will not function properly even with them, so plan accordingly.

PAPERWORK AND RESIDENCE RULES

Great Britain makes it easy for U.S. citizens to plan lengthy stays. Americans can reside in Great Britain up to six months without a visa. However, if you intend to stay longer or move permanently, you'll need a visa. If you are at least sixty years old, you can apply as a Retired Person of Independent Means. You must prove that you can support yourself with a minimum annual income of at least £25,000 (about $37,000 at the current exchange rate), and you must be able to support any dependents. The tricky part about the rule is that you must show a close connection with the United Kingdom, such as having relatives living there. You must intend to make your main home in the United Kingdom.

You are required to apply for Entry Clearance and pay applicable fees before you arrive in the country; the fees change monthly. Because medical care is socialized and more or less free in Great Britain, authorities hesitate to admit anyone who might be a burden on the state medical system. Anyone who plans to stay in Great Britain for longer than six months must be examined by a medical inspector at the border. Admission to the country can be refused on medical grounds.

You'll need your passport, two recent passport-sized photos, and application fees (in the form of a check or money order), which vary depending on what type of visa you're seeking; the fees are nonrefundable. You may have to go through an interview, and you will probably be asked for additional documents such as evidence of funds. Allow at least three months to process your application.

For further information, contact the British Embassy in Washington, D.C., or the British Consulate closest to you. Or check the Internet at www.britain-info.org/consular/visas.

Pets

For decades Britain has been the bane of pet lovers (including its own citizens who travel) due to the onerous regulations requiring six months' quarantine for any pet coming from outside the country. Fortunately the laws are gradually being revised to incorporate a "doggy passport" and tattooing system that will enable some pets to enter Great Britain without the quarantine.

In any case, you must obtain an import license six to eight weeks before your scheduled arrival. A health certificate must be issued fifteen days or less prior to your departure for Great Britain and normal dog and cat vaccinations must be current. Do not have your pet revaccinated for rabies before departure because that shot must be administered within twenty-four hours of arriving in Britain.

At the present time, dogs, even those that have their "passport," can enter only through specific entry ports so it's still not always convenient to travel with your pet. Before you plan a move, check the British Embassy or Consulate nearest you for the most up-to-date regulations.

GETTING THERE AND GETTING AROUND

Great Britain is well served by numerous airlines, including British Airways, Delta, Air Canada, American Airlines, Continental Airlines, United Airlines, and Virgin Atlantic. The country is well known for its "bucket shops" or ticket consolidators who sell charter trips at amazingly low prices, making London one of the least expensive starting points for a trip virtually anywhere.

Within the country, BritRail trains connect most main cities and regions. London's Underground subway system and bus service enable you to avoid frayed nerves from driving in the city. But if you want to avoid feeling like a sardine, avoid rush hours! Various discounts apply to public transportation, especially for seniors, so be sure to ask about available options when you purchase your tickets.

A BUCKET-FUL OF TRAVEL OPPORTUNITIES

If you want to travel often, one of the lovely benefits of living in Great Britain is easy access to London's "bucket shops." These are ticket consolidators that vie with each other to see just how low the prices can go, with amazing deals on airline tickets and package holidays to destinations worldwide.

Driving

The British take great joy in cars and driving. As an American your biggest obstacle will be adjusting to driving on the "wrong" side of the road. Just take it easy at first and remind yourself constantly to stay on the left—especially after a short break or circling the roundabouts—until it becomes second nature.

In London and nearby suburbs, you can manage well—and will avoid traffic jams and parking hassles—by using public transportation. If you choose to live in the country, you'll probably want a car. Technically, you're allowed to bring a car into Britain without customs duty and tax if you've owned the car for at least six months prior to arriving. Just because you can doesn't mean you should. Your car must meet British safety standards, and you're likely to spend more time and money bringing the car up to standards than it's worth. Sell your car in the United States, and buy or lease one in Great Britain. The bad news is you'll have to learn to drive from the "passenger" side.

Third-party insurance is mandatory. A good record from your prior insurer will help lower the cost. Of course, cars must also be registered.

You can drive on a valid U.S. driver's license or an international license for up to a year. At that point you'll have to pass a British driving test in order to get a British license.

MANAGING YOUR MONEY

Your cost of living in Great Britain will be about 20 percent or more than comparable costs in the United States. The actual costs depend on where you choose to live. Your budget will inflate considerably more in high-priced London than in that charming small village in Scotland. Housing makes up the largest chunk of the cost differential. Food and sundries will also be a bit more costly. Filling the car's gas tank will give most Americans a panic attack when they figure the price of gas (petrol) at over $4.60 a gallon.

You'll pay for your purchases with the British pound, which is divided into one hundred pence. It wouldn't be terribly confusing except that you must also get used to the fact that the British have various names for a single currency item. A pound is also a "quid." And pence can be abbreviated as "pee." "Tuppence" is two pence, and "shilling" means five pence. Well, eventually, you'll get the hang of it.

Great Britain will not adopt the common Euro currency that will officially be distributed on January 1, 2002, but it may opt to join later.

Opening an Account

Other than learning to spell "check" as "cheque," the banking system in Great Britain will seem familiar. You can easily open a checking account at the main English banks or through the post office. The main difference in managing your checkbook will be that the bank won't keep records of your checks once they're cleared and returned to you.

Privacy is important to bankers here, and your account information will be held very closely. In fact, the island of Jersey is one of the top offshore investment centers. If you plan to invest, however, be sure to investigate as carefully as you would in the States.

Many Americans keep most of their funds in the United States, transferring money as they need it or accessing cash via automatic tellers. The U.S. card goes in and the British pounds come out.

Taxes

As in most European countries, Great Britain has a high rate for taxable income. However, as a retiree you won't be working in Great Britain, may not have a high income, and may be paying your taxes in the United States. In the latter case, you won't be taxed twice for the same income thanks to an agreement between the United States and Great Britain.

A 17.5 percent value-added tax (VAT) is assessed on most goods and services sold in Great Britain. This is refunded to visitors, but if you become a resident, obviously you will pay the full tax.

Great Britain has capital gains taxes, but these do not apply to the sale of a home. If you make other investments that do well, you'll pay a 25 percent capital gain on gains over $8,000. Additional taxes include a local council tax, inheritance taxes, stamp taxes, and a variety of social security and corporate taxes if applicable.

STAYING HEALTHY AND SAFE

Britain offers good, inexpensive health care, and emergency care will be provided free. If you become a resident, after six months you may be entitled to National Health Service (NHS) coverage. The NHS offers free or very low-cost medical and hospital care. That's the good news. However, the NHS is under fire for long delays in arranging nonemergency care. To get around the problems, most Brits carry additional health insurance, enabling them to use private hospitals and clinics.

Your U.S. health insurance may or may not cover you overseas. If it does, you may want to continue with your current company for the first year or two that you live in Britain, until you are firmly established as a resident. If you decide to go with a private British company, consider one of the three largest private health insurance companies in the country:

BUPA (British United Provident Association)
Russell Mews
Brighton, Great Britain BN1 2BR
Phone: (44) (0) 1273 208 18
www.bupa.co.uk

Western Provident Association
Rivergate House, Blackbrook Park
Taunton, Somerset TA1 2PE
Phone: (44) (1823) 625 000
www.wpahealth.org.uk
It offers a wide range of health insurance plans, depending on age.

PPP Healthcare
Phillips House, Crescent Road
Tunbridge Wells, Kent TN1 1PL
Phone: (44) (1892) 772 002
www.ppphealthcare.com

(For other expatriate insurance providers, see Chapter 25.)

Dental care is not fully covered by the NHS though some treatments are partially covered. The same system applies, in that some dentists also treat patients under private plans. Many British do not practice preventative care with regular checkups so you may have to request this on your own.

If you take a prescription medicine, bring a supply with you and a sample prescription with the generic name for the medication. You can't use that prescription, but it will tell a British doctor exactly what you're taking so he can issue a new prescription. Pharmacies, called "chemists," operate on a rotating schedule so their coverage extends after normal working hours.

Security

Crime in Great Britain is low. The exception is large cities, where the numbers of burglaries, street robberies, and car thefts have risen. Take normal precautions. You won't have to worry much about drive-by shootings, however. They're uncommon—mainly because there isn't much to shoot *with*. Great Britain strictly controls firearms. Even mace and pepper spray are considered weapons. If you're concerned about self-defense, the local authorities suggest carrying a personal alarm or a whistle.

The major concern recently has been terrorist bombings and scares, especially in London. For current travel warnings, contact the U.S. State Department or check their Web site at www.travel.state.gov.

FOR MORE DETAILS

Below are some resources to help you further investigate a long-term stay in Great Britain.

Official Sources

British Consulate General
845 Third Avenue
New York, NY 10022
Phone: (212) 745-0200
Fax: (212) 754-3062

British Embassy
3100 Massachusetts Avenue, NW
Washington, DC 20008
Phone: (202) 588-6500

British Tourist Authority in Chicago
625 N. Michigan Avenue,
   10th Floor
Chicago, IL 60611
Phone: (800) 462-2748

British Tourist Authority in New York
551 Fifth Avenue, 7th Floor
New York, NY 10176-0799
Phone: (800) 462-2748

Cornwall Tourist Board
Pydar House, Pydar Street
Truro TR1 1EA
Phone: (44) (187) 227 4057

Immigration Advisory Service
County House, 190 Great Dover Street
London SE1 4YB
Phone: (44) (0) 207 357 7511
Fax: (44) (0) 207 403 5875

U.S. Embassy
24 Grosvenor Square
London W1A 1AE
Phone: (44) (171) 499 9000

Internet Connections

BritainUSA
www.britain-info.org

British Tourist Authority
www.visitbritain.com

London Index
www.londonindex.co.uk

Property for sale or rent
www.ukpg.co.uk

Short-term rentals
www.barclayweb.com

Background Reading

Culture Shock! Britain
by Terry Tan
Graphic Arts Center Publishing, 1991

The New London Property Guide 2000/2001
by Carrie Segrave
Mitchell Beazley, 2000

Notes from a Small Island
by Bill Bryson
Avon Books, 1997

8

Ireland

Remember the song lyrics about "People who need people are the luckiest people in the world"? That goes double if they live in Ireland. Warm, welcoming Ireland does the heart good. Feeling at home here is easy when the people you pass smile and wave just for the pleasure of it.

The pastoral countryside is picture-postcard lovely. That's true even through the frequent mist. The undulating hills are a blanket of green velour polka-dotted in white sheep. On the west's Dingle Peninsula, craggy cliffs rise above the sea with walking paths for the intrepid hiker. Villages and small harbors compete with the thriving modernity of the capital, Dublin.

Life moves at a placid pace here. Part of the pleasure is sharing time for unhurried conversation whether on the street or, more likely, in one of the countless social venues known as pubs. The lilting Irish accent

Highlights

- Amazingly hospitable people
- Pubs, beer, and tall tales to enjoy with them
- English with a lilting accent
- Lush green countryside
- (And gentle drizzle!)

and traditional storytelling skills make for enjoyable listening—if not for absolute truth when the tales become taller than a leprechaun.

This is not to say that Ireland is "ye olde sod." Far from it. These days, the overwhelming color of Ireland is green, not just the landscape but also the country's thriving economy. It wasn't always this way. The Irish have seen their share of suffering and emigration due to famine and poverty. It's a different world here now. New cars are ubiquitous. Homes are well tended. Computers and telecommunications are state of the art.

THE BASICS

Most people call the island west of Great Britain "Ireland." In fact, the island is split into two parts: The Republic of Ireland and Northern Ireland. There are vast differences in economy between the two areas, plus the euphemistically titled "troubles" are still present in the northern section despite efforts at peace. Since most retirees prefer tranquility, the Ireland of this chapter concerns only the Republic of Ireland.

Though Ireland is now prosperous and thoroughly modern, for centuries the country struggled. The country's rebirth has been dramatic and relatively quick. A full member of the European Union (EU) since 1973, Ireland has undergone a period of astonishing economic growth. The result is an amazing improvement of living standards in Ireland, which have been rising for the past two decades. EU funds have helped upgrade the country's physical infrastructure and industry, further tourism projects, and expand training and employment programs.

THE "CELTIC TIGER" ROARS

Ireland's economic turnaround has succeeded in turning the tide from emigration to immigration. The country's population has reached its highest level since the 1881 potato famines, when waves of Irish left for better lives elsewhere. Their descendants are returning home to a modern economy, a low 4.3 percent unemployment rate, and a country thriving on its communications prowess.

Climate

It's not called the Emerald Isle for nothing. The well-known mist keeps Ireland truly bright and gemlike. However, the climate is mild with few extremes in temperature. Winters are generally snow-free since temperatures average about 40°F. Summers are usually cool, averaging about 65°F.

Language

Technically, the Irish speak English, but their literary heritage instills the desire to embroider it with a flair far beyond that of any other English speakers. You'll understand them, of course, but there are times when you'll wonder whether they're trying to entertain you or themselves with their tales!

We won a trip to Ireland years ago and loved it. [Eventually] we bought a cottage and moved there. The weather is not so bad, actually, when you compare it to New York and Connecticut. For gardening it's superb.

Kernochan Bowen, Cork

YOUR NEW LIFESTYLE

How will you fill your days? Here's an overview of activities and interests that are part of daily life in Ireland.

Food and Drink

Hearty stews and fish and chips—and beer, of course—are served in the countless pubs that cater to families in every town and village through-out the country. In large cities, especially Dublin, you'll find an array of international restaurants serving continental and ethnic cuisine. Talented cooks can be found even in out-of-the-way villages. We were served what could arguably be called our best meal in Ireland at a simple farmhouse. Even better, when we raved about the mushroom soup, our hostess insisted on sharing her secret recipe the next morning in a cook-ing lesson.

Arts and Entertainment

Ireland is revered for its literary history. Great writing has always been the norm, from the vividly illustrated ninth-century *Book of Kells*, displayed at Dublin's Trinity College, to works by a host of literary luminaries including, but not limited to, novelists James Joyce *(Ulysses)*, Jonathan Swift *(Gulliver's Travels)*, and Bram Stoker *(Dracula)*, Nobel Prize–winning poet Seamus Heaney, and playwright George Bernard Shaw.

Irish folk music and dance stands out with distinctive verve. The fly-ing feet of Celtic step dancing, as made famous by the internationally famous *Riverdance* company, takes the breath away just watching it.

IS THAT A LEPRECHAUN OR A LAUGHING IRISHMAN?

The Irish combine a strong Catholic faith with a sense of magic and mys-ticism. The country is pockmarked by holy wells and fairy rings, and story-tellers love to spin tales by a fireside. Everyone's heard about leprechauns, those little people who guard treasure from us humans. Of course, no one believes in them. (But if you see a fellow about two feet tall scurrying away with a bright kettle of gold, you might as well follow him.)

Outdoor Life and Sports

Soccer is popular, as is the local sport of hurling, which is a cross between soccer and field hockey. Naturally, with all those green hills and parklands, hiking is popular. Horseback riding, horse racing, sailing, and great fishing are other popular sports.

Shopping

Ireland has large shopping centers and many smaller shops. Most stores are open from 9:00 A.M. to 5:30 P.M. though small ones may close early one day a week. Large shopping centers stay open until 9:00 P.M. several nights a week. In Dublin opening hours are longer, with a few twenty-four-hour shops.

Weaving and woolens are two crafts that provide both warmth and aesthetic pleasure. Some craft shops even provide on-site weaving demonstrations. You'll have a tough time limiting yourself when it comes to choosing among the beautifully patterned wool sweaters and woven throws.

SEEING RED

Being in Ireland is like seeing the world through rose-colored glasses. Whether you're on the street or in a busy store, you may think you're at a clone convention where everyone has strawberry blond locks and bright red freckles. Of course, not every Irishman or woman is a redhead; it just seems that way.

Social Life

It's true that life in Ireland revolves around the pub. An American may immediately conjure up images of the stereotypical pint-swilling Irishman. That's because we think pubs are merely bars. In fact, Irish pubs are family oriented. They serve as a virtual community center, where you can meet your neighbors and share simple, hearty meals. In the evenings, many pubs offer entertainment ranging from professional singers and musicians to anyone who happens to feel like taking the stage that evening.

The people of Ireland have an international reputation for hospitality, but until you set foot here you can't imagine just how hospitable.

Strangers wave at you along country roads. New friends share stories and offer fresh-made tea and scones. And, if you're like us and just can't parallel park in a tight spot beside a pub, you may finally succeed only to be rewarded by a round of applause and the offer of a pint.

WHERE TO LIVE IN IRELAND

Outside of Dublin and a few other large cities, Ireland is a country of charming small towns and villages. If you want to live here, it's best to narrow your focus down to the region that appeals to you, then explore it. A quick overview of several areas follows, starting with the capital.

Dublin

Dublin is a popular place to live, and it's easy to see why. Unlike many cities that can be forbidding with their hustle bustle and high-rises, Dublin is a comfortable city that offers parks, good shopping, restaurants, and entertainment. It's the capital—as well as the cultural hub—of the Republic of Ireland. Of course, since it's popular, it's also more costly than living in the Irish countryside.

That said, homes and apartments are available throughout Dublin. Temple Bar is a restored Bohemian area smack-dab in the middle of the city. Ballsbridge is an upscale residential and commercial area with tree-arched streets just south of downtown. Farther south are villages such as Blackrock, Dalkey, and Killiney, which are served by the Dublin Area Rapid Transit (DART). Also on the DART, but to the north of Dublin, are the suburbs of Clontarf, Howth, and Sutton.

The average monthly rent for a small house in the greater Dublin area ranges from $775 to $1,300, and apartment rents run from $525 to $1,050 depending on quality and nearness to downtown. Most small towns and the countryside are less expensive. A four-bedroom, semi-detached home with a terraced property a short distance to town was listed to buy for $112,000.

The Southeast

Wicklow, the city, sits at the edge of the sea, about twenty-seven miles south of Dublin. County Wicklow also features the low Wicklow mountains and parklands, which create popular green spaces for Sunday strolls. A three-bedroom bungalow on a corner site a short distance from the sea was for sale for $146,000.

The Southwest

The Dingle Peninsula on the far west of Ireland is a bastion of tradition. It's here that Irish is still the official language. Villages are scattered about amid the hills, nothing very far from the sea.

Farther south and east is Kinsale, which is best known for its beautiful harbor, elegant boutiques and art galleries, and restaurants that have given the town a reputation for gourmet cuisine. Kinsale's upscale character makes it expensive compared to many of the other small Irish towns. Near the harbor, a three-bedroom, two-bath apartment could cost upwards of $300,000.

Kenmare is a pretty, small town and it has a quieter charm than the more blatantly tourist-oriented areas, such as Killarney with its hordes of tourist buses.

County Cork attracts many new settlers with its picturesque coastal towns. The climate is another draw. County Cork is milder than many other regions in Ireland, and the beaches, fishing, and beautiful scenery combine to create a hospitable lifestyle. Cork also boasts an international airport, important for expatriates who want to travel to the continent or entertain visiting friends and family.

Due to its increase in popularity, prices are rising in Cork. A three-bedroom home with a coastal view would cost about $300,000. A two-bedroom apartment goes for about $100,000.

SETTING UP HOUSE

Ireland's raging prosperity has created an influx of returning Irish and new immigrants. The result is a housing shortage, especially in Dublin, and areas of high employment. Most likely you'll have to visit in person to find accommodations, and leave plenty of time to find long-term lodgings.

Though housing may be different from what you expect in the United States, you can be comfortably installed. Heating is probably the most important issue in this damp climate. Older homes may not have central heat, and electric heating is expensive. Adjust your expectations or look for modern accommodations to meet your needs.

Finding a Rental

You can find houses and apartments for rent furnished or unfurnished; furnished housing generally includes all that's necessary as far as appliances and furniture are concerned. Unfurnished rentals include carpets and kitchen equipment.

To find housing, check classified listings in local newspapers or use a rental agency, which will charge a fee for their service. Most property owners require a deposit equivalent to one or two months' rent, and rent will then be due each month. Legally, you must receive a written rental agreement.

Buying a Home

The resurgence of the Irish economy has increased home prices dramatically in recent years. However, the advantage to being retired is that you can choose a location more for its charm and affordability than for convenience to a job center. As mentioned above, Dublin has the highest housing costs. The 1999 Irish Auctioneers and Valuers Institute's online site listed the average new house in Ireland as costing $119,313, but the average price in Dublin was considerably higher at $157,530. If you choose another location, such as County Cork, the average price drops to $113,045. County Galway's average is $112,228, Limerick's is $100,160, and Waterford's is $104,856.

Resale homes are more costly than new ones, with the average cost being $132,260. Dublin prices are, of course, higher.

To purchase a home, you'll make a bid based on the seller's asking price. Though not an auction, be aware that others may also be making offers, which can lead to higher prices and doubts as to whether you'll get the home. Before you sign, be sure to have an attorney review all offers and contracts.

Purchase costs include a stamp duty ranging from 0 to 9 percent based on the purchase price (the higher the house price, the greater the percentage of stamp duty), legal fees that will be approximately 1.5 percent of the home price, plus survey and valuation fees.

If you meet the financial criteria, banks and building societies will make mortgage loans of up to 90 percent of the purchase price, with the normal repayment period being twenty years.

Utilities and Infrastructure

Water: Water from the mains in Dublin and most of Ireland is safe to drink. However, in houses that use a storage tank system, water from the tap may not be potable.

Electricity: Electricity is delivered at 220 volts, 50 hertz, which is incompatible with North American appliances. You'll need plug adapters and transformers. The latter will be useless for televisions since broadcasting systems differ overseas. VCRs are also different, though if you have a multisystem VCR that accepts all types of tapes, you may be able to use it. Electrical plugs do not match U.S. appliances either so you'll need adapter plugs. In general, you'll want to purchase electronic items and large appliances after you arrive.

Communications: Telephone service is highly sophisticated in Ireland. The country has developed advanced digital telecommunications and serves as an international telecommunications center. Naturally, the Internet is fully up to speed here. Postal services are efficient. Mail is delivered Monday through Friday, but not Saturday or Sunday. Post offices are located in most cities and towns, train stations, and airports. The post office provides more than stamps. It offers savings plans, currency exchange, applications for TV and dog licenses, and a host of other services.

Time Zone: Ireland is on Greenwich Mean Time, the same time zone as Britain. That makes it five hours ahead of Eastern Standard Time in the United States. Daylight savings time occurs from spring through autumn.

Weights and Measures: Ireland uses the metric system.

MOVING PLANS

You're allowed to bring belongings, including household items, to Ireland with no tax or duty provided that you've owned them for a minimum of six months. Talk to the Irish Embassy about the proper forms.

You can import a motor vehicle duty- and tax-free provided it meets certain requirements. Basically, it must be a personal vehicle brought in within twelve months of your move, and you must prove you've owned it for at least six months prior to the move. The vehicle cannot be sold or hired out for twelve months following its registration in Ireland. As with most countries abroad, however, it's easier to avoid the hassles of conforming to import and vehicle requirements by selling your car in the States and buying one in Ireland.

PAPERWORK AND RESIDENCE RULES

You can live in Ireland for up to ninety days with your passport being the only entry requirement. Americans who want to stay longer than ninety days must make their request prior to the end of those ninety days.

To make the request, you'll need your passport, four passport photos, and financial forms showing that you have enough funds to support yourself for the time you intend to be in Ireland. Take these to the Aliens Registration Office, Police Office, Harcourt Street, Dublin 2, or to the police superintendent's office in the Irish town nearest to you. You will most likely be granted the extension, especially if you have relatives in Ireland.

If one of your grandparents was born in Ireland, you can apply for Irish citizenship. Unlike some countries, Ireland permits dual citizenship, so you can retain your U.S. citizenship as well. For those of you who want to travel or do business in any other country in the European Union, an Irish passport eases the way. Even if you don't have an Irish grandparent, if you legally reside in Ireland for four years out of eight you can apply for citizenship.

Pets

As an island without rabies, Ireland maintains strict controls over animals entering the country. Dogs and cats are the only permitted pets, and they usually face a mandatory six-month quarantine period. Regulations are currently being changed with a program to permit entry to pets with a microchip proving their compliance with strict antirabies requirements. Before you get too relieved by this news, be aware that it's difficult to find rental housing that accepts pets. All this should discourage you from bringing Fido. If you still plan to do so, then you'll need two official (and separate) health certificates, proof of immunizations for common diseases dated at least 30 days prior to entry but not more than 180 days, and an import permit. Contact the Irish Embassy or the Department of Agriculture, Kildare Street, Dublin 2, for current regulations and application forms.

GETTING THERE AND GETTING AROUND

The Irish carrier, Aer Lingus, and other international airlines fly into Ireland's international airports in Dublin, Cork, and Shannon. Most cities and towns in Ireland are connected by train or bus, though sometimes you have to travel to Dublin to make connections.

In metropolitan Dublin, DART (Dublin Area Rapid Transit) trains and buses serve the city and nearby suburbs.

Driving

The Irish drive on the left so take time to adapt and constantly remind yourself of this before pulling out of a parking lot or side street. Otherwise, driving is relatively easy, though slow. There are few motorways; most roads are two lanes that wend among towns and the countryside. Signs are clear when you find them although you'll contend with Irish spellings and signposts when you're on the Dingle Peninsula.

You can drive in Ireland on a U.S. license for a year after your arrival. Then you must get an Irish driver's license, which requires U.S. drivers to pass a driver's test. You'll start with a provisional license, good for two years. You'll need to provide a passport or birth certificate, two passport-sized photos, and an eye-test report. Everyone over the age of seventy must pass a medical exam every three years to maintain their license.

Automobile owners must register their vehicles with the local licensing authority and pay an annual motor tax calculated by engine size. Drivers are required to have third-party liability insurance; comprehensive insurance, though recommended, is not mandatory. Insurance is expensive and costs more for left-hand drive vehicles than right-hand drive ones. You must display a disc on the windshield that shows you've paid your insurance and road tax; these are checked at random, and fines apply if it's missing or invalid.

CONSIDER THIS AN ENTERTAINMENT TAX

To support the television programming in the country, Ireland taxes televisions. You'll be charged about $105 for color sets annually . . . and, yes, it is enforced. Just think of it as a way of cutting down on all those commercial breaks.

MANAGING YOUR MONEY

The unit of currency in the Republic of Ireland is the Irish pound, also called the *punt*. It's divided into one hundred pennies. Ireland also uses the euro, as currency for bank transactions and foreign exchange. The euro will be issued as notes and coins in January 2002, at which point the Irish pound will be withdrawn from circulation over a six-month period.

A local bank account can supply you with checks (spelled "cheques" here) and an ATM card. Checking accounts are called *current* accounts. Charges can be high, but you can avoid them with the required minimum balance. Be sure to check the exact regulations. Remember that even though the language is English, dates are written European style on checks; i.e., the day is first, then the month, then the year.

You can use your ATM card from a stateside account to withdraw funds in Irish pounds, which is one of the easiest and lowest-fee ways to transfer funds. This is especially helpful if you want to keep your money, including Social Security automatic deposits, in your U.S. account.

Your cost of living here will be close to that in the United States, except for fuel, which costs three times as much in Ireland. If you want to cut costs, live in a small town or the countryside. Dublin is the most expensive location, mainly due to the expense of accommodations.

Taxes

If you decide to live in Ireland full-time, you'll be responsible for paying income taxes there. You won't pay double for both Irish and U.S. taxes since a tax agreement between the United States and Ireland credits the taxes paid in one country.

Income-tax rates in Ireland are high. Income tax is 28 percent, increasing to 46 percent when your income exceeds 23,000 Irish pounds. Certain deductions apply depending on your family status. Property taxes are not charged on property valued under $140,000 and is proportional based on property value from that point up. Other taxes include capital gains, excise tax, annual road taxes, vehicle registration, and a value-added tax on some goods and services. Note that the value-added tax of 12.5 percent applies if you live in Ireland, but if your retirement living is of short duration and you return to the States it can be reimbursed.

A SNAKE-FREE ENVIRONMENT

Legend has it that in the fifth century St. Patrick banished all the snakes from Ireland. They went into the sea and drowned—and the island is snake free to this day.

STAYING HEALTHY AND SAFE

No special vaccinations are required for Ireland, and there are no special health concerns in moving there. Medicare does not cover retirees in Ireland. If you have U.S. health-care insurance of another sort, check whether it will cover you overseas and if so, for how long. If your insurance covers you at all, chances are it will be just for emergency care and for a limited length of time. A few plans, notably Blue Cross/Blue Shield, are transferable to an Irish counterpart. International expatriate insurance policies are another option if you need coverage. (For listings of some expatriate insurance companies, see Chapter 25.)

If you become a legal resident of Ireland, you will pay a social insurance tax, which entitles you to free public hospital services through the Department of Health. Individuals whose incomes meet established guidelines may be eligible for no-charge access to general practitioners through government-run programs.

Public services may require a wait, however. If you want to use private services, you can apply for private health insurance, such as Voluntary Health Insurance (VHI), to supplement public coverage. The system offers a range of plans depending on how comprehensive you want your coverage to be. You must join before the age of sixty-five. Once you have the insurance, however, there is no discrimination on the basis of age, and your premiums do not increase with age. For more information contact the Voluntary Health Insurance Board, VHI House, Lower Abbey Street, Dublin 1; Phone: (353) (1) 872-4499.

Security

The Republic of Ireland is a safe country, with relatively little crime, especially in rural areas. Take normal precautions in large cities and tourist areas by watching where you walk and protecting your valuables.

FOR MORE DETAILS

Below are some resources to help you further investigate a long-term stay in Ireland.

Official Sources

Embassy of Ireland
2234 Massachusetts Avenue, NW
Washington, DC 20008
Phone: (202) 462-3939
Fax: (202) 232-5993

Irish Tourist Board
345 Park Avenue
New York, NY 10154
Phone: (212) 418-0800

U.S. Embassy in Ireland
42 Elgin Road
Ballsbridge (Dublin)
Phone: (353) (1) 668-7122
Fax: (352) (1) 668-9946

Internet Connections

**Government of Ireland/
Department of Foreign Affairs**
www.irlgov.ie/iveagh

Irish Emigrant News
www.emigrant.ie

The Irish Guide
www.theirishguide.com

The Irish Times
www.Irishtimes.com

Irish Tourist Board
www.ireland.travel.ie

Property search
www.iavi.ie

Relocation service
www.corporatecare.ie

Background Reading

Buying a Home in Ireland
by Joe Laredom and
  David Hampshire
Survival Books, 1999

*Choose Ireland for Retirement:
Retirement Discoveries for
Every Budget*
by Patti Cleary
Globe Pequot Press, 1999

Culture Shock! Ireland
by Patricia M. Levy
Graphic Arts Center Publishing,
  1995

*Ireland: True Stories of Life in the
Emerald Isle*
edited by James O'Reilly
Travelers' Tales, Inc., 2000

*O Come Ye Back to Ireland: Our
First Year in County Clare*
by Niall Williams and
  Christine Breen
Sophia Books, 1989

*Round Ireland with
a Fridge*
by Tony Hanks
St. Martin's Press, 2000

9

New Zealand

Conjure up an image of pristine seas, lush forests, vineyards, and incredibly beautiful vistas. Add modern cities, charming small towns, and friendly people. In two sentences, that is New Zealand.

What it isn't, is Australia. It's amazing how many people lump them together. It's true that Australia and New Zealand are relatively close together, and since New Zealand is smaller, it's easy to consider the country to be an adjunct to Australia. But don't say that to a New Zealander! Even though the two countries share a British Commonwealth heritage and are neighbors in the Pacific, they're distinct in government, geography, and culture.

Highlights

- **Pristine countryside**
- **Low cost of living**
- **Casual and comfortable lifestyle**
- **Friendly people**
- **A sailor's paradise**

THE BASICS

New Zealand consists of two main islands southeast of Australia, which are quite simply called the North Island and the South Island. Between them lies twenty miles of the Cook Strait. These, and smaller island off-shoots, are surrounded by the Pacific Ocean on the north and east and the Tasman Sea, which lies between New Zealand and Australia. The total size of New Zealand is roughly equivalent to the state of Colorado.

The islands had a volcanic birth that created mountainous areas, which alternate with several sections of plains. The principal mountains on the North Island occur on the eastern side. On the South Island, the Southern Alps extend from the southwest to the northeast.

Politically, New Zealand is an independent democracy, but as a member of the Commonwealth the country recognizes Queen Elizabeth II as its head of state. The prime minister is the executive head of the government. The capital is located at Wellington, though Auckland has nearly three times the population.

English is the official language and is spoken throughout the country. Maori is a second official language though it's rarely used except by Maori natives for traditional ceremonies. Most of New Zealand's citizens originally came from Europe, and of those, most were from another island—Great Britain. The indigenous Maori make up about 13 percent of the population. The remainder of the population are Polynesians who immigrated from Pacific islands and eastern Asia.

The society is a secular one. More than half of the people consider themselves as Christian including Anglicans, Presbyterians, Roman Catholics, Methodists, and Baptists, but they aren't regular churchgoers. About 1 percent of the population are Hindu or Buddhist.

THE NAME GAME

A Dutchman by the name of Abel Janzoon Tasman discovered New Zealand in 1642. He didn't get greedy and name the entire country for himself. He settled on naming the island of Tasmania.

Climate

New Zealand is in the Southern Hemisphere so seasons are reversed there. Summer occurs from December through February, fall is March through May, winter is June through August, and spring is September through November. Although New Zealand has four seasons, they are all temperate. Winter is short and mild, and temperatures rarely fall below freezing except in the mountains.

At the capital, Wellington, the average temperature is 68°F in January and 42°F in July. In Auckland, the January average is 74°F, with July averaging 46°F. As befitting an island, however, rain is common and abundant throughout most of the country.

WHEN IS A KIWI NOT A KIWI?

North Americans think a kiwi is that small green fruit that's delicious in salad. It's also the name for a bird found only in New Zealand (possibly because it can't fly!). It's the nation's national emblem. By extension, "Kiwi" is an idiom for a New Zealander. And on the stock exchange, the New Zealand dollar is referred to as the Kiwi.

YOUR NEW LIFESTYLE

How will you fill your days? Here's an overview of activities and interests that are part of daily life in New Zealand.

Food and Drink

Its British background lends New Zealand a tradition of big breakfasts and meat and potato meals. Fish and chips are popular, too, but restaurants in large cities are enormously varied, including Indian, Greek, Thai, Chinese, and Mexican among some of the more popular cuisines. Fruit and dairy products are plentiful. New Zealand wines have won awards internationally.

Arts and Entertainment

The Maori culture brings an interesting element to local arts in the form of tribal legends, painting, sculpture, pottery, music, and dance. Most large cities sponsor art galleries and museums, and among the more notable are the Auckland City Art Gallery and Auckland Museum and the Wellington City Art Gallery and New Zealand Portrait Gallery.

In literature, several New Zealanders are popular internationally, including teacher and novelist Sylvia Ashton-Warner, short story writer Katherine Mansfield, and the prolific mystery writer, Ngaio Marsh.

Outdoor Life and Sports

With its large wilderness areas and parks, New Zealand is a paradise for the active. Naturally, being an island country, water sports such as sailing, fishing, and swimming are extremely popular. Rugby is the most popular sport, and New Zealanders follow the exploits of the national team, the All Blacks, passionately. Soccer and cricket are also favorite active and spectator sports. The sport-loving New Zealanders enjoy many other sports as well including golf, tennis, horseback riding, and skiing.

Shopping

The quality of shops and products is high, and you can find virtually anything you need in the large supermarkets. Be sure to try the fine wine and cheeses. For decorative items for your home, look for Maori wood carvings, pottery, sheepskin or leather goods, hand weavings, or bone carvings. In stores, the Goods and Services Tax is already included in the marked price.

Social Life

New Zealanders are casual and friendly. Unlike some more formal cultures, when meeting someone, a New Zealander will soon be on a first-name basis, and invitations to visit at home appear soon after. The most popular form of entertainment is the barbecue.

WHERE TO LIVE IN NEW ZEALAND

New Zealand's two main islands are separated by twenty miles across the Cook Strait. Each island has its own pleasant residential areas, and most people live in urban centers, in or near the main cities. Coastal areas are also popular, as are some of the newer "lifestyle" developments that offer parklands and planned communities. Here are a few of the options.

Auckland (North Island)

The largest city and center of commerce, Auckland is a cosmopolitan city on the Hauraki Gulf. North and south of the city is a magnificent swath of coastline providing wonderful beach areas, a beautiful harbor, and a nickname: the City of Sails. Auckland is home to the America's Cup, yachting's greatest trophy.

The city is sophisticated with art galleries, museums, theaters, and restaurants. As a multicultured city, Auckland combines Polynesian and European cultures. Such a beautiful city does not come cheaply. Auckland is the most expensive place to live in New Zealand. But all things are relative. Properties in Auckland may be expensive for New Zealand, but they're reasonable compared to most large cities elsewhere in the world. To check some properties online, try Harcourts Real Estate at www.harcourts.co.nz.

Wellington (North Island)

Located on the southwest part of the North Island, Wellington sits beside a deep harbor, surrounded by wooded hills. New Zealand's capital, it's compact in size and is easy to get around. Buses help make driving unnecessary, but when you do drive you'll find few traffic jams.

The city offers a vast array of superb restaurants, many with marvelous views of the harbor or city, charming cafés, shopping, and entertainment. The New Zealand Symphony and the Royal New Zealand Ballet are located here, plus several other dance, drama, and musical groups. New Zealand's Te Papa museum reveals the nation's history. Less than an hour's drive away is the Kapiti Coast, a recreational haven of beaches and mountains. In fact, Wellington is such an entertaining place that it's popular as a weekend destination for other New Zealanders.

Hawke Bay (North Island)

If you're a lover of wine and sunny skies, you may want to explore Hawke Bay on the east coast of the North Island. It's one of the sunniest regions in New Zealand and is known for its chardonnay and cabernet sauvignon wines. Many of the vineyards are open for wine tastings. Several have cafés and restaurants. If you like art deco, the main city in the area, Napier, has the greatest concentration of art deco buildings in the world. The Art Deco Walk is open year-round.

Christchurch (South Island)

Located on its east coast, Christchurch is the largest city on the South Island. Despite being a main island center, Christchurch has retained a small-town feeling of peace and tranquility. It's laced with tree-lined streets, gardens, and nineteenth-century buildings. Nearby areas are rural, but Christchurch offers sophisticated

I have a funny requirement when looking for a place to live, work, or retire. I look to see whether or not avocados grow there. You see, avocados like it warm, with lots of sunlight. So do I. So if they grow there, I know I'll at least like the weather. Avocados grow very well in northern New Zealand.

Rick Rule, North Island

options, including fine theater, shopping, and restaurants—plus an historic tram that transports you hither and yon in the city center. The International Antarctic Centre is located here. A fair number of artists have also settled here, and there are a number of museums and art galleries.

SETTING UP HOUSE

Most New Zealanders own their own homes, but renting makes more sense for an American retiree since strict immigration policies tend to limit stays to a long-term sojourn rather than a permanent move. The only reasons to purchase would be if you had a reason to return periodically or you plan to rent your property when away.

Finding a Rental

Even if you eventually succeed in residing in New Zealand, rent before taking the major step of buying property. That way you'll become familiar with specific areas and be sure that life in New Zealand suits you. Some furnished apartments are available, but houses are usually rented unfurnished. If you need to supply furniture you can rent it, but buying reasonable secondhand furniture may actually be less expensive.

One unique option is a motor home. New Zealanders love the outdoor life, and motor homes (and camping) are extremely popular. If you want to spend several months traveling the country, you can easily hire a comfortable motor home to serve as your accommodations.

Buying a Home

The national median sales price for a residence in New Zealand is NZ$172,000, or just a bit over $76,000. Of course, home prices are higher in main centers than in provincial towns. Auckland is the most expensive, with the median price of about $110,000. Wellington is the second-most expensive, and other cities drop lower. Coastal areas are more expensive than inland property.

Rural land is being organized into subdivisions; they are close to an urban center but with a country feeling and lower prices. One example is a new residential development in Newhaven, just outside Auckland, which offers three-bedroom, two-bath homes set around parks for $70,000 to $130,000.

Utilities and Infrastructure

Water: Tap water is safe, but don't drink from rivers and lakes.

Electricity: Electricity is 230–240 volts, 50 hertz. You'll need converters or transformers to use North American appliances. You'll also need plug adapters to fit the three- or two-pin plugs.

Communications: New Zealand is a modern country with up-to-date postal and telecommunications services. Most public phones take cards, not coins. Cards can be purchased from news agents and booksellers.

Time Zone: New Zealand is twelve hours ahead of Greenwich Mean Time.

Weights and Measures: The metric system applies.

MOVING PLANS

Customs requirements are strict in New Zealand. To avoid problems with customs, bring prescription drugs in their original containers and keep your doctor's prescription with them. Do not bring handguns; any other firearms require a permit from the police.

With the strict immigration laws, you'll likely limit your stay to anywhere from three to nine months, in which case you won't need to move more than your personal items. If you have approval to reside in New Zealand, you can import your household goods and a motor vehicle free of customs duties and taxes provided you have personally used the items. You must have owned your car for at least a year. For more information, contact New Zealand customs; their Web site is www.customs.govt.nz.

PAPERWORK AND RESIDENCE RULES

You'll need a current passport to visit New Zealand, but that's all you need to enjoy a stay there without a visa for up to three months. For longer stays, apply for a visitor's visa, which allows you stay up to nine months within an eighteen-month period. After nine months out of the country, you can apply for another three-month stay.

If you want to reside in New Zealand for a longer period, be advised that it will be difficult at best, and maybe even impossible. Immigrating to New Zealand is restricted unless you have family there, you can prove that you are an entrepreneur starting a business, or you are a worker with the requisite amount of experience that will contribute to the country. The latter eligibility is based on the General Skills application that rates employability. If you're over age fifty-six, the General Skills application for residence is not accepted. Other requirements for immigration include English language skills, acceptable health, good character, and sufficient personal funds to support yourself and any dependents. You can apply from inside or outside the country, but first contact the New Zealand Immigration Service to ascertain your chances before filling out any forms since fees are nonrefundable.

Pets

Cats and dogs are subject to strict entry regulations. You must have a Permit to Import prior to your pet's entry. Among other requirements, your pet must be more than nine months old, have a health certificate, and have a microchip or permanent tattoo proving its identity. An animal is not eligible to enter the country until six months after blood testing. If you intend to take your pet with you, request the full paperwork and requirements from the New Zealand Embassy or Consulate nearest to you or contact the Ministry of Agriculture and Forestry, 101-103 The Terrace, P.O. Box 2526, Wellington; Phone (64) (4) 474-4100.

GETTING THERE AND GETTING AROUND

New Zealand's three international airports are located at Auckland, Wellington, and Christchurch. The main international airline is Air New Zealand; other international airlines fly there, including the Australian airline Qantas and major U.S. carriers. Flights from the United States are usually nonstop and overnight.

Domestically, air and train services connect the main cities. Between the islands, transportation is by ferry or by air. The main domestic airlines are Air New Zealand, Ansett New Zealand, and

Mount Cook Airlines. Buses, taxis, and shuttle services provide transportation within the major cities.

Driving

Like the rest of the Commonwealth, New Zealanders drive on the left side of the road so be alert, especially at traffic crossings. All signs are posted in kilometers, with the speed limit being 100 km/h (about 60 mph) on open highways and 50 km/h (about 35 mph) in residential areas. A current U.S. driver's license or an International Driving Permit is valid in New Zealand for up to twelve months.

You can rent a car through major car rental companies such as Avis, Hertz, or Budget, or at local companies.

MANAGING YOUR MONEY

Currency is the New Zealand dollar, abbreviated NZ$, which divides into one hundred cents. New Zealand does not restrict the amount of foreign currency brought in or out of the country, but if you carry cash over NZ$10,000 you must complete a Border Cash Report. You can exchange foreign currency at banks or Bureau de Change kiosks in international airports and large cities. Usually you'll get a better exchange rate simply by accessing cash via an ATM. Just make sure you have a four-digit PIN. ATMs are commonly found in banks, malls, and main shopping streets throughout the country. Banks are open from 9:30 A.M. to 4:30 P.M. Monday through Friday. All major credit cards are accepted in New Zealand.

The cost of living is reasonable compared to the United States. Certainly, any place where a fresh lobster dinner can be had for $10 or less can't be all bad. It's difficult to estimate average yearly expenses due to variables based on personal taste in accommodations and lifestyle, but in general, living costs in New Zealand will be less than in the United States.

Taxes

With the strict immigration laws, chances are you won't be residing permanently in New Zealand. Therefore, most taxes that apply to residents won't apply to you. However, you will pay a 12.5 percent Goods and Services Tax, which applies to purchases and is included in the displayed price. Unlike some countries, American visitors cannot claim back this New Zealand tax when leaving the country; however, items shipped from New Zealand to a U.S. home address will not be charged the Goods and Services Tax.

STAYING HEALTHY AND SAFE

Medical facilities in New Zealand are modern and efficient. Accident victims receive free care. Residents and citizens of Australia and the United Kingdom, and those holding residence permits valid for two years or more, receive free treatment for emergencies and major problems, maternity care, and dental treatment for children under age eighteen. However, North Americans are responsible for health care costs incurred. Your U.S. Medicare will not cover you in New Zealand so you will need private insurance while visiting or living there. (For a few options, see Chapter 25.)

Security

New Zealand is one of the safest countries in the world. Violent crime is unusual, and the most serious problems tend to be theft from cars or camper vans. The islands have no snakes or dangerous wild animals so you can enjoy the beautiful outdoors without listening for slithering and snorting sounds.

Some areas of the country are susceptible to seismic activity so check the conditions where you intend to stay. Choose housing that meets safe standards, and be aware of the best procedures in case the earth starts rocking and rolling.

FOR MORE DETAILS

Below are some resources to help you further investigate a long-term stay in New Zealand.

Official Sources

New Zealand Consulate General
Los Angeles
Phone: (310) 207-1605

New Zealand Embassy
37 Observatory Circle, NW
Washington, DC 20008
Phone: (202) 326-4800

U.S. Consulate General in Auckland
4th Floor, Yorkshire General Building
Corner Shortland and O'Connell Street
Auckland
Phone: (64) (9) 303-2724

Internet Connections

New Zealand Embassy
www.nzemb.org

New Zealand Immigration Service
www.immigration.govt.nz

New Zealand Tourism
www.newzealandtourism.com

New Zealand Tourist Board
www.immigration.govt.nz/visit

Background Reading

Live and Work in Australia and New Zealand
by Fiona McGregor and Charlotte Denny
Vacation-Work, 1999

STRETCHING YOUR
BUDGET

I f the budget's a tad tight when you retire, you can always downsize your lifestyle, giving up splurges, a roomier house, dinners out, regular golf, or the travel you dreamed of during those years chained to a job. But where's the fun in all that lovely free time if you're spending it counting pennies?

Some retirees count pesos or colónes or escudos instead. They've discovered that those currencies go a lot further than their U.S. dollars. For them, the secret to enjoying a low-cost retirement is to live overseas in a country with a low cost of living. Americans without affordable health care even find that they can get good care and prescription medicines at a fraction of U.S. prices in certain countries.

Mexico is a prime example of a low-cost destination for retirees. Some sections of Mexico are rapidly becoming southern suburbs for legions of American retirees on fixed incomes, especially those from western and north-western states. Their base is in Mexico, but the proximity enables them to visit back and forth with friends and family. Costa Rica is another popular option, along with a host of other countries that offer low-cost options for exploring the world.

Of course, you don't have to be hard-pressed for cash to enjoy living in one of these sunny havens overseas. The low cost of living may simply be a pleasant side benefit, while your retirement stash grows for a few extra years undisturbed. You may even be pleasantly surprised to discover that when you return to the States, you're better off than when you left!

10

Belize

Yes, the truly tropical ambiance still thrives on the beaches of Belize. That speck of a country on Central America's Caribbean coast, next to Guatemala and south of Mexico, is a paradise of azure seas, palm trees, and Mayan ruins. The coastline is two hundred miles long and many areas are not heavily populated so if you're looking for that magnificent Caribbean view, it's still possible to find an afford-

Highlights

- Sunny, subtropical paradise
- Incredible snorkeling and scuba diving
- English speaking
- Affordable living
- North American retiree incentives
- Friendly people

able spot. Settle down with a beach blanket, and don't forget a snorkel mask or scuba gear. Just off the coast is the largest barrier reef in the Western Hemisphere (second largest in the world) thriving with colorful fish.

THE BASICS

Belize is an independent state within the British Commonwealth. Formerly called British Honduras, Belize is a democratic country that became independent in 1971, though it maintains traditional English common law. The country has a prime minister, a house of representatives, and a senate. There are two main political parties—the People's United Party and the United Democratic Party—both of which are similar in ideology and tend toward the political center. Queen Elizabeth II is the titular head of state, but she is represented locally by a governor general. The capital of Belize is Belmopan, but the largest city (and former capital until 1970) is Belize City.

Belize encompasses almost nine thousand square miles, much of which is covered by mangrove swamps and islands along the coast. In the south the land rises, and the highest point is 3,700 feet at Victoria Peak. Most of Belize is forested with mahogany, cedar, and logwood though savannas serve as a rich agricultural base for sugar and citrus fruits.

The majority of the people are Roman Catholic, but about a third are Protestant.

Climate

The climate is subtropical with temperatures usually in the 80s or 90s with temperatures dropping in the winter to the 60s or 70s. In the mountains the temperatures are lower, especially in winter when the thermometer can read as low as the 40s. Be prepared for high humidity, though it's offset by refreshing breezes on the coast.

Language

The official language is English, and all legal documents are written in English. Spanish is common. Other languages include Creole—which combines English and West African—Garifuna, and Mayan.

YOUR NEW LIFESTYLE

How will you fill your days? Here's an overview of activities and interests that are part of daily life in Belize.

Food and Drink

Fresh is best in Belize. Enjoy just-caught sea bass or lobster for your lunch, and it won't cost you a fortune. A seafood meal, even including lobster, will go for about $14. Or cook it yourself after a trip to see the fishermen at the dock. Local markets are filled with bananas, mangoes, and other produce at low prices.

Arts and Entertainment

Belize is not Broadway. Don't expect to find a lively nightlife. But then, that's not what the residents are here for. The entertainment is found under blue skies and in the clear seas. The cultural history is largely Mayan, and spectacular temples and their remnants are waiting to be explored. National parks are showcases of natural wildlife. For more civilized viewing, the Belize Zoo is located in Belmopan, between Belize City and San Ignacio.

Outdoor Life and Sports

Scuba diving, snorkeling, swimming, sea kayaking, boating, and fishing are part of daily life in Belize—and no wonder. The longest barrier reef in the Western Hemisphere is located just off its shores. If you're feeling waterlogged, then take to the land for hiking, horseback riding, or jungle treks.

Shopping

Learn to shop the open-air markets and seafood cooperatives for the freshest ingredients for your meals. Grocery stores can be found, but not the large chain stores you're accustomed to in North America. Shops are closed on Sundays and with no Wal-Mart just around the corner, you'll be hard-pressed to find the exact widget you want, but you'll get to know your local merchant well. And just think of the beautiful views saved by the lack of massive development!

Social Life

Belize is known for its racial harmony, tolerance, and friendliness. The people of Belize are welcoming to North Americans, and you'll also find friends among the other Americans, Canadians, and Europeans who visit or live here. The society is varied, with people of Indian, African, Mayan, and Chinese heritage.

A "KEY" TO CORRECT PRONUNCIATION

Islands in Belize are called *cays,* but don't pronounce the word like a woman's name. Say *key,* as they're called in the Florida Keys.

WHERE TO LIVE IN BELIZE

Islands and the sea that surrounds them are the siren call to Belize. Below are a few of the more popular locations.

Ambergris Cay

The largest island in Belize, Ambergris Cay is the most developed of the islands. It's the most popular destination for tourists as well as for many of the snowbird expatriates so you'll find an array of low-rise hotels and guest houses. The island is a short boat trip or a twenty-minute plane ride from the Belize mainland.

San Pedro is the main town. It's the sort of place you might imagine from forty years ago, with colorfully painted houses, small shops, and a relaxing pace. The San Pedro library is so relaxed that its books are available to one and all with nary a library card needed. Traffic jams are few unless they're caused by the golf carts and bikes on the roads. Bicycles are the principal means of transportation. Just offshore is the amazing barrier reef, and there's no shortage of dive shops ready to help you take advantage of it.

Naturally, the tourism aspect makes Ambergris Cay more expensive than any other place in Belize (though still less expensive than Florida or the more built-up Caribbean islands). A two-bedroom apartment will rent for $500 to $1,500 a month. If you want to purchase a home, condos and houses range in price from $80,000 to over $500,000. For example, a two-bedroom condo would cost anywhere from $125,000 to $250,000 depending on its location near the sea or the beachfront.

Placencia

The Placencia peninsula is located on the southern end of the Belize mainland. It includes two villages and several hotels designed for tourism. The area sits between the Caribbean beachfront and a lagoon. Many expatriates are beginning to buy properties and build homes here so real estate prices are starting to rise, especially for the beachfront properties. The lagoon side is less expensive, but Caribbean lots cost $50,000 or more. That's expensive for some areas of Belize, but have you looked at waterfront lots in the States lately?

Corozal

Close to Mexico on Corozal Bay is the town of Corozal. Here you'll find an extremely inexpensive and peaceful lifestyle. Be aware that peaceful means there isn't a lot to do here except enjoy the sea and the sunny weather. You could find an up-to-date rental house for $400 to $700 a month. Property is reasonable to purchase. A typical Belize-style home here could cost under $30,000. New North American–style homes with three bedrooms are available for $75,000 to $200,000. Or purchase a lot and build your own home.

SETTING UP HOUSE

The typical Belize-style home is small and relies on fans and ocean breezes for cooling. North American–style homes are available with the full enchilada of several bedrooms and air conditioning. It's up to you and your budget to choose.

Finding a Rental

Furnished accommodations are available in Ambergris Cay and in any of the areas built for tourists, which are scattered throughout the country, like Cayo in western Belize, where you'll find cottages and hotels. You might look in older resort areas where the properties are being converted to condominiums. Many of the units are sold and then rented out when the owners are not using them.

Buying a Home

Foreigners are able to purchase property in Belize with very few restrictions. Sales of land on some cayes require approval for sale to foreigners, but otherwise you can purchase a half acre or less of land inside a town or ten acres or less outside town limits. Just to be safe, check before you make a purchase offer to ensure that you have the right to the property, and insist on title insurance.

Multilisting of properties does not really exist in Belize as it does in North America so visit several real estate agents. You can also look around at For Sale signs, agents' brochures, and Internet sites, though some of this information may not be current.

Mortgages are available, but at steep rates of about 14 percent or more. You may want to pay cash, arrange for a loan through another source outside Belize, choose developer financing, or convince an individual seller to finance the loan. Unless you're a citizen, you'll pay a 10 percent transfer fee when you purchase property.

Utilities and Infrastructure

Water: Tap water in Belize City is purified, but many people stick to bottled. It's essential anywhere outside the city.

Electricity: Electricity is provided at 110 volts, the same as in North America. Towns are supplied with electricity, but the back country is still rustic. In any case, electricity is very expensive and its delivery can be interrupted during tropical storms so many people have a generator.

Communications: Mail service is good. Belize Telecommunications Ltd. provides the phone service, and you can even log on to the Internet.

Time Zone: Belize is on Central Standard Time, which is six hours behind Greenwich Mean Time. The island does not observe daylight savings time.

Weights and Measures: Belize uses metric measures.

MOVING PLANS

When you first come to Belize, bring your bathing suit and not much more. You'll want to test the waters, so to speak, by renting furnished accommodations until you decide whether you want to stay.

PAPERWORK AND RESIDENCE RULES

Belize's retiree program is specifically designed to entice United States citizens (along with Canadians and Brits) to establish residence here. Retirees can't work, but any income they receive from outside the country is free of taxes. To qualify for the program, you must prove you have $1,000 a month in pension or Social Security income, or have an income of $2,000 a month, to be deposited in a Belize bank. You'll pay a one-time fee of about $700 when you apply. For information on the retiree program, contact the Belize Tourist Board.

If you don't qualify as a retiree, you can apply to enter Belize through the normal immigration department, which requires more paperwork and has specific residency rules. Since many North Americans only live here part-time, they simply renew their entrance permits for up to the permitted maximum of six months each year.

Pets

Belize has no pet quarantine. However, you must show that your pet's inoculations are up to date and provide a health certificate signed by a veterinarian. For the forms and more information, contact Belize Immigration well before your departure.

GETTING THERE AND GETTING AROUND

Belize City airport welcomes a number of international airlines, including American Airlines and Continental Airlines. Local airlines serve the country internally. Buses run inside Belize City and from Belize City to the main towns. Taxis serve towns and resort areas, but they're not metered so ask the fare before getting in.

Driving

The lack of extensive public transportation makes driving here essential. If you're intending to live or travel to less developed areas, consider getting a four-wheel-drive vehicle. It will be essential for the Belize backcountry.

WHICH DOLLAR IS THAT?

The name is the same, but the Belize dollar is worth half the U.S. one. When asking prices, make sure that you know which currency is under discussion!

MANAGING YOUR MONEY

Technically Belize has its own currency, the Belize dollar. However, the U.S. dollar is accepted throughout the country at a fixed rate of two Belize dollars to one U.S. dollar. Since the U.S. dollar is the more accepted currency worldwide, you'd do well to simply use that. In fact, most expatriates leave their funds in the United States and simply transfer funds when they need them.

The cost of living can vary widely. If you kick back and go with the flow of cooling ceiling fans in a typical Belize home and buy fresh local produce, you can live on under $1,000 a month. If you choose to live in an upscale expatriate resort area and can't give up frosty air conditioning and imported foods, then your budget will be considerably more.

Taxes

Belize has an 8 percent sales tax on most goods and services except for a few essentials in the food and medical categories. If you enter Belize under the retiree program, you can bring $15,000 worth of household goods, a car, and a boat (even an airplane, if you are of a mind) free of import duties. The personal income tax ranges according to income with the highest rate at 25 percent. There are no capital gains or estate taxes.

STAYING HEALTHY AND SAFE

Belize does not require any specific inoculations for entry into the country, and there are no serious epidemic diseases here. If you're planning extended jungle stays while you're in the country, antimalaria tablets are recommended.

As with any country outside the United States, Medicare will not cover you here. Neither will most U.S.-based insurance policies. You'll need to apply for insurance from a local company in Belize or through an international expatriate insurance carrier. (For some options, see Chapter 25.)

Since English is the main language, you won't have any language-barrier concerns when seeking medical attention. Many of the physicians and dentists were trained in the United States, and care is amazingly inexpensive. A general office visit usually costs less than $12, and prescriptions are vastly less expensive than in the United States. Belize City has a well-staffed hospital and doctors. District towns and larger villages have hospitals or clinics. Specialists are in short supply, however, and the most sophisticated treatments will not be found. Most American expatriates head north for serious medical conditions, taking the short flights to Miami or Houston to use U.S. insurance or Medicare.

Security

Serious crime doesn't seem to affect the expatriate in Belize, though robberies, muggings, and shootings are far too common in the lower rent districts. Be aware of your surroundings and take precautions. Don't leave your property unprotected. Many expatriates have fences or burglar bars, and ensure that a housekeeper or security guard watches the house when they are away.

Hurricanes are a fact of life here. The hurricane season runs from June through November, though most storms arrive after September. Pay attention to warnings and be prepared to take steps for your safety in case of severe weather.

FOR MORE DETAILS

Below are some resources to help you further investigate a long-term stay in Belize.

Official Sources

Belize Tourist Board
421 Seventh Avenue, Suite 1110
New York, NY 10001
Phone: (800) 624-0686

U.S. Embassy
2535 Massachusetts Avenue, NW
Washington, DC 20008
Phone: (202) 332-9636

Internet Connections

Ambergris Caye
www.ambergriscaye.com

Belize Net
www.belizenet.com

Belize First e-zine
www.turq.com/belizefirst

Background Reading

Belize First Guide to Mainland Belize
by Lan Sluder
Equator, 2000

Belize in Focus: A Guide to the People, Politics and Culture
by Ian Peedle, edited by James Ferguson
Interlink Publishing Group, 1999

Belize Retirement Guide: How to Live in a Tropical Paradise on $450 a Month
by Bill Gray and Claire Gray
Preview Publishing, 1999

Hidden Belize
by Stacy Ritz
Ulysses Press, 2000

11

Costa Rica

One day, umpteen years ago, before my own adventures overseas, my hairdresser returned from a vacation to Costa Rica. She spent the whole haircut raving about the place . . . and by the next haircut, I was told to find a new hairdresser. My hairdresser would be trimming her expenses in Costa Rica.

She's not the only one. Ameri-

Highlights

- Laid-back, relaxed lifestyle
- Friendly, welcoming people
- Warm, semitropical climate
- Incredible national parks, flora, and fauna
- Affordable living

cans have discovered Costa Rica in droves. (Thus raising what years ago was bottom-line pricing to very affordable.) They've come to enjoy the stunning white and black sand beaches, lush rain forests, dramatic coral reefs, stunning mountains, and clear rivers and streams. They get to enjoy all this scenic magnificence virtually nonstop thanks to spring-like temperatures year-round. And they've met people who are friendly and enjoy a laid-back lifestyle.

THE BASICS

The Republic of Costa Rica is tucked between Nicaragua and Panama in Central America. Despite its small size (19,652 square miles or approximately the size of Massachusetts), Costa Rica's long, narrow dimensions provide it with lengthy coastlines on both the Caribbean Sea and the Pacific Ocean. The country is a democracy and has a relatively stable government, which is another draw for Americans. Costa Rica is divided into seven provinces, each of which is headed by a governor appointed by the president. The government has four branches, the executive, legislative, judicial, and the electoral tribunal. The president and legislators are elected for four-year terms and cannot be reelected.

Some consider Costa Rica to be the Switzerland of Central America since it remains neutral in the area's politics. It has abolished its army and has chosen to spend the extra money on social projects instead.

Some of the Costa Rican culture evolved from Mayan civilization. Most of the people these days have a European heritage, plus there are South and Central American immigrants. A minority are Native Americans, blacks, and ethnic Chinese. The vast majority of the people are Roman Catholic but the Constitution provides for religious freedom.

Chapter II

> **WHAT'S IN A NAME?**
>
> In 1502, Christopher Columbus visited Puerto Limón and got the impression that the land was rich in gold. Thus he named the country "rich coast," or Costa Rica. He was wrong about the mineral content but right if you consider the country's natural attractions.

Climate

For most of the year, temperatures in Costa Rica stay comfortably in the mid 70s, varying little from one month to the next. The average maximum temperature in January is 70°F; in June it's 79°F. The rainiest months are September and October, but these are followed by a relatively dry winter. Summer showers are frequent but tend to pass by quickly.

Language

As in most of Central America, Spanish is the official language, but the influx of tourists and residents from the United States has encouraged English, which is widely understood. If you want to immerse yourself in language studies in Costa Rica, you'll have no problem doing so. Countless schools, including branches of many U.S. universities, offer programs. A long list is available on the Internet at www.studyabroad.com.

> **YOU SAY TOMATO, I SAY . . .**
>
> Though Costa Ricans speak Spanish, they have the habit of ending words with the affectionate diminutive "–tico" rather than the more common Spanish version "–tito." Thus the familiar name for the locals: Ticos.

YOUR NEW LIFESTYLE

How will you fill your days? Here's an overview of activities and interests that are part of daily life in Costa Rica.

Food and Drink

Costa Rican food is much like that in Mexico or Spain. Black beans and rice is a dietary staple, along with tamales, tortillas, and empanadas. Beef with vegetables and rice with chicken are common. As befitting a country with long coastlines, the fresh seafood can be excellent. With the tropical climate, fresh fruits and vegetables are delicious and available throughout the year. A popular break in the afternoon is for coffee—naturally, since Costa Rica is a major producer of the beans.

Arts and Entertainment

The National Symphony Orchestra and the National Dance Company perform seasonally in San José. Theater groups work in Spanish, but occasionally plays are produced in English. American movies are popular and, unlike many countries, they're usually shown in the original English with Spanish subtitles, rather than being dubbed. The tickets cost about half what you'd pay in the States. American newspapers such as *USA Today* and the *New York Times* are widely available. In addition, the English-language paper *Tico Times* is published in San José specifically for the English-speaking population.

Outdoor Life and Sports

National parks and nature preserves are a big part of Costa Rica's splendor, and they have done well to protect the country's flora and fauna. Visit the Rain Forest Aerial Tram and view the waterfalls, orchids, and amazing variety of colorful birds from above. The beaches and barrier reef offer some of the best snorkeling in the Caribbean.

Soccer, called *fútbol,* is the national sport, popular with amateur and professional players and spectators. Baseball, basketball, swimming, and tennis are also popular, along with a wide variety of other sports. Golf is a sport of the so-called wealthy, which includes American retirees who, even if they've moved here for the low cost, usually have more income than the average Costa Rican.

Shopping

The largest shopping areas are located where the majority of the people live, near San José. Supermarkets have a wide range of foods, and leading chains stock some North American brands but these are extremely high in price compared to local products.

Clothing is not necessarily a good value; it's expensive and not always of high quality. It's difficult to find a good selection of sizes, especially for North Americans who tend to be larger than native Costa Ricans.

Social Life

Costa Rica has a well-organized network of North Americans who reside here and have developed social organizations, most of which meet in San José. The English-language *Tico Times* is a handy reference for groups and their meeting times and places. Free seminars that share tips on health care, property ownership, and other topics of interest to new residents are held every month at the Hotel Irazú.

The local people in Costa Rica are friendly and are accustomed to American tourists and expatriates. If you make an effort, you will make friends. As in many Hispanic cultures, the daily customs here are more traditional, polite, and relatively formal. People use professional titles and *Señor* or *Señora* rather than first names until they're well acquainted. People tend to be more formal in dress, especially in San José. American retirees may be more casual overall, but they save shorts and other beachwear for the seaside.

WHERE TO LIVE IN COSTA RICA

The majority of retirees settle in the capital city initially, and most of them stay there or in the nearby suburbs. Some, however, head to the coast.

San José

The capital and largest city is San José, and the majority of the native population lives in or near it. They're doing so to be near their jobs, but foreign retirees settle here as well. The main reason is that San

José provides access to the range of restaurants, shops, parks, entertainment, and social life that retirees plan to enjoy.

The University of Costa Rica, the American–Costa Rican Cultural Center, and other universities are located in the eastern suburb of San Pédro. Those cultural advantages, plus an array of good housing, make this section of the city popular with both natives and expatriate Americans. Ciudad Caríari, east of the city, also offers a wider choice of new homes.

Many retirees choose some of the more elegant residential suburbs farther outside San José, such as Escazu, west of the city. The area features a full complement of services for daily living, including shops of all types, restaurants, and entertainment plus the Costa Rica Country Club. Housing developments include townhouses and individual homes at prices that are still reasonable.

English-speaking families often reside in the neighborhoods of Caríari, Los Arcos, and Bosques de Doña Rosa (all part of the Hotel and Club Caríara Resort) since one of the best English-language schools in the country, the Costa Rican Academy is located there.

Coastal Living
Though the coasts are less populated with retirees, those who prefer beachside living have several choices. The more popular coast for retirement living is along the Pacific side. Retirement communities are well established here, offering comfortable amenities and a ready-made batch of North American playmates.

The Caribbean coast is less expensive than the Pacific side, but there are reasons: It's more remote and it is hotter and more humid. The provincial capital and port city of Puerto Limón is located on the Caribbean coast, however. Just three hours' drive from San José, Puerto Limón is a lively city, which has attracted its own large community of expatriates. The other side of the coin is that the city is crowded and has a higher crime rate than other areas. Additional Caribbean coast options are the smaller villages south of Puerto Limón, such as Cahuita, Manzanillo, and Puerto Viejo de Limón.

> **TICO TIME**
>
> If you're a Type-A personality with a ceaseless desire to check your watch, don't come to Costa Rica. The pace is slow and punctuality is a word little understood. A small store or business may say they open at 9:00 A.M., but if the owner oversleeps, hey, 9:45 is OK with them!

SETTING UP HOUSE

An array of apartments, townhouses, and individual houses are available in San José and the suburbs. Larger homes tend to be located in the suburbs and often have separate maid's quarters. Since petty crime is a concern in Costa Rica, garages are welcomed as a security measure against theft and break-ins.

Most housing is roomier than you'll find in European countries. Parquet flooring is common, but central heating is not. In a country with eternal spring (but rainy seasons), most homes have porches or patios that are covered or enclosed.

Finding a Rental

Furnished or unfurnished houses and apartments are available, though unfurnished accommodations are easier to find. You may have to supply your own large appliances. Many unfurnished apartments and homes do not include a stove and refrigerator in the rental. Furnished accommodations do include appliances but may not include small appliances, linens, and such. A roomy apartment or small house will cost $500 a month or less.

Leases are usually for three years, and rent is paid in advance. At leasing you'll pay a month's rent and a security deposit, which is usually equivalent to a month's rent.

The English-language publications, *Tico Times* and *Costa Rica Today*, are excellent places to start looking for a rental. If you can manage

Spanish, you may find that local papers such as *La Nación* target locals and thus have lower prices than ads to Americans.

Buying a Home

The low prices in Costa Rica will soon tempt you to buy property. However, be aware that some of those low advertised prices of $40,000 are not for the type of place that most North American retirees would find to their liking. Most expats pay $100,000 or so for more amenities, like running water. I josh, but not overly. Just be sure to check that impulse to buy, and rent first to try out the location and get a better feel for the housing market. If you decide to purchase a home, talk with people already living there to see whom they would recommend as a real estate agent. There are many fly-by-night agents, and you'll want a professional. When you find a property that interests you, hire a lawyer to review the contract and do a title search.

Utilities and Infrastructure

Costa Rica has most of the amenities you're looking for, though they may not all be quite as efficient as what you're accustomed to in the United States.

Water: Water is purified and safe in San José and most other cities. In rural areas, if you're not sure of the quality, choose bottled water.

Electricity: Electrical current is 110–120 volts, 60 hertz, the same as in North America. Plugs are also the same so you can use appliances from the States. However, the electricity is unreliable so you'll want surge protectors for sensitive electronic equipment.

Communications: The telecommunications system is modern and the Internet is in use here, but cyberspace hasn't found its way into the general community.

Time Zone: Costa Rica operates on U.S. Central Time. The country does not observe daylight savings time.

Weights and Measures: The metric system is used in Costa Rica.

MOVING PLANS

Although North American appliances will work in Costa Rica, any of them that don't arrive with you on the plane must go through customs. You won't need air conditioners, but you might appreciate a small electric heater to take off the chill at night. Don't bring your car. Not only will you have to ship it, the customs and other charges are so extravagantly expensive that it's better to sell yours in North America and purchase a new or used one in Costa Rica.

PAPERWORK AND RESIDENCE RULES

Costa Rica puts out the welcome mat for retirees. You can live in Costa Rica for up to six months a year on a free tourist visa. If you want to live in the country longer, you can apply for resident status. The requirements are many but not particularly complicated. Among other things, you'll need a copy of your passport, birth certificate, marriage certificate (if applicable), application form, a police statement of good conduct from the States, and several passport-size photos. You must have at least $600 a month in income from a pension or retirement plan, and the funds must be converted into colónes at a government bank. Are you an early retiree with no pension yet? You can enter on a *rentista* program by showing an outside source of income that generates at least $1,000 a month.

After two years under these temporary resident programs, you can apply for permanent residency, which has few restrictions; you can even work if you care to. To obtain residency, health tests are required, including blood, lung, and HIV tests. These must be performed in Costa Rica. If you want to start a business, you can also qualify as a resident based on your investment in the country. If you reside in Costa Rica permanently for five years, you can apply for citizenship. This does not cause you to lose your U.S. citizenship.

One group that can help you settle in is the Association of Residents of Costa Rica. They provide advice, documents, and contacts; recommend lawyers, real estate firms, and other professionals; and generally help newcomers in countless ways. A provisional membership of $60 enables you to use the association's services when applying for residency.

Contact the organization at Apartado 1191-1007, Centro Colon, San José; Phone: (506) 233-8068; Fax: (506) 233-1152.

Pets

Domestic pets, including dogs and cats, can enter Costa Rica, but you must submit the proper paperwork and ensure that your pet meets the country's health requirements. Your animal will need an official International Health Certificate, which must be certified by a Costa Rican Consulate. Your local veterinarian can provide the official paperwork that ensures your animal is healthy and is up-to-date on the required vaccinations. Your animal's shots must be more than 35 days old, but less than 180 days old before departure. To ensure that there are no problems with your pet's official entry, contact the nearest consulate as soon as you know you're going to Costa Rica and request all forms and the most current regulations.

GETTING THERE AND GETTING AROUND

You'll probably arrive in Costa Rica at the international Juan Santamaria airport, which is ten miles northwest of San José. Costa Rica Airlines/LACSA, Aero Costa Rica, and major international carriers serve Costa Rica from the United States and Europe. Small domestic aircraft provide transportation within the country. Buses are inexpensive and the system is extensive, being the most common form of transportation within and between cities. Taxis are relatively inexpensive when compared to those in North American cities.

Driving

If you live in San José, you can use public transportation, but you may still want a car for travel in the countryside. You can import your car to Costa Rica, but you'll pay a heavy tariff and surcharges. Between the hassle and the fees, it's easier to simply purchase a car in Costa Rica. In fact, if you intend to drive outside the San José area, you may want a rugged, four-wheel-drive vehicle. Auto insurance is mandatory and must be purchased from the National Insurance Institute, which is run by the government.

You can drive on a valid U.S. driver's license for the first three months, then you must have a Costa Rican license. Another option is to use an International Driving Permit. You're also required to have your passport with you when driving. Seat belts are required for the driver and front-seat passenger.

Drivers are independent souls (often literally since Costa Rica has one of the world's highest accident rates), who sometimes seem to obey their own set of traffic rules, which may not be the ones posted. Drive defensively and, even when there's not another car in sight, be cautious since roads are often rutted and pocked with potholes.

The Costa Rican Automobile Association offers emergency road service and is affiliated with AAA in the United States. For more information on driver's licenses, contact Dirección de Transporte Automotor, Avenida 18 Calle 5, San José; Phone: (506) 227-2188.

MANAGING YOUR MONEY

Remember that $600 a month you had to prove as income to become a resident *pensionado*? Yes, you can live on it. The average Costa Rican family manages on less than half that. In reality, you'll want to budget more than that. You should live comfortably on $18,000 to $24,000 a year. Housing costs are rising in San José (hmmm, those Americans are increasing the demand). However, utility bills are next to nothing since the weather requires neither heating nor air conditioning.

You'll need colónes in Costa Rica, but U.S. currency is also accepted in some areas. Checks are relatively new in banking here and are not accepted as readily as in the States. Most people use cash. If you need to exchange dollars for colónes, Banco Central de Costa Rica has a currency exchange office at the San José International Airport. Or simply withdraw cash from an ATM that accepts your network, such as Cirrus. Most banks have them. Major credit cards are accepted in Costa Rica, though some merchants may add a surcharge to purchases. You'll find state-owned banks and private banks in Costa Rica as well as some international banks.

Taxes

If you live in Costa Rica for a few months, you can forget about filing a tax return there. However, if you live in Costa Rica for more than six months in the tax year, you are considered a resident and must file a tax return. You will pay taxes on Costa Rican income that exceeds 111,000 colónes, about $400. The tax rate ranges from 10 to 25 percent depending on various deductions, salary ranges, and whether or not you are self-employed.

A 15 percent sales tax is levied on several types of merchandise, excluding some basic necessities, services, and real estate. Imports are liable for a 1 percent surcharge except for medicines. A consumption tax ranges from 5 to 75 percent on imported products. The tax on vehicles is among the highest at 45 percent. You'll pay property taxes in Costa Rica, but housing is low-cost and so are the taxes, usually about 1.25 percent of assessed value. There is no capital gains tax on real estate or securities.

STAYING HEALTHY AND SAFE

Costa Rica's health standards are among the highest in Central America, and in some areas it matches that of the United States—but not in all. Though water is often purified in the large towns, hotels, and some individual homes, you may prefer to drink well-known brands of bottled water. If you're in a rural area and really in doubt, then use bottled water for ice and brushing your teeth as well. The heat, sun, and insects may present problems so be prepared with sunscreen and insect repellent.

Costa Rica's health care system is one of the best in Central America, at prices that seem too good to be true. San José offers the most and best choices for medical care, including the Clínica Biblica or Clínica Católica; in other areas you'll need to look harder for good medical choices. Many of Costa Rica's medical professionals speak English and received their training in the United States. Ask for a list of English-speaking doctors and dentists at the U.S. Embassy.

Medicare does not cover you overseas, but the Caja Costarricense de Seguro Social, which is Costa Rica's state-sponsored network of hospitals and clinics, is available to foreign residents and visitors as well as to locals. You can join by paying a small monthly fee based on your income. An alternative is to buy health insurance from the state Instituto de Seguro Nacional, which offers private care through more than two hundred doctors, hospitals, labs, and pharmacies. Even if you opt for private care, you may be surprised at how low the costs are. It's estimated that surgery here costs 60 to 70 percent less than in the United States.

If you need specific prescription drugs, bring them with you. Common drugs are available, but certain brands are not.

Security

From a personal safety standpoint, Costa Rica is relatively safe. However, you should take normal precautions such as avoiding remote locations. And if the low cost of living allows you to live extremely well here, don't flaunt it in public with money, expensive jewelry, and fancy electronic gear.

Unemployment has not hit pickpockets so watch your cash, credit cards, and passport. Don't leave valuables on view in a car. Break-ins and car thefts are on the rise so most people insist on a garage or well-fenced and locked area for overnight parking.

FOR MORE DETAILS

Below are some resources to help you further investigate a long-term stay in Costa Rica.

Official Sources

Costa Rica Consulates General

Atlanta
1870 The Exchange, Suite 100
Atlanta, GA 30339
Phone: (770) 951-7025

Chicago
185 N. Wabash Avenue, Suite 1123
Chicago, IL 60601
Phone: (312) 263-2772

Los Angeles
1605 West Olympic Blvd., Suite 400
Los Angeles, CA 90015
Phone: (213) 380-7915

Miami
1600 N.W. Le Jeune Road, Suite 102
Miami, FL 33126
Phone: (305) 871-7487

New Orleans
World Trade Center Building
2 Canal Street, Suite 2334
New Orleans, LA 70130
Phone: (504) 581-6800

New York
80 Wall Street, Suite 718
New York, NY 10005
(212) 509-3066

Tampa
2200 Barker Road
Tampa, FL 33605
Phone: (813) 248-6741

Costa Rica Embassy
2114 S Street, NW
Washington, DC 20008
Phone: (202) 234-2945
Fax: (202) 265-4795

U.S. Embassy
Apartado 920-1200
Pavas, San José
Phone: (506) 220-3939
Fax: (506) 232-7944

Tourism and Resident Sources

**Association of Residents
of Costa Rica**
Apartado 1191-1007
Centro Colon, San José
Phone: (506) 233-8068
Fax: (506) 233-1152

**Costa Rica
Tourist Board**
Phone: (800) 343-6332
U.S. infoline: (800) 343-6332

**Oficina de Turismo
(Tourism Office)**
Apartado 777
1000 San José
Phone: (506) 223-1733
Fax: (506) 225-1452

Internet Connections

Costa Rica Tourist Board
www.tourism-costarica.com

Costa Rica Travel
www.costarica.com

Embassy of Costa Rica
www.costarica.com/embassy

World Travel Guide
www.wtgonline.com/country/cr/gen.html

Background Reading

Choose Costa Rica for Retirement
by John Howells
The Globe Pequot Press, 2000

The Costa Rica Handbook
by Christopher P. Baker
Avalon Travel Publishing, 1999

Living Overseas in Costa Rica
by Robert Johnston
Living Overseas Books, 2000

**The New Golden Door to Retirement
and Living in Costa Rica**
by Christopher Howard
Costa Rica Books, 2000

**Your Guide to Retiring to Mexico,
Costa Rica and Beyond**
by Shelley Emling
Avery Penguin Putnam, 1996

12

Honduras

In many ways Honduras is paradise lost. It's off the tourist track and not yet discovered by most travelers and retirees. That's the good and the bad news because, unlike areas of Mexico or Costa Rica in which North Americans have created a comfortable infra-

Highlights

- Scenic beauty
- Inexpensive lifestyle
- Sailing, diving, and fishing paradise

structure, the retiree in Honduras has to be a more independent sort. Honduras is not (yet) for the masses.

Even Americans who enjoy coming here for the peace and quiet will admit that Honduras is often better chosen as a place for part-time retirement. It's a great place to zone out on the beach, but you might eventually want a few more activities in your daily life. Retirees often return to the States periodically to enjoy more entertainment options and variety. But if you are looking for gorgeous beaches, astounding natural beauty, a warm climate, and an amazingly inexpensive lifestyle relatively close to the United States, then this is your spot.

THE BASICS

Honduras has a democratic government, with a more open society and less class structure than most of its Latin American neighbors. As with any developing country, the infrastructure and amenities are still unevenly distributed. The available services vary depending on the town and its tourist attractions. Some places barely meet adequate standards while others meet American expectations, specifically in the resort communities built for tourists.

The scenic beauty is expressed in diverse ways, from beach vistas to mountain landscapes to abundant agricultural lands. These riches, along with the Mayan ruins in Cobán and coral reef skin-diving off the Islas de la Bahía on the Caribbean, attract visitors. However, it's the lack of major tourism in Honduras that attracts those independent-minded Americans who choose to stay.

The country is bordered on the west by Guatemala, on the south by El Salvador, and on the east and southeast by Nicaragua. Numerous archaeological sites attest to the rich Mayan heritage in Honduras. The Spanish also colonized the country. Today, the 5.5 million people who live in Honduras represent an ethnic mix of native Indian, Spanish, and other nationalities. The majority of the populace is Roman Catholic.

For the most part, Honduras subsists on an agricultural economy. A third of the land is farmland, and the main crop is and always has been bananas. American companies have established their branches and business interests. Over the years other exports, including coffee, citrus fruits, beef, cotton, and wood, have been added to the economy. Today the urban population is increasing, especially in the capital of Tegucigalpa and in the industrial city of San Pedro Sula.

WHAT'S IN A NAME?

Tegucigalpa (pronounced phonetically tay-goo-see-gahl-pah) was originally named "silver mountain" by the Spanish who discovered it. The full name is a bit of a tongue twister, even to native Hondurans. They solve the problem by calling it "Tegus" for short.

Climate

A relaxed, outdoor lifestyle is a natural result of Honduras's weather. The climate is a tropical one and varies very little in temperature throughout the year. The specifics depend on altitude. The mountains are cooler; the coasts and valleys are very hot. It can be a tad cooler in the rainy season of January and February. March and April are the hottest months.

The capital, Tegucigalpa, sits in a sheltered valley with a springlike climate most of the year. January highs are in the mid 70s with lows in the mid 50s. April highs are in the low to mid 80s, and lows are in the 60s. Mountain areas are cooler, while the coastal islands, including the Bay Islands, are hotter throughout the year but enjoy ocean breezes.

Language

The official language of Honduras is Spanish. But American plantation interests have been here a long time so English is commonly spoken. The Hondurans have good feelings toward Americans and are willing to help out even if your Spanish is less than perfect. Three language schools in Copan Ruinas offer a unique chance to learn on-site with a one-to-one teacher to student ratio. The schools are the Ixbalanque Spanish School, the Guacamaya Spanish School, and the Copan Spanish School.

YOUR NEW LIFESTYLE

How will you fill your days? Here's an overview of activities and interests that are part of daily life in Honduras.

Food and Drink

The fishing areas of the north coast, including the Bay Islands, supply fresh red snapper, lobster, shrimp, and conch. Definitely try the conch stew and chowder. You won't be lacking for your hamburgers and steaks here either, thanks to the country's numerous cattle ranches. To go with your main dish, expect to have fried plantain or yucca, beans, cabbage, rice, cheese, or warm tortillas.

Restaurantes in cities and larger towns may serve a variety of haute cuisine. Local specialties served in small cafés will be less expensive. Town markets sell fresh local produce to take home for your own menus.

> We fit the description of Americans retiring in Honduras, but we are working harder than ever in one sense, with less stress from commuting, etc. We are developing a nine-acre piece of beachfront into a resort hotel and housing subdivision. Most gringos here have retired from their jobs. Some have a pension and do not need to work, but many have some project going.
>
> Bill and Cathy Service, Bay Islands

Arts and Entertainment

Popular Caribbean music includes the merengue, salsa, and reggae; American music is also heard frequently. Traditional "punta" music is based on a strong drumbeat, with singing, dancing, and conch shell blowing added. In main cities, modern movie theaters feature first-run films. U.S. cable television is available in main cities or via satellite TV in areas not served by cable. Honduras has various museums, most of which showcase the local flora and fauna. Sandy Bay on Roatan is a cultural center that includes the Roatan Museum, the Institute of Marine Sciences with dolphin shows, the Carambola Gardens, and Tropical Treasures Bird Park.

Outdoor Life and Sports

Water sports are big in Honduras. Sailing and fishing—both lake and deep-sea fishing—are popular. The barrier reef is the site of excellent scuba diving and snorkeling.

Soccer is the national sport of Honduras, and the national soccer stadium is in Tegucigalpa. The baseball stadium can also be found there. Honduras is a good place for hiking, but if you're into more civilized sports, country clubs have swimming pools, tennis courts, and golf courses.

Shopping

Shopping malls and supermarkets are located near the main residential areas and offer ample parking. There you'll find products similar to those you're accustomed to in the States. Shop local markets for the freshest produce, fish, and meats. Native crafts to collect include wood carvings, palm mats and baskets, leatherwork, and ceramics. Prices are fixed in large stores, but when shopping at a local outdoor market feel free to barter.

Most shops close for lunch; they are usually open Monday through Friday from 8:00 A.M. to 12:00 P.M. and from 1:30 P.M. to 6:00 P.M. Stores often stay open all day on Saturday but may close earlier at 5:00 P.M.

Social Life

Most of the social life in Honduras revolves around religious celebrations and local festivals plus the casual socializing provided by common interests in diving and sports. Upscale developments for tourists offer restaurants, bars, and discos, where friends can gather.

WHERE TO LIVE IN HONDURAS

Below are a few areas to consider when looking for your ideal location in Honduras.

Tegucigalpa

Tegucigalpa is the capital and largest city in Honduras. As such it offers the most amenities for daily life. The weather's ideal too. The city is located in a mountain valley in Honduras's central highlands, with warm, springlike weather year-round.

Tegucigalpa is a modern city, but fortunately it has retained much of its colonial charm from earlier days as a mining center. Parks and historic architecture dot the original city center. The city began as two separate cities, Tegucigalpa and Comayaguela, which grew together, but they're very different in personality. Comayaguela offers cheaper housing, but there's a reason: It's more unsavory and to be avoided after dark. You'd do better to reside in the Tegucigalpa side, which has more charm and better neighborhoods.

The business center is at Boulevard Morazan. That's where you'll find the most upscale shops and restaurants. Five universities are also located downtown. From Tegucigalpa you can take excursions throughout Honduras to old Spanish towns and nature parks.

The Bay Islands

The Bay Islands consist of three islands: Roatan, Guanaja, and Utila. The islands used to rely on fishing plus banana and pineapple plantations, but these days the tourists help support them. Since this area of Honduras is the most highly developed with modern amenities, the Bay Islands are most frequented by Americans. The destruction of 1998's Hurricane Mitch hit this area's tourism industry hard and, in fact, devastated much of the country. However, the area is starting to renew itself. The islands can be accessed by air, and Roatan and Utila can be reached by ferry service. The daily ferry from La Ceiba to Roatan takes less than two hours.

Roatan is the largest and most developed of the three Bay Islands. A paved road connects the most important communities, including Coxen Hole, French Harbour, Sandy Bay, and various resort developments. Roatan is lush, rather mountainous, and a diver's paradise. The island is surrounded by a barrier reef teeming with aquatic life.

Roatan has a variety of furnished apartments and resort homes for rent. An upscale one-bedroom apartment on the beach was advertised for $1,200 if rented monthly. One of the main housing communities is the gated Palmetto Bay, with its own white sand beach, pool, boardwalks through landscaped gardens, and a restaurant. Due to foreign money, these homes are on the high end for Honduras, with prices from the low $100,000s to $300,000 or more. A three-bedroom, two-bath home, completely furnished with stunning views, was advertised for $195,000. A two-bedroom, two-and-a-half-bath cottage, fully furnished in a residential resort community on the beach was going for $128,000. Other upscale developments include Parrot Tree Plantation and the Mayan Princess.

The smallest Bay Island, Utila, is closest to the mainland, just a fifteen-minute flight or short ferry trip over. It's known for its lovely beaches and superb diving.

Guanaja has some high-end resort hotels, but the island is not very developed.

> Right now, Roatan does not offer the luxury that you may be used to in North America. There are no Wal-Marts or Home Depots. What it does offer is a different lifestyle. Most people fall in love with the island and its way of life. You can still be connected with the "real world and Wall Street" if you want, but you get to choose.
>
> Matt Halliday, Roatan

San Pedro Sula

The second-largest city in Honduras, San Pedro Sula, is a bustling commercial center, much of it involved in the business of bananas. The city is located in the northern part of Honduras, about 150 miles from Tegucigalpa. The main entry point is San Pedro Sula International Airport, with flights from several spots throughout the United States.

Despite its agricultural leanings, San Pedro Sula is a main commercial center and a cosmopolitan city with a symphony orchestra, multiplex movie theaters, international restaurants, and excellent shopping. The cathedral, built in the relatively recent 1950s, is the city's central highlight, but markets on the northwest and southeast of town are popular for shopping trips. The Guamilito market near the central plaza has a wide selection of Honduran handicrafts.

Because San Pedro Sula is smaller and less populous, it tends to be less expensive than other areas. Quiet residential neighborhoods in the city provide housing that's unbelievably reasonable. A four-bedroom, three-and-a-half-bath home, completely furnished, was offered for $125,000. An air-conditioned three-bedroom, two-bath home close to schools and shopping was offered for $55,000.

Copan Ruinas

The quaint town of Copan Ruinas is named for the Mayan ruins of Copan nearby. The ruins are the number one tourist draw in Honduras, attracting thousands of people every year. Tourism also means that there's a good road leading to San Pedro Sula, which is the closest city three hours away and the location of the region's main airport. Bus service connects Copan Ruinas with San Pedro Sula, and some small planes fly directly to Copan Ruinas from Guatemala City.

> It [Copan Ruinas] met all our criteria. Small town, nice climate, few mosquitoes, no crime, three hours—a reasonable drive—to San Pedro Sula, where there is shopping and all services.
>
> Howard Rosenzweig, Copan Ruinas

You'll want to go to San Pedro Sula for major shopping since Copan Ruinas is not particularly well stocked with shops. One American entrepreneur has opened La Casa de Café, the only bed-and-breakfast in Copan Ruinas, and he raves about the friendly people, low crime, and cobblestone streets. Prices here are much less expensive than land on the beach or the Bay Islands, and a small expatriate community has already bought properties here.

SETTING UP HOUSE

You'll find an array of tourist hotels and furnished apartments for short-term living while you test the waters in Honduras. For long-term rentals, individual homes will usually be of brick and masonry, often with inner patios. Apartment complexes are also available.

Finding a Rental

Modern apartment complexes in Honduras offer one- to three-bedroom units that are fully equipped with appliances and are centrally located. You can also rent an individual home in residential areas. Costs in

Honduras, outside the tourist resorts, are what they were in Mexico before the influx of Americans populated many of those resort areas and colonial towns. You can find an unfurnished one- or two-bedroom apartment for as little as $250 a month. A basic furnished apartment starts renting at $300 and up. Beware that prices in the top tourist spots on Roatan will be much higher. Furnished one-bedroom villas on the beach are advertised for vacationers at $500 a week or $950 a week for a three-bedroom unit with a full-time housekeeper. Do the math and you could get sticker shock at the $2,000- to almost $4,000-a-month cost. Fortunately you won't need to pay those prices if you shop around for residential rentals instead of glitzy tourist lodgings.

Buying a Home

Foreigners are permitted to own property in Honduras, but be especially wary if you decide to buy property here. Make sure that the person selling the property is really entitled to convey the title to it. They must have a *Dominio Pleno* (General Warranty Deed) that conveys property to a private citizen. Much of the property in Honduras is government land that has been provided for farming or building but which will revert to the government later.

Be careful about purchasing in coastal areas and on the Bay Islands. The Honduras constitution restricts or outright prohibits foreigners from owning land in coastal and border areas, but certain other laws permit it with restrictions. The whole situation is up in the air. Be careful about taking the word of real estate agents with something to gain by selling you a property. Before deciding to buy, check title rights and your right as an American to purchase the property. Also contact the U.S. Embassy in Tegucigalpa for their current recommendations on the legal implications of purchasing property.

That said, Honduras presents opportunities to purchase property at prices that Americans will find unbelievably low. Even the property taxes are low, ranging from 0.3 to 3 percent a year. An acre of land can be purchased for as little as $5,000. Of course prices vary widely. Beach lots and property on the more tourist-oriented Bay Islands will run much higher with half-acre, ocean-view lots priced from $38,000 to $57,000. On the mainland a home or condo can be found for $40,000 to $60,000 and up. Again, the Bay Islands would cost much more.

Multiple listing services do not exist in Honduras so you'll need to speak to several different real estate agents to review their offerings. If you don't speak fluent Spanish or the agent doesn't speak English, find a reliable person to translate. As in any place where you don't understand the system, be cautious. Real estate agents in Honduras often work solely with foreign buyers, and some may not be trustworthy. Check them out and look at enough properties to assure yourself that the prices they quote are not inflated.

Be sure the property has a clear title. In fact, property titles should be double-checked. In the past squatters have laid claim to properties owned by U.S. citizens. One real estate firm in Honduras with agents who speak English is Re/Max Bay Islands, French Harbour, Roatan Island, Republic of Honduras, Central America; Phone: (504) 455-5379; Fax: (504) 455-5226.

You cannot arrange title or deed insurance in Honduras so retain a lawyer you trust to advise you and to investigate any property you're interested in buying. Get an estimate from the lawyer before retaining him, but expect to pay about 1 percent of the purchase price for legal services.

To finalize the property purchase, you'll work with a *notario,* or notary, who is the equivalent of a Honduran attorney and performs most of the services involved in a real estate transaction. Don't sign anything without first having an accredited attorney review it carefully. (Some people who have completed law school can open a legal office but are not accredited.) Also, the *notario,* who may be knowledgeable about Honduran law, may not know the ramifications of you, as an American, making the purchase. Ask the American Embassy for a list of reliable lawyers.

Utilities and Infrastructure

Living conditions can be comfortable in Honduras, with certain exceptions. This is, after all, still a developing nation.

Water: Do not drink the tap water. Do not even brush your teeth with it or use ice cubes made from it. As in other developing areas, use bottled, boiled, or otherwise purified water to avoid disease. Some fresh water is provided via roof catchments into cisterns.

Electricity: Electricity varies in Honduras at 110, 120, or 220 volts, 60 hertz.

Communications: The phone system is relatively modern; Celtel is the main network provider for mobile phones. Cellular phones operate on the same standard as in the United States. Internet service is available, and two main providers are Hondudata and NetSys. Cyber cafés can be found in the main towns. Postal service lacks the efficiency you may expect. Incoming mail from the United States rarely reaches its destination.

Time Zone: Honduras is on Central Standard Time, which is six hours behind Greenwich Mean Time. The country does not observe daylight savings time.

Weights and Measures: Honduras uses the metric system.

MOVING PLANS

You can stay up to ninety days in Honduras simply by getting a visa and having it renewed twice. You'll want to rent furnished property for such a short stay. If you decide to reside in Honduras longer and have the proper residence visa, you can import all your personal property free of charge. This may include an automobile and the personal property of your dependents as well.

PAPERWORK AND RESIDENCE RULES

To visit Honduras, your passport should be valid for at least six months past your date of arrival in the country. You don't need a visa to visit Honduras for up to thirty days, and the permission can be renewed through the Honduran Immigration Service for a total of up to ninety days. If you don't want to reside full-time in Honduras and plan to travel outside the country often, you can just leave the country; when you return you can stay another thirty days without a visa, with renewals for up to three months.

Honduras is encouraging retirees to settle there. To stay longer than three months, apply for a residence visa at a Honduran Embassy or Consulate. You'll need to show a passport valid for at least one year from the date of your application, a birth certificate, a certificate of good health, a good-conduct reference from your U.S. police department, three passport photos, and proof of financial independence. Your income must be $600 or more a month if you're applying as a *resident pensionado,* i.e., retiree, and $1,000 per month if your status will be *resident rentista,* with income from a foreign source. After three consecutive years of residence, you can apply for Honduran citizenship.

Pets

Rover does not face any quarantine or import permit requirement in Honduras. Just make sure that he has a valid rabies shot given less than twelve months prior to entry into the country. He'll also need a current health certificate. If you plan to bring a pet, check with the Honduran Embassy before traveling to ensure that you have the most current regulations.

GETTING THERE AND GETTING AROUND

Honduras has four international airports, one each in Tegucigalpa, San Pedro Sula, La Ceiba, and Roatan. The principal airlines serving the country are American, Continental, Copa, Lacsa, Taca, and Isleña Airlines. Be aware that Honduran airlines are under scrutiny by the U.S. Federal Aviation Administration, which categorizes Honduras's civil aviation authority as not meeting international aviation safety standards.

Local bus services are inexpensive, and they run in and between major areas. However, avoid traveling at night. There are very few railroads in Honduras. La Ceiba on the north coast is one of the few areas with rail lines.

Driving

A network of paved highways connects major cities and resort areas in Honduras. Some of the roads are among the best in Central America, but many are in bad condition due to poor maintenance and the aftermath of Hurricane Mitch. Many secondary and private roads are simply dirt-packed. It doesn't take much to imagine their condition during the rainy season! In fact, flooding and mudslides can adversely affect even major highways at times. Throughout the country, some bridges, washed out by Hurricane Mitch, still present problems during bad weather.

If you plan to drive a long distance, learn the route and drive only during daylight hours. Roads are inadequately marked and you could be a potential target for crime. The U.S. Embassy advises against car and bus travel after dark. Be careful driving near border areas at any time, even high noon, to avoid any armed bandits in those sections.

MANAGING YOUR MONEY

Living in Honduras is so inexpensive it's difficult to imagine what you will do with your money. You can dine out, enjoying a five-course meal for $10 to $15. To live in Honduras, a couple retiring there must prove they have a minimum income of $600 a month, though as an American you may want to live a bit more upscale so count on $1,000 a month for two people.

The monetary unit in Honduras is the Lempira, abbreviated Lp. However, the U.S. dollar is used in foreign commerce. Honduran banks and savings and loans are up to date with modern services, including credit card services. Some national banks are affiliated with international banks. Lloyds Bank serves the country, and Citibank has a local subsidiary called Banco de Honduras.

It's almost impossible to cash personal checks in Honduras. It's also difficult to transfer funds, especially in the Bay Islands where banking facilities are limited.

Taxes

Retirees to Honduras who live on foreign income, such as Social Security and pensions, do not pay income taxes on that income, regardless of the amount.

STAYING HEALTHY AND SAFE

To stay healthy in Honduras, be extra careful about what you eat and drink. As mentioned before, do not drink the tap water. Don't even open your mouth in the shower. Wash fruits and vegetables with an iodine solution. Dysentery and stomach parasites are common. Take precautions against malaria in coastal areas. Typhoid and tetanus vaccinations are recommended.

Over twenty-five hospitals and clinics provide Honduras with adequate health care, some even meet high standards. Private hospitals are a better choice than the public hospitals, which are lower in quality. Complex surgery can be performed in Honduras, but many retirees who need care for serious maladies, such as cardiac conditions, return to the United States for care in Miami, New Orleans, or Houston, which are each about two hours away by air. Returning to the United States also means you can use Medicare, which does not cover retirees out of the States. (For other insurance options, see Chapter 25.)

Most Honduras physicians have been trained in the United States. A visit to the doctor costs about $5 to $10 and most expect an immediate cash payment. A private hospital room costs about $340 a day. Since Medicare will not cover retirees in Honduras, you'll need private health insurance.

Pharmacies in major towns use a rotating schedule to ensure that one establishment is open at all hours. Prescription drugs cost 50 to 90 percent less than in the United States, and many of them are available over the counter.

We do feel safe here, but there is petty thievery. Very little violent crime here, [but] unless you have a watchman, you may need to put bars on the windows. A good watchdog will do, and those living here year-round rarely get bothered. We have had no trouble for five and a half years.

Bill Service, Bay Islands

Security

The crime rate has traditionally been low in Honduras, but robberies and pickpocketing are rising. As in many countries, most of the crime occurs in the largest cities, in this case, Tegucigalpa and San Pedro Sula.

Outside of the major cities, you'll find it much more tranquil. Crime is low in the small towns. The U.S. State Department warns that cross-border bandit groups and antipersonnel mines exist near some border areas so it's not recommended that you drive in these areas or travel off the beaten path. In fact, some highway robbers have preyed on tourists coming from San Pedro Sula Airport. Some residents feel that the reports are exaggerated and overly cautious, and that actual problems are minimal. The best advice is to be aware of your surroundings, learn your way around, and know enough Spanish to be familiar with the news reports. If in doubt, err on the side of safety. Generally, Honduras is reputed to be among the most peaceful and tranquil of the Central American nations.

FOR MORE DETAILS

Below are some resources to help you further investigate a long-term stay in Honduras.

Official Sources

Embassy of Honduras
3007 Tilden Street, NW
Washington, DC 20008
Phone: (202) 966-7702
Email: embhondu@aol.com

U.S. Embassy
Avenida La Paz, Apartado Postal No. 3453
Tegucigalpa, Honduras
Phone: (504) 236-9320
Fax: (504) 236-9037

Internet Connections

Honduras News
www.honduras.com

Honduras Resources
www.honduras-resources.com

Honduras This Week
www.marrder.com/htw/

Information Guide
www.hondurasnet.com

Roatan Online
www.stic.net/roatan/roatanonline

Background Reading

Live Well in Honduras
by Frank Ford
Avalon Travel Publishing, 1998

Moon Handbooks: Honduras
by Chris Humphrey
Avalon Travel Publishing, 2000

13

Mexico

When we first explored Mexico with an eye on retiring there, we were amazed. We had known that Americans were retiring south of the border, but never had we envisioned the size and impact that the expatriate communities were having on the country, especially in Guadalajara, beside Ajijic's Lake Chapala, and in the artistic town of San Miguel de Allende.

Highlights

- Low cost of living
- Convenient to the United States
- Active expatriate community
- Mayan and traditional Spanish culture

Of course, when we thought about it we realized the benefits: an extraordinarily low cost of living, proximity to the United States, lovely weather year-round, and a fascinating culture to explore. And as a second language, Spanish is the easiest to master.

Mexico may not be everyone's enchilada. There are challenges and trade-offs to living there. Contemporary Mexico is not as modern as the United States, but the country is more advanced than most Americans imagine, especially in the areas where American retirees have settled. Among the low-cost options, Mexico is the closest to the United States, and hordes of American retirees have already prepared the way. Plus, the country offers a unique culture that combines aspects of Mayan and Spanish history. Whether you crave the cultural life of Guadalajara, the Old World style of a colonial village, or a seaside retreat, Mexico offers a choice for everyone.

THE BASICS

Mexico is located on the southernmost part of the North American continent, sharing borders with California, Arizona, and Texas. On the south are Guatemala and Belize, so Mexico literally forms a bridge between North and South America. The Pacific Ocean is on the west. On the east are the Caribbean Sea and the Gulf of Mexico. Mexico is about three times the size of Texas, but unlike Texas, it encompasses a wide range of geographic features from tropical jungles to cold volcanic mountain peaks to arid desert.

The country is strongly Roman Catholic, with 89 percent of the population belonging to the church. Six percent of the people profess

to be Protestant. Although Catholicism is integral to the Mexican culture in its holidays and beliefs, the government is secular. The constitution guarantees freedom of worship.

Climate

It's called "sunny Mexico" for a reason. Mexico is very dry, though some areas in the south and the Yucatan have more rainfall. In the highly populated inland areas the average temperatures hover nicely around the mid 70s year-round, with low humidity and moderate rainfall. In other words, it's most people's idea of the ideal climate. Winters tend to be drier and summers rainier farther south. Mexico City gets an hour of heavy rain almost every afternoon from April through July.

Language

You may manage just fine without knowing Spanish, provided you live in an area where American retirees have already made inroads. However, to feel truly at ease you'll do well to learn some of the language. At the very least, take an evening course or a cassette course before you leave home. Then take some lessons when you arrive to speed up your learning curve. If you're in the central area, the Instituto Míguel de Cervantes in Guanajuato offers a wide range of classes from novice to advanced. Contact the school at Apartado Postal #406, Guanajuato, Gto 36000 Mexico; Phone: (52) 473-2-80-69 or check their Web site at www.spanish-immersion.com. The Instituto Allende in San Miguel de Allende was begun by an American and has become one of the most famous Spanish language schools in the world. For information, contact Instituto Allende, Ancha de San Antonio #20, San Miguel de Allende, Gto 37700, Mexico; Phone: (52) 415-2-01-90; or check the Web site at www.instituto-allende.edu.mx.

Speaking of Web sites, a host of Spanish sites can help you learn and perfect your Spanish. The Tecla site, presented by the Spanish Embassy Education Office in association with London's Birkbeck College, offers superb Spanish texts and activities for intermediate to advanced students at www.cec-spain.org.uk/Pub/tecla.html.

YOUR NEW LIFESTYLE

How will you fill your days? Here's an overview of activities and interests that are part of daily life in Mexico.

Food and Drink

A typical Mexican menu includes *frijoles*—beans to you—with breakfast, lunch, and dinner. Don't despair, though, the more cosmopolitan areas offer everything from pizza to fine French cuisine. If you cook at home, you'll find a choice of fresh foods available at local markets for excellent prices. Especially the oranges. The fresh-squeezed juice is one of my all-time favorites and once got me through a case of the flu in fine form.

The biggest challenge to preparing food yourself will be to adapt to the water problem by learning to fix fruits and vegetables with care and using boiled or bottled water. It's a technique that retirees who live there have adopted, and they tell us that the system soon becomes second nature.

ORANGE JUICE BY THE SACK

Fresh-squeezed orange juice, sweet and delicious, is sold on street corners in small plastic bags tied at the top with a straw slipped in to sip from. It's a wobbly package to hold but it works, as long as you don't untie it!

Arts and Entertainment

Exuberant music, dancing, and extravagant costumes all come together on stage in Mexico's Ballet Folklorico. The extravaganza rivals the best Broadway productions and is not to be missed. The Ballet Folklorico company travels the world, but it's even better when seen at home in Guadalajara.

Fiestas are giant parties that range across the calendar, usually based on religious celebrations and historical events. Most are family oriented. One of the more unusual is the *Día de Los Muertos,* or Day of the Dead. It's often celebrated with skull-shaped candy and trips to the cemetery, where families picnic to "share" the day with long-gone relatives.

For English language reading, the major U.S. papers are sold in Mexico (though sometimes a day later). Various expatriate groups put out locally produced English-language newspapers. Many bookstores, including the Sanborn chain, stock English-language books.

Outdoor Life and Sports

Fútbol, the Spanish name for soccer, is closely followed in Mexico. Along the coasts, you can enjoy all the water sports, including sailing, swimming, snorkeling, scuba diving, and just plain reposing on the white sand beaches. Metropolitan and tourist areas offer a range of popular retirement sports, including golf and tennis.

A HEAD FOR GOOD LUCK

My husband bent down low, and the five-year-old girl, dressed in her best Easter finery, bopped him on the head with an egg. She giggled, and he thanked her before she skipped off. Of course, these are not your normal gooey or hard-boiled eggs. These have been carefully hollowed and stuffed with colorful confetti. So don't yell "Assault and battery" at Easter in Mexico. The crack on your skull doesn't hurt and supposedly brings you good luck.

Shopping

Many retirees will swear by their Mexican Wal-Mart for the basic necessities, but you'll find more interesting shopping in local markets and boutiques. Look for bargains on Mexican silver. In fact, it's difficult to find a place without a silver shop, especially in Guadalajara, where it seems the guards stand on every block protecting the jewelry stores!

Pottery, embroidered fabrics, brightly colored dolls, and textile paintings are all terrific buys and a cheery way to brighten your home.

Social Life

Newspapers, magazines, and social groups help the retiree get acquainted with the local lifestyle and residents. English-language publications include *The News, Guadalajara Reporter,* and *El Ojo Del Largo.* The American Society of Jalisco—Avenue San Francisco 3332, Colonia Chapalita, Guadalajara, Jalisco, Mexico; Phone: (52) 3-121-2395; Fax (52) 3-121-0887—holds get-togethers and offers Spanish and other classes. The American Library in San Miguel de Allende provides more than reading material; it's the social hub for Americans living in the town.

WHERE TO LIVE IN MEXICO

You've heard of Mexico City and many American expatriates live there, mostly for business or government interests. It's notably absent on this list, however. Despite its cultural amenities, it's difficult to imagine a retiree preferring Mexico City because of its pollution and congestion. There are many other choices that offer a better quality of life. One of the most popular areas in Mexico, the Colonial Heartland, is known for its variety of historic colonial towns and the sunny, springlike climate. The Colonial Heartland includes Guadalajara, San Miguel de Allende, and Guanajuato. If the beach is more your thing, there are two sides to seaside living in Mexico: the Pacific and the Caribbean. Take your pick.

Guadalajara and Environs

Guadalajara offers a more gracious, less crowded lifestyle than the capital, Mexico City. It's also generally safer, certainly less polluted, and offers a more temperate climate year-round. Guadalajara is a mecca for retirees since it offers a wide range of amenities and entertainment, while maintaining the traditional charm of a typical Mexican city with historic buildings and tree-lined parks. The outskirts are popular places with affordable housing, especially in the western part of the city.

South of Guadalajara are the towns of Ajijic and Lake Chapala. Though they're about an hour's drive from the city, retirees treat them as suburbs of Guadalajara, visiting the city often for shopping and entertainment. These quieter areas offer the opportunity to become part of a smaller community. Americans have become so common here that a wide range of groups meet for social events, theater, and bridge.

Prices are still amazingly low though they're increasing as the area gains popularity with Americans. In Lake Chapala, the average furnished rental house with two or three bedrooms goes for $600 to $700 a month.

A newly remodeled two-bedroom, two-bath home (one with Jacuzzi) with a living area, spacious kitchen, and screened-in terrace and garden with pool was listed for purchase at $139,000. New two-bedroom, two-bath condominiums in a gated community with pool and clubhouse were offered completely furnished right down to the toaster and cable TV for $83,000.

San Miguel de Allende

I almost hesitate to recommend San Miguel de Allende. Not because it's not a good location, but perhaps because it's too good. Thousands of American retirees and snowbirds have ballooned the population, making this a minisuburb of the States.

The town is a protected historic site, ensuring that the beautiful old buildings and charming central square retain their character. The arts thrive here as attested to by its dozens of art galleries. Of course, this is also home to the Instituto Allende, known for its superb art and Spanish language courses.

Guanajuato

An up-and-coming town that offers a charming alternative to San Miguel is Guanajuato. The town is defined by its river, the Rio Guanajuato, and its position on a hill, where narrow roads wind through and around the central area. As in San Miguel, Guanajuato is a university town, though here the school is more for the native population than for American retirees looking for extra courses.

Housing is more reasonable here than in San Miguel, not due to lack of charm but to a lesser influx of "rich" Americans. Unfortunately, the same effect is starting to be felt in Guanajuato as more Americans move in.

The Pacific Coast

The Pacific coast offers palm trees, lovely beaches, and the good weather to enjoy them year-round. Some areas are packed with tourists, but that doesn't mean you can't find your own spot of paradise. Mazatlán is a popular place with American retirees, so it's ideal for the person who wants a ready-made set of new friends who speak English. The area includes a variety of excellent choices in housing; prices are higher here, however, than in small, less popular areas.

Puerto Vallarta became famous when Elizabeth Taylor and Richard Burton's stayed there while filming *Night of the Iguanas,* but the town offers a lot more than Hollywood history. While the new section lacks charm, the old town has plenty of it plus reasonable prices. New planned developments with large houses and amenities are springing up in areas just outside Puerto Vallarta. Acapulco offers retirement living near the beach along with city attractions, and it's more affordable than you might think. For a more typical Mexican lifestyle, check out the many smaller towns along the coast, including San Blas and Boca de Tomatlán.

The Yucatan Peninsula

The Mexican Caribbean offers more up-to-date living, and higher prices to go with it because the area was developed with American wallets in mind. English is widely spoken there, and you can even use dollars. Cancun was created as a world-class resort from the ground up starting in 1970. It's one of the few areas in Mexico with a decent and safe water treatment system. You'll find white sand beaches, aqua seas, Mayan ruins, and lively entertainment. Of course, you'll also find that the scenery is obscured by high-rise hotels, condos, and time-share apartments.

Mérida and Valladolid are two towns that offer more historic character than the tourist-built resorts of Cancun. Mérida combines the charm of yesteryear with modern amenities, including an international airport. The town includes Colonial architecture, tree-lined streets, and green spaces. Valladolid is a colonial town. Either one will offer better value for housing than you'll find in Cancun. Even so, the Yucatan peninsula in general tends to be pricier than Mexico's inland areas.

SETTING UP HOUSE

Regulations in Mexico forbid foreigners to buy property within sixty-two miles of the Mexican border or thirty-one miles of the sea. Therefore, many retirees—especially snowbirds with the dream to live in a beach community—rent their accommodations rather than purchase property. Inland, however, the low prices in colonial Mexico often entice Americans to purchase property. If you're tempted, rent first in order to familiarize yourself with the area you've chosen before taking the major step of purchasing.

Finding a Rental

Mexico is accustomed to retirees landing here from the United States. You'll find a good choice of furnished rentals at prices that will make you believe in early retirement. Check the classified ads in the English-language papers, and in the local Spanish-language papers for even better deals. In areas heavily populated with expatriates, such as Lake Chapala, local stores often have bulletin boards packed with ads for rentals.

If you intend to stay for a long period, then you may want to find an unfurnished place and buy furnishings. Furniture isn't costly, and the accommodations and your monthly cost will be less overall. For the best deals, lock in your long-term deal before the snowbirds arrive in winter.

Leases are usually made for a year and require a cosigner. They must be based on pesos, not dollars. Rent is paid monthly in advance. A security deposit of one or two months' rent is common.

One tricky part of renting a property in Mexico is ensuring that you have phone service. It takes forever and a day to get a phone installed so if one's available it's usually advertised as an amenity. If you can't get a phone installed immediately, buy a cell phone. If you're renting a home, make sure it has a reliable source of water.

Buying a Home

Prices in Mexico encourage some Americans to purchase sooner than they otherwise might. It's always best to rent in an area first, then do your homework by studying the places you're most interested in. Talk to other retirees about their experiences there. Many Americans have purchased property in Mexico and are happy with the results. But recently some retirees in Baja found out the hard way that their long-term land leases were actually "owned" by other people. They were in danger of losing the homes they'd built.

You'll need more than one real estate agent to help in your search for property since multiple listing services do not thrive in Mexico. Some real estate agents are not certified so make sure that your real estate agent is reputable by asking for references from other expatriates. Get professional aid before purchasing property in Mexico. Have a builder or professional appraiser review the property before making the offer. Find a good attorney to help you understand the contracts and set up a will to protect your rights. Make sure any home you purchase has phone service and a reliable water supply.

Utilities and Infrastructure

Water: The water in Mexico is notorious and is the major concern of Americans who are considering living here. The solution: Just don't drink it. Bottled water is found throughout Mexico. In a few tourist areas, such as Cancun, the water plants are newer and designed for safe drinking. In other areas, expatriates report that it soon becomes a habit to purify or filter their water and to keep bottled water handy for drinking, brushing their teeth, and cooking.

Electricity: No difference here. Mexico delivers electricity at 110 volts, 60 hertz, which is the same as in the United States and Canada.

Communications: The telephone system in Mexico has greatly improved though it is still not as good as in the United States. Cell phones are popular, and this is a solution if you're without a phone at home (it takes eons to have one installed). A cell phone is also handy if you travel by car and need to call someone for assistance. If you already have a cell phone in the United States, you may be able to use it in Mexico but the roaming charges will make calls much more expensive. If you want to stay connected online, Internet service providers are available. Mail service is notorious for its inefficiency. It's highly unreliable so don't trust it for sending important mail and parcels; use international courier services or Mex-Post, an independent company. Discourage family and friends in the States from sending parcels and gifts; the packages will be subject to high duty and bureaucracy.

Time Zone: Most Mexican clocks are set six hours later than Greenwich Mean Time, the same as U.S. Central Standard Time. However, Baja California Sur, Sinaloa, and parts of Nayarit are an hour behind that, in Mountain Standard Time. Daylight savings time is in effect between April and October.

Weights and Measures: Mexico uses the metric system.

MOVING PLANS

You can tote your small electrical appliances to Mexico because the wall plugs, voltage, hertz, and broadcast system are identical to the rest of North America.

Cars are more expensive in Mexico than in the United States so Mexico strictly regulates their entry to prevent their illegal importation and sale. Recently, Mexico has even begun collecting deposits of up to $800 for U.S.-registered cars. If you're going to live in Mexico under an FMT or FM3 visa and maintain a U.S. or Canadian driver's license, you can bring in a car subject to special permission. Many expatriates just buy a new or used vehicle in Mexico. If you do, plan on air conditioning and ensure that the vehicle has the power to manage the high altitude of areas such as Mexico City.

Most Americans who retire to Mexico sell their furnishings in the States and rent furnished housing or buy furnishings, which are inexpensive in Mexico. Do not bring firearms without applying for a permit. Possessing one without proper authorization could land you in jail for up to thirty years. For more information on import regulations, contact the nearest Mexican Consulate.

PAPERWORK AND RESIDENCE RULES

As a retiree who does not intend to work, you're free to visit Mexico for up to six months on a Tourist Card, known as an FMT. The FMT is available when you enter Mexico as long as you provide proof of U.S. citizenship, such as your passport, birth certificate, or a voter registration card. The easy thing about the FMT is that it's renewable. You can hop across the border to the United States and then reenter Mexico for another six months. This system comes in handy if you're making short visits to see whether you want to retire permanently to Mexico.

The classification of *"no rentista"* is applied to foreigners who want to live in Mexico but who have income from overseas sources. That's you if you're retired and living on funds from the States. This requires an FM3 visa. You'll need to apply at the consulate in person with a valid passport and two front-view passport-size photos. Be prepared to show proof of a monthly income of $1,000 plus an additional $500 per month for each family member. The FM3 allows you to take household goods and a car into Mexico without paying duty.

If you want to live in Mexico permanently, you'll need the FM2 visa, which requires proof of a minimum of $1,800 per month in income and $900 a month for each dependent. Permanent residents can take advantage of specific tax savings. If you want to become a Mexican citizen, you do not need to renounce your U.S. citizenship. For details, contact the Mexican Consulate.

Pets

Dogs, cats, and parakeets can enter Mexico with their owners without concerns over quarantine. However, you'll need to be prepared with several documents describing your animal's health and vaccinations. Among them is a health certificate issued by your veterinarian within 10 days prior to entry into Mexico. You'll need proof that all common vaccinations are up-to-date, and an original rabies certificate must show that the vaccination was given more than 30 days but fewer than 180 days prior to your pet's arrival. You may also need to obtain an import permit when you arrive. For details, write or call the Mexican Embassy or Consulate nearest you.

GETTING THERE AND GETTING AROUND

You can arrive in Mexico via several airlines, including Mexicana, Continental, and American. They fly in and out of the country daily with connections to regional destinations at Mexico City.

Inside the country, public transportation is inexpensive and generally efficient. Mexico City's Metro system is quick and quiet, with beautifully designed stations, but avoid the overcrowded rush hours.

Mexico's bus system is amazingly inexpensive and convenient. First-class buses offer comfortable reclining seats, soft drinks, and snacks, and often show movies en route. Buses other than first class are less expensive, but they're crowded and noisy. You may not even find a seat. They're fine if you're just traveling a short distance within the city, but for anything longer, it's worth it to choose a first-class bus.

Train travel is generally below standard—and below that of the first-class buses—though a few lines are being upgraded around Mexico City. Taxis are not expensive but be wary, especially in Mexico City. Take a taxi from an approved area or call a reliable company since problems have occurred with rogue drivers who prey on unsuspecting tourists with high prices or worse.

Driving

Mexico features more than five thousand miles of well-maintained toll roads, including five major routes that crisscross the country. You can operate your North American car in Mexico, but you'll receive a logbook to present to customs each time you cross the border. Carry liability insurance when driving in Mexico; otherwise, the Mexican police are empowered to arrest you until all claims are settled. Foreign policies will usually not cover you in Mexico so arrange a policy with a well-known Mexican insurer such as Lloyd, Sanborns, or Asemex.

Carry a valid U.S. or Canadian driver's license or an International Driving Permit in Mexico. After you move there, you can obtain a Mexican license; it's usually a fairly simple process. Always carry your current driver's license, insurance papers, and proof of ownership.

Local roads are often rough and poorly marked, and some areas have problems with cattle wandering onto the warm asphalt, or even bandits, so know where you're heading and avoid driving at night, especially long distances or in unfamiliar areas.

The Mexican Tourism Secretariat maintains a fleet of mechanics in green trucks (Green Angels) that patrol main highways. Service is free, except for parts and gasoline. The angels stop working each evening at nine, so plan accordingly.

DOUBLE-CHECK YOUR CHECKS

If you're in the habit of making small goofs in spelling, better order the large economy supply of checks. In Mexico, any errors made on a written check will invalidate it. Even if you initial the change, a bank can't accept it.

MANAGING YOUR MONEY

Mexico is one place where you may actually live on a Social Security check since $1,000 a month permits a comfortable life. If you have anything more, you'll live very well indeed.

The unit of currency is the peso (shown as $ or P), divided into one hundred centavos. The peso has stabilized recently; nevertheless, most Americans here keep their money in dollars and access it periodically when they need cash. ATMs make this easy to do. They're widely available and offer an excellent rate of exchange when your withdrawal comes out in pesos. Just make sure that you have the four-digit PIN required and use a common access system such as Cirrus.

To pay rent and daily expenses, you may want to open a checking or savings account in a Mexican bank; however, checks are not widely accepted in stores. Banking is similar to the U.S. system, but you need to show proof of living in Mexico to have a checking account. To open an account, be prepared to show your FM3, a housing contract in your name, and a local bill showing your full name and address.

Taxes

If you move to Mexico, you can import personal and household belongings with no import tax. Pensions from abroad are exempt from income tax in Mexico. Other income will be taxed if you become a resident; however, you'll receive credit for taxes paid in the United States to avoid double taxation. If you're a non-resident (meaning you live in another country more than 183 days a year), you'll pay tax only on income from Mexican sources. A series of personal deductions apply.

Property taxes in Mexico are a real bargain at just .08 percent of the assessed value of the property, and they get lower if you pay your total annual bill in advance. A value-added tax adds 10 to 15 percent to many goods and services although most groceries are not taxed. An annual car tax is based on the size and age of the car. There is no inheritance tax in Mexico.

STAYING HEALTHY AND SAFE

Worried about rising medical costs or a monthly insurance premium that rivals your mortgage payment? Mexico's national health insurance costs about $300 a year. You must have a medical review and wait six months after you apply for coverage. People with serious or preexisting problems can be rejected. However, specialized services aid expatriates in their applications and will do their best to ensure a favorable decision. Ask other Americans in your area for advice before applying if you think there may be a problem.

Medicare won't cover treatment in Mexico, but some retirees go back to the States for serious conditions. You may not need to, though. If you must pay for care, most medical costs are 30 to 50 percent lower than in the United States. Hospitals and clinics in major cities or areas with large groups of Americans tend to offer the best care and most extensive service. Many are actually staffed by doctors and dentists trained in the United States who speak English. One hospital was even begun by an American living in San Miguel. Hospital de la Fe in San Miguel has an excellent reputation. Care tends to be personal in Mexico and many expatriates rave about it. And doctors in Mexico still make house calls! Naturally, good medical care is limited in small towns and the countryside.

Prescription drugs cost considerably less in Mexico than in the United States, as much as 30 to 60 percent less. Many drugs that require prescriptions elsewhere are available over the counter here. Pharmacies *(farmacias)* are identified by a green cross. They can fill U.S. prescriptions or you can ask a Mexican physician to supply a prescription.

If you stay in the normal tourist and residential areas, you won't need any special inoculations against tropical diseases. However, if you have questions, ask your doctor. To prevent *turista*, the fever and diarrhea that attacks travelers, drink only purified water and avoid salads, uncooked vegetables, or undercooked meats. Mosquitoes and gnats are prevalent in coastal areas and the Yucatan lowlands. Use insect repellent and if you intend to be in such areas, ask your doctor whether you'll need malaria shots. Scorpions exist in Mexico. Be aware, and if you are bit see a doctor. By the way, pest control services are readily available.

Security

Mexicans are family oriented and highly religious. Crime rates, including violence and property theft, with the exception of certain areas such as Mexico City and tourist areas, are significantly lower than in the United States. Be careful in some southern Mexican states such as Chiapas, where rebels are making their voices heard with violence. Their protests are aimed at the government, not at Americans, but avoid getting in the middle of it.

FOR MORE DETAILS

Below are some resources to help you further investigate a long-term stay in Mexico.

Official Sources

Consulate General of Mexico
27 East 39th Street
New York, NY 10016
Phone: (212) 217-6400
Fax: (212) 217-6493

Mexican Embassy
911 Pennsylvania Avenue, NW
Washington, DC 20006
Phone: (202) 728-1600

**Mexican Government
Tourist Office**
450 Park Avenue, Suite 1401
New York, NY 10022
Phone: (212) 755-7261
Fax: (212) 755-2874

Mexican Ministry of Tourism
60-61 Trafalgar Square
London WC2N 5DS
England
Phone: (44) (171) 839 3177

Sanborns Insurance Services
2009 S. 10th Street
McAllen, TX 78503
Phone: (800) 222-0158
Email: info@sanbornsinsurance.com

**U.S. Embassy
(Embajada de Estados Unidos)**
Paseo de la Reforma 305
Col. Cuauhtémoc 06500
Mexico, DF
Phone: (52) 5209-9100
Fax: (52) 5511-9980

Internet Connections

Mexico Connect
www.mexconnect.com

Mexico Links
http://quicklink.com/mexico/

Mexico Ministry of Tourism
www.mexico-travel.com

Travel Guide
www.go2mexico.com

Virtual Mexico (info on retirement and relocation)
www.virtualmex.com

Background Reading

Choose Mexico for Retirement
by John Howells and Don Merwin
Globe Pequot Press, 2001

*Live Well in Mexico: How to
Relocate, Retire, and Increase
Your Standard of Living*
by Ken Luboff
Avalon Travel Publishing, 1999

Travelers' Tales: Mexico
edited by James O'Reilly and
  Larry Habegger
Travelers' Tales Inc., 1994

*Your Guide to Retiring to Mexico,
Costa Rica and Beyond*
by Shelley Emling
Avery Penguin Putnam, 1996

14

Portugal

Portugal is warm and sunny, with astoundingly beautiful shore-lines and southern beaches, charming mountain villages, and friendly people, *and* it's affordable. The mystery is why the country is relatively undiscovered by North American retirees. For years the British, Germans, and Dutch have made Portugal their playground, importing the English language, favorite foods, and their native customs—not to mention the accou-trements of luxury in subdivisions, supermarkets, and golf courses. In the more popular areas, including the Algarve, the influx of expatriates occasionally masks Portugal's native charms with upscale development and high-season traffic jams. But don't be discouraged. There are many lovely areas of Portugal in which to enjoy the mélange of enchanting villages, cosmopolitan cities, and historic sites that recall the country's seafaring, Spanish, and Moorish past.

Highlights

- Temperate climate
- Superb beaches
- Most affordable living in Western Europe
- Moorish and Roman history

The few American retirees here speak fondly of the country, the people, and the almond trees that blanket the countryside with snow-white blossoms in February.

THE BASICS

Portugal is tucked in the far southwestern corner of the European continent. In centuries past, the country's neighbors had a habit of visiting and then taking it over. (Some might say the invaders are comparable to today's northern European tourists, but they carry charge cards rather than spears.) Archaeological remains attest to Roman, Celtic, Moorish, and Spanish rule.

Portugal was once the poorest nation in Western Europe, but the country is making remarkable strides since it became a member of the European Union in 1986. EU funds have subsidized essential infrastructure improvements, raising general living standards and increasing tourism. The modernization is a mixed blessing. On one hand, it's raised the quality of life and brought Portugal further into Europe's mainstream; on the other hand the increased amenities have encouraged rampant development, especially on the sunny Algarve coast, and increased prices. Nevertheless, Portugal is still the most reasonable of all Western European countries in which to live.

Climate

Portugal's weather is temperate for the most part. Variations depend on the specific location. In the north, relatively cool Atlantic beaches are juxtaposed with stretches of vivid green landscape, thanks to healthy rainfalls. Lisbon and its coastal area enjoy a temperate climate ranging from a cool 57°F in winter to a pleasing 75°F in summer. Sun worshippers who want a respite from long, cold winters head to the far south where the Algarve region boasts an average of 3,300 hours of sun each year. Of course, August in the Algarve can be sweltering with highs in the 90s—one reason the pool suppliers do very well. Inland, the mountain areas suit those who are not adverse to cooler weather since temperatures drop as the altitude rises.

Language

You'll hear English spoken often in the tourist areas of the Algarve thanks to all those Brits and Germans in the area. Ditto for Lisbon with its business and tourism interests. Because many Portuguese have worked in France, a more prosperous country, French is also commonly spoken. However, if you intend to stay, learn some basic Portuguese. It will help you adapt and fully explore the less-beaten paths.

Ahh, there is the rub. Portuguese is one of the more difficult languages to master, especially since its pronunciation employs guttural sounds that defy description. Reading Portuguese is easier; it's a Romance language derived from Latin with roots that borrow from Spanish, French, and Italian.

We return to the Northern Virginia area about once a year to visit the children and grandchildren. It's my impression that the pace in the United States has increased and people are under a lot of pressure. [One morning] I went to Staples and bought two desk calendars, but the girl rang up three. The man behind me burst into a tirade. The staff opened another register for him. The lady behind him carried on a conversation with an invisible person. I am glad I live in Portugal!

Gilbert Wells, Azenhas do Mar

YOUR NEW LIFESTYLE

How will you fill your days? Here's an overview of activities and interests that are part of daily life in Portugal.

> ### WHERE'D ALL THAT DRIED COD COME FROM?
>
> For centuries Portugal has been known for its fishing and seafaring skills—yet the most popular dish here is based, not on the fish fresh from the local nets, but on dried cod. What's stranger is, the dried cod here is usually imported! There is a seafaring history to the dried cod, though. Its use harkens back to fishing days when it kept well for sea voyages.

Food and Drink

Dried cod is virtually the national dish of Portugal. Every cook has their favorite blend for creating *bacalao,* a mix of shredded dried cod, onion, garlic, potato, eggs, peppers, and any other desired ingredients. For fresh fish, nothing beats the simplicity of a thick tuna steak or grilled sardines. Pork is the meat staple in Portugal, and it's extremely delicious and tender. A range of other cuisines can be found, from Spanish to French to Italian to Chinese, especially in the larger towns. Wine can be downright cheap, and much of it is delicious; some is absolute nectar. Porto is famous for its port wine.

Arts and Entertainment

Hand-painted Portuguese tiles *(azulejos)* are a delight to the eye and serve as both an art form and everyday decoration. Vivid, hand-designed tile work covers entire walls in plazas, churches, and homes.

The melancholy *fado* songs are Portugal's unique offering to music. The style began centuries ago but has remained popular with

After visiting a few times I decided to move over here and try living for a while. It's very nice. One can get along fine without speaking the language if one is a bit outgoing.

Don Price, Cascais

modern variations. Local festivals are popular events that range around the calendar, often in concert with religious holidays.

Portuguese television offers a variety of channels. With satellite access you can receive English-language programming such as CNN, the BBC, and movie channels.

SINGING THE PORTUGUESE BLUES

Fado is Portugal's unique sound. The word literally means "fate," and *fado* lives up to its name with lamenting, mournful lyrics and a sorrowful tone. If you want to hear the real thing, look for a club or presentation known for traditional music. Some *fado* music events put on for tourists lose a lot in translation.

Outdoor Life and Sports

Portugal is a beach-lover's paradise—and that includes all the sports that go along with it—from sailing and swimming to fishing, wind-surfing, and beach blanket dozing. Upscale golf and tennis resorts are found in the more popular areas though many of them require a plump retirement income; golf fees in the ritzy Algarve resort areas begin at $100 and up for eighteen holes.

As in most of Europe, soccer, called *futbol*, is popular. Horseback riding is practiced in several areas, but don't expect to do much biking. Between high-speed highways, rutted dirt side roads and interior hills, the choice of bike paths leaves much to be desired.

Shopping

Shop till you drop and be amazed at the savings on handcrafted items in Portugal. Embroidery, knit sweaters, hand-painted pottery, copper ware, and vividly painted tiles are lovely and amazingly low priced, especially when you get away from the coast and the tourist routes. For daily needs, fresh food markets are common in every town. Giant supermarkets, though still a relative novelty in some areas, are making their presence felt.

Social Life

Americans gather at a variety of recreational clubs devoted to golf, archaeology, bridge, tennis, and yachting. It should be noted, however, that these are more commonly found in the Lisbon area. One American in Sintra notes that there are not more than five Americans there. However, a new club, Americans in Portugal, has been meeting in Cascais. The American Club of Lisbon is well established, but most of the members are Portuguese, as are the luncheon speakers. In the Algarve, you'll have a lively social life if you want it, but your English will largely be spoken with the Brits, Germans, and Dutch.

WHERE TO LIVE IN PORTUGAL

From the lively cosmopolitan city of Lisbon to charming small fishing villages, living in Portugal can be very pleasant. Here are just a few locations that might fit your idea of paradise.

The Algarve

I have a soft spot for the Algarve, mainly because of the powdery beaches that go on for miles, punctuated here and there by natural rock formations that look like giant sculptures in the sand. The Algarve is the southern coastal area of Portugal. The small towns are charming, and even the main city of Faro appeals with its port and array of interesting shops and restaurants.

We investigated Italy, Spain, and Portugal. The last place we checked was Portugal [the Algarve], and it happened to be February with the almond blossoms in bloom. That did it. We decided to stay.

Anne Berra, Albufeira

The area gets its name from the Moorish term *al-Gharb*, meaning "the west." It's dotted with historic sites and small villages featuring charming whitewashed houses. Of course, the area has been discovered by tourists so August traffic snarls all the way to the beach. Most retirees here grin and bear it and wait for September to arrive.

Years ago this area was a real steal for property. Not so anymore, though it's still possible to find deals if you're patient and don't plan to live in a posh development. One couple rented for three years until just the right property came on the market and bought their three-bedroom home with a faraway ocean view for under $100,000 from another American couple—in their eighties—who were heading back to the States. Prices at the Algarve's status-heavy golf resort and seaside properties reach to the skies, starting at $200,000 and going up.

Lisbon and Environs

The capital of Portugal, Lisbon is a sophisticated city with a popular commercial and tourist trade. The city attracts many expatriates for its combination of cosmopolitan and quaint attributes. The main boulevard, Avenida da Liberdade, cuts a wide tree-lined swath past cafés, shops, and offices. Though more expensive than country living, Lisbon is still more reasonable than most capitals.

Lisbon enjoys moderate temperatures year-round, and living here gives you access to the nearby Atlantic coast as well as to city amenities. The international populace ensures a supply of English-language entertainment, good health care, and interesting clubs. Lisbon's international airport makes travel easier for visits from friends and relatives and for your own retirement trips.

Many expatriates prefer to live in southwest Lisbon, surrounded by its architecturally interesting nineteenth-century buildings, residential attitude, and convenient restaurants, shops, and health clubs. Lap, Estrela, and Rato are a few suburbs in this area.

Restelo, just west of Lisbon, is an exclusive and expensive area near the River Tejo. North of Lisbon are modern apartment buildings, many of them rather charmless high-rises, but easily connected to the city via Metro and bus. An urban renewal project has created new apartments and shopping areas in the northeast section of Lisbon.

A line of coastal cities near Lisbon are popular with expatriates. Cascais houses thousands of international residents, especially the British. It has developed into a favorite tourist destination. The resort town of Estoril has modern accommodations available in new condominiums and villas, plus older, renovated villas. Sintra is in the mountains, just eighteen miles northwest of Lisbon. It offers a more rural atmosphere though still within range of the city. Commuter trains from Sintra take about forty minutes to reach Lisbon. Rentals are more often houses than apartments.

Costa Verde

In the northwestern corner of Portugal, as far away as you can get from the tourist hordes of the Algarve, the Costa Verde lives up to its name as the "green coast." The rolling hills are lush with the most verdant green imaginable, contrasted with the blue Atlantic and pale sandy beaches.

The area is known for its fine wines and port. Though not as warm as the Algarve, the weather along the Costa Verde is mild. The average year-round temperature hovers between 49°F and 68°F. The Costa Verde is easily accessible by means of the international airport at Porto. It is also within an easy drive of northern Spain and southwestern France, making it convenient for forays into other parts of Europe.

SETTING UP HOUSE

Arranging for accommodations can be as simple as finding a furnished apartment in a tourist area or as complicated as finding and renovating a ruin of a house (with nothing more than lovely old stones and a view!) into your dream home.

Finding a Rental

Monthly rents depend on the location's popularity. You'll pay more in the Algarve and Lisbon than in the Costa Verde or in Portugal's interior. Furnished properties normally include all basic appliances, though not necessarily extras such as a dishwasher or microwave. Older apartments may not have central heating, and air conditioning is rare. Leases are usually for one or five years. When signing a lease, you'll be expected to pay two months' rent and a security deposit equal to a month's rent.

Relocation consultants can help you find rental housing in Portugal for a fee. Or check out the listings in real estate agents' offices. Also review the classifieds in the newspaper *APN (Anglo Portuguese News)*, or ask around in the expatriate community.

Buying a Home

Real estate offices have boomed in the popular areas of Portugal, but not all are equally reliable. Ask other expatriates for recommendations. Plan to use more than one agent in order to see a wide range of offerings since properties are not computerized and shared.

The restrictions on property purchase can be complicated, not just for expatriates but for the Portuguese too. For example, to avoid overbuilding in some areas, regulations may require you to find a property that already had a house on it—even if just one standing wall is left. Talk to the professionals about current regulations.

When you find your dream property, you'll pay a property transfer tax, which is about 15 percent of the selling price. The transfer tax is not charged on land or on apartments that cost less than $55,500.

Utilities and Infrastructure

Water: Tap water is generally safe, though many expatriates prefer bottled or spring water.

Electricity: Electricity is 220 volts, 50 hertz. Electrical plugs usually have two round pins. Adapter plugs and converters or transformers will be required for U.S. appliances. Be sure to use a surge suppresser for computers and other sensitive electronic appliances.

Communication: You'll find a post office in most towns, but the mail, *correios,* is slow. International overnight mail services are generally limited to the Lisbon area; in the countryside, expect delays. Portugal Telecom provides phone service, and it's much improved in recent years, but expensive. However, competition for long-distance service has significantly lowered rates and the trend will hopefully continue. Local calls are metered, even for Internet connections, which makes that expensive. Internet service providers are readily available, though cyber cafés are not common.

Time Zone: Portugal operates on Greenwich Mean Time, so it's five hours earlier than the United States.

Weights and Measures: Portugal uses the metric system.

MOVING PLANS

You can bring your household items, including furniture, to Portugal if you're establishing residence and you have used the items for a year in your previous residence. Your small appliances will need adapter plugs and converters or transformers to convert from the North American 110 volts to Portugal's 220 volts. However, don't bring a North American television to Portugal; the broadcasting system is different.

You're allowed to import a car, but don't try it. You must transport it, register it in Portugal, and pay customs duties. It will be much easier to sell your car in the States and purchase a good new or used car in Portugal.

Make sure you have your residence permit in hand before you import your household belongings. If you don't, you will not get customs approval, and if that happens you'll be responsible for costly storage fees. Check with the Portuguese Consulate and follow all regulations. Then check again.

PAPERWORK AND RESIDENCE RULES

Americans can stay in Portugal for up to sixty days on a valid U.S. passport. If you want to stay longer, you'll need a visa. If you plan to reside in Portugal for more than six months, apply to the Portuguese Consulate for a residency visa, which takes up to six months to be approved. If you're approved, you will be given permission to enter Portugal but will have to get a permanent residency card from the Servico de Estrangeiros once you arrive.

Pets

To enter Portugal, your canine and feline friends must show original documentation proving they've had their vaccinations more than 30 days but not more than 180 days before departure. Your pet must be accompanied by an International Health Certificate signed by a veterinarian no more than ten days before departure, endorsed by the USDA Federal Veterinarian, and legalized by the Portuguese Consulate. You must also obtain an entry permit in Portugal. When you start planning your own entry, be sure to request full information from the Portuguese Consulate on current pet regulations since they are liable to change.

GETTING THERE AND GETTING AROUND

A number of international airlines serve Portugal, among them the Portuguese national carrier TAP, British Airways, Delta, KLM, Lufthansa, Swissair, and TWA. Flights arrive at one of three international airports—Lisbon, Porto, or Faro.

Airlines, train, and bus service link main cities within the country. Lisbon has a Metro transit system, trams, and taxis, all of which are reasonably priced.

Driving

The current debate is whether Portuguese or Greek drivers are Europe's most dangerous. It's common to be driving peacefully down the road and see a car flying straight toward you as it passes another car. One resident taught us to drive based on the rule of "hugging the breakdown lane. That way you can get over to the right faster if someone's coming toward you." The roads range from multilane superhighways to pitted dirt tracks. At least the speed demons can't go quite as fast on dirt.

If you live in Portugal, regulations call for you to have a Portuguese driver's license within three months of arrival. You must trade in your former license, and you'll need to show a residence visa. The process includes getting a translation of your American driver's license through the American Consulate, undergoing a medical exam, and making a visit to the regional transportation center.

If you choose to buy a car, third-party liability insurance is mandatory. The car registration process can be helped by Autómovel Clube de Portugal for a fee. The car must be inspected and a tax sticker affixed to the windshield, showing that you've paid the road tax.

MANAGING YOUR MONEY

For cost of living, Portugal is the least expensive country in the European Union. Roughly speaking, most goods and services cost about 15 percent less than in the United States. You can live on $20,000 a year if you live very basically. Or you can spend well over that in some of the Algarve's plush expatriate communities that are being developed with million-dollar homes.

Portugal's unit of currency is the escudo, broken into one hundred centavos. Prices are written with a dollar sign between the figures, for example a price of one hundred escudos, twenty-five centavos would be shown as 100$25. A thousand escudos is called a *conto*, though don't look for a bill by that name.

The euro is now being used in Portugal also. You'll see euro prices noted in stores, on checking statements, and on bills. The physical currency will be issued in January 2002, following which escudos will gradually be withdrawn.

Portuguese bank services are modern. You can open either a foreign or a residence account if you have a Portuguese residence card. Checks from local banks are accepted, as are traveler's checks. Credit cards are commonly accepted. Your bank account will also enable you to receive a Multibanco card, which is an electronic debit card useful for making purchases or paying bills. Many bills, especially utilities, are paid by direct debit in Portugal.

You can exchange dollars for escudos at banks or exchange bureaus, though the latter tend to have worse exchange rates. One of the easiest and most financially favorable ways to access escudos is to use your bank card tied to international systems such as Cirrus to withdraw money from an ATM. You can use a credit card to withdraw funds too, but this method incurs an expensive cash advance fee; save this for an emergency.

Taxes

If you're a Portuguese resident, you'll pay personal income tax on your income wherever it's earned. A tax treaty between Portugal and the United States, established in January 1996, prevents double taxes if you already pay taxes in the States.

A value-added tax applies to most goods and services purchased in Portugal. An annual road tax on cars is based on the number of cylinders and the age of the car.

STAYING HEALTHY AND SAFE

Medicare is not valid outside the United States, and few American health-care plans offer coverage in Portugal. Most expatriates buy medical insurance policies through one of the providers based in Europe. (For a list of some expatriate insurance providers, see Chapter 25.) It may even be possible to join Portugal's low-cost national insurance.

Public health-care costs are very affordable by U.S. standards, but most expatriates prefer private care; public hospitals can be crowded and are sometimes mismanaged. Many health-care providers in Lisbon and in the main tourist areas speak English. The British Hospital in Lisbon has a completely English-speaking staff.

Pharmacists in Portugal are extremely helpful and can prescribe for minor ailments. Pharmacies *(farmácias)* rotate their hours of operation to ensure coverage; hours are posted in the window and usually in a local paper.

Security

Aside from the crazy drivers, Portugal is generally safe from a personal standpoint. However, pickpockets know how to prey on the unwary in tourist locations so be on your guard. When you leave your home or apartment, lock up and use normal precautions to not advertise your departure.

FOR MORE DETAILS

Below are some resources to help you further investigate a long-term stay in Portugal.

Official Sources

American Club of Lisbon
Rua Castilho 38
E. Lisbon

Embassy of Portugal
Consular Section
2125 Kalorama Road, NW
Washington, DC 20008
Phone: (202) 328-8610
Fax: (202) 462-3726

**Portuguese National
Tourist Office**
590 Fifth Avenue
New York, NY 10036
Phone: (212) 354-4403

U.S. Embassy
Avenida Das Forças Armadas
1600 Lisbon
Phone: (351) (1) 727-3300

Portuguese Trade and Tourism
1900 L Street, NW
Washington, DC 20006
Phone: (202) 331-8222

Internet Connections

Discover Portugal
www.geocities.com/Paris/4118/index.html

Real estate information
www.cite.pt

**Portugal accommodations,
health directories, leisure, and
search engines**
www.portugalvirtual.pt

Welcome to Portugal
www.portugal.org

Background Reading

Note that these books have a British orientation; some facts will not
pertain to other nationalities.

Buying a Home in Portugal
by David Hampshire
Survival Books, 1999

Living and Working in Portugal
by Sue Tyson Ward
Trans-Atlantic Publications, 2000

CULTURAL HIGH POINTS

Every country is culturally interesting in its distinctive way, but some have captured the imagination for centuries based on a thriving heritage of art, architecture, music, and an intense joie de vivre.

The countries chosen here are all fascinating and happen to be neighboring countries in Western Europe. But each one is unique, with its own language, customs, vistas, and cities to explore. It's easy to develop an interest in perfecting the language, enjoying the cuisine, and enveloping yourself in the daily lifestyle in each of these lands.

From France's vineyards to Italy's hill country, Germany's Black Forest to Spain's sunny coast, explore one, or even better, settle in one and use it as a base from which to explore the others!

15

France

France calls itself the "divine hexagon," a loving and patriotic tribute to its shape and varied charms. The country is proud of its artistic, linguistic, and gourmet endeavors. Rightly so. France has a rich heritage and a *trés agréable* lifestyle that attracts retirees like bees to honey. I mean that literally, if you count the local honey found in the outdoor markets—not to mention the sea-

Highlights

- Artistic and cultural riches
- Cuisine above the call of duty
- Wine by the gallon at pint-size prices
- Central Western European location

sonal produce like fresh asparagus, the rich cheeses, and the glorious wine. Yes, food is one of the special joys of this country where only fresh will do and restaurants change the silverware between each course to avoid any conflict of flavors!

THE BASICS

France is the largest country in Western Europe and is extremely varied in geography, from the sandy Atlantic beaches to craggy northern cliffs, from the Alps's highest peak, Mont Blanc, to the palm-lined Riviera shores. The incredible richness of culture encompasses Basque, Italian, Celtic, and German influences in the border regions.

The dominant religion in France is Roman Catholic. Every city, town, and village of any size is dominated by its cathedral and churches (yes, usually more than one). The saints' days are even listed in the local paper. In actuality, most people do not attend church regularly and the society and government are secular. Other religions represented include Protestant, Islam, and Judaism.

Climate

Winters and summers tend to be mild in France. In the winter, the average daytime temperature is 40°F throughout most of the country; the Riviera is warmer with a high of about 55°F. Of course, it's much colder in the Alps. In Paris, winter months are gray and rainy. Spring can also be cool and damp. Late summer and early fall bring the nicest weather.

Visit France in both winter and summer before taking up permanent residence. Paris may be gay when café tables are set up in the sun outside and the streets are filled with vendors and performers, but it can be wet and miserable during the winter. (However, with the museums, shops, and cafés, you might not notice!) The countryside is idyllic and lovely, but you may find some areas to be too tourist-packed in summer or too sleepy and silent in winter.

> I can see the Spanish border from my living room. This area has a microclimate and is one of the sunniest places in France. We've met a lot of people around the area and are very well integrated.
>
> Mike MacDonald, Sorede

Language

I know people who've managed to live in France without ever really learning the language, but I'd advise you to try. Unlike some countries, such as Germany, where English is widely spoken, English isn't so common in France. That said, be aware that most French people understand more English than you realize—they just are embarrassed to speak it—so be careful what you say where they can hear you!

Paris offers more language training than anyone would ever need, including the granddaddy of French language and culture, Alliance Française. Other schools include Berlitz, L'Institut Catholique de Paris, Accord, and countless smaller language clinics and conversation groups. Outside Paris, all the major cities and most towns of any size have classes available or you can find a private tutor. If you go the private tutor route, be sure that the person has training.

YOUR NEW LIFESTYLE

How will you fill your days? Here's an overview of activities and interests that are part of daily life in France.

Food and Drink

You could wax poetic about French cuisine. The French take their food and wine seriously. You will too once you become a devotee!

Each region has its specialties, all of them delectable. The cheeses are my personal downfall. With 365 to choose from, it's a challenge to compare them all.

Local produce is not only delicious, it's reasonable if you stick to the items in season. Even restaurant meals can be an excellent value, provided you don't go in for Michelin stars or the latest hot spot with a view of the Eiffel Tower. Wherever you dine, *le menu* offers a set meal of two or more courses for a price that's better than purchasing each item individually.

Arts and Entertainment

Wherever you are in France, the historic, cultural, and scenic sites can keep you busy. You don't have to be in Paris. Even the tiniest village has its piece of history, be it in the form of a fifteenth-century chapel or a Roman bridge.

If you're a movie buff, large cities often have theaters showing films in the original language version. Look for the initials V.O. for *version originale;* V.F. means it's dubbed into French.

Painting is a joy in France and art clubs abound, though joining one is not necessary when you can just pull a drawing pad and pencil out of your pocket and draw a village scene.

For English-language programming on television, you'll need satellite or cable that offers NBC, National Geographic, CNN, the BBC, and movie channels. If you want to play videocassettes, be aware that the European standard is different than that in the United States. You can't play U.S. tapes on a French system and vice versa. You can, however, buy a VCR that works on both the PAL/SECAM and NTSC systems.

Though you can find English-language books in several Paris bookstores, they're extremely expensive. Shopping online at amazon.com.uk is a better idea.

Outdoor Life and Sports

By far the most popular sport is football, or *le foot,* which is what Americans call soccer. The night that "les Bleus" won the World Cup was like the Fourth of July and the Super Bowl rolled into one.

Boules, also called *pétanque,* is played throughout France wherever a patch of flat dirt can be found. Players roll or toss steel balls at a smaller wooden ball, earning points for those who get closest to the target.

Other popular activities include skiing—both downhill and cross-country—tennis, biking, swimming, hiking, horseback riding, hunting, and fishing.

Shopping

The quality and freshness of local produce makes shopping for the day's dinner an adventure in good taste. It could even convert you to spinach; it did me!

Large cities, especially Paris, have full-service department stores and specialty boutiques enough to keep the inveterate shopper happy for years. Small towns, of course, have a more limited selection, but most are fully equipped with the basic shops needed for daily living. In many areas, shops and services are offered by mom-and-pop operations, a big difference from the big-chain shopping you may be used to. Get acquainted with your local merchants, and you'll discover that the level of personal service is extraordinary.

Social Life

Americans and British are spread throughout France, though there are large pockets in Paris, Provence, the Southwest, and the Dordogne. Try not to limit yourself to those areas. If you can speak a little French, you'll find that the French people are warm and welcoming. One genial group is Accueils des Villes Française. A national organization with six hundred branches in towns throughout France, it welcomes newcomers, French and foreign alike, and offers a range of classes (sometimes including French) and social activities at extremely affordable prices. Your French town hall *(mairie)* can tell you whether there's a branch nearby or you can contact Accueils des Villes Françaises, Union Nationale, Secretariat Administratif, 20 rue du 4 Septembre, 75002 Paris; Phone: (33) (01) 40 17 02 36.

WHERE TO LIVE IN FRANCE

At first France appears to be homogenous, but a closer look reveals an amazing diversity. From Celtic Brittany to Germanic Alsace to the Italian southeast to the Basque regions to the traditional pure French-speaking center of the country, each area offers a microculture to explore.

Paris and the Ile de France

I'm not a city lover by nature, but even I admit that Paris is the most liv-able, most culturally rich city in the world. It's full of surprises and beauty, with museums and shopping that's unsurpassed. For an American, the city offers social life in English with countless clubs, the American Library, and English-language films and entertainment.

The catch? Paris doesn't come cheap. You'll have to downsize your housing plans drastically compared to most other places you could live in France, or anywhere else for that matter. But if you're willing to do that—or if money is no object—then Paris is a gem.

Housing costs in Paris depend greatly on which *arrondissement*, or section, of Paris you're investigating. Naturally, the most convenient, central areas are the most costly. The prime areas are the 6th, 7th, 16th, and 17th *arrondissements*. Rentals run the gamut from a small studio for under $700 a month to two bedrooms in the 6th *arrondissement* for $1,700 a month and on up. To purchase a small two-bedroom apart-ment with a living room, galley kitchen, and one bath can cost $160,000 or much more.

Many expatriates live in the west and northwest parts of the city near the international schools. These areas include Neuilly-sur-Seine and Boulogne-Billancourt.

The South

Provence and the Côte d'Azur are extremely popular, and for good reason. The weather tends to be sunnier and warmer than other areas, except when winter's harsh northern mistral wind blows. Only around Nice are you protected from it. The landscape and architec-ture are equally sunny, rich in ochre and lavender and gnarly silver-green olive trees. The area is popular with everyone, but especially with expatriates and tourists from all points, resulting in summer traffic jams and high prices.

The largest towns in the Côte d'Azur are Nice and Cannes. Both are jam-packed with luxury high-rises. The airport in Nice provides direct flights to the United States. Inland, Aix-en-Provence is a charming old town known for its tree-lined main street and fountains. The surrounding area is mostly made up of other small towns, still expensive but a little less so.

The Southwest
The region called Languedoc-Roussillon covers Toulouse and Albi, along with the beautiful Mediterranean from Perpignon to Nimes. This area may be south, but it's not protected from the cold mistral wind that chills the area to the bone in winter. It is a lovely place, however, and Toulouse is a sophisticated upmarket city, home to France's aerospace industry. It's packed with wonderful restaurants and boutiques, but is just a short jaunt to the Pyrenees. The university town of Montpellier is another city worthy of consideration.

The North
Normandy and Brittany have a special place in my heart. Perhaps it's due to the warm welcome Americans still receive here more than fifty years after the liberation. But how could anyone not love this rolling green countryside of stone villages, craggy cliffs, and charming small fishing ports. The weather isn't the sunniest in France, but if you don't suffer from seasonal affective disorder at the sight of clouds, you'll love this beautiful area. It's one of the lowest cost regions in all of France and is just a few hours' drive from Paris.

The Center
The Loire Valley is having a resurgence. The area is agricultural (read vineyards!), but it's just an hour by the speedy TGV fast train to Paris. Building the TGV line has led Parisians to discover the region for weekend retreats in the country. Prices are still reasonable, however. You can

rent a renovated two-bedroom, one-bath house in a small village for $700 a month.

An inexpensive area, farther to the south, is the Massif Central. Rural in character, the area is great for the outdoor lover with smaller cities and a wilder and more extensive countryside.

SETTING UP HOUSE

Housing in France is as varied as the apartment in Paris, the plush villa in Provence, or a renovated farmhouse anywhere in the countryside. Take your time to scout out what suits your lifestyle best.

Finding a Rental

Housing prices depend on where you want to live and your budget. In Paris, the best place to start looking for an apartment or house (or anything else for that matter!) is *France-USA Contacts (FUSAC)*. The publication is targeted toward expatriate Americans and is distributed free every month in English-language bookstores and other places where expatriates gather. Its large classified section includes apartments for sale, rent, and sublease. You can have it mailed to you in the States for just the postage fee. Contact *FUSAC* at 3 rue la Rochelle, 75040 Paris; Phone: (33) (01) 45 38 56 57; or P.O. Box 115, Cooper Station, NY 10276.

Outside Paris, check the local papers or get one of the major real estate magazines; *De Particulier á Particulier* is found on most large newsstands for just FF15 (about $2.50). The American Church in Paris publishes *The Paris Free Voice,* which also has ads for apartments. It's free from the American Church, 65 Quay d'Orsay 75007, Paris; Phone: (33) (01) 40 62 05 00. (This church is also a good place to meet fellow expats and to make connections.)

The Women's Institute for Continuing Education (WICE) and the American Cathedral have bulletin boards that may list rentals. Also check local boards in small shops or pass the word to other expatriates that you're looking for a place. Check the Internet. We found our original rental there; it was a summer home owned by a couple who weren't able to use it that year.

Unfurnished apartments are naturally less expensive than furnished ones, although both are available. If you opt for an unfurnished apartment, you can pick up essentials at flea markets and rummage sales. Or if you'll be staying awhile, you can import your own furniture.

Most unfurnished apartments have three-year leases, though furnished home leases can be shorter. You can't be evicted without a court order, and you can never be evicted in winter (October through March), even if you don't pay your rent. Once you have signed a lease and moved in, you don't have to give up your unfurnished apartment or house unless you want to (furnished apartments are excluded from this law).

Make sure that the lease or written agreement on the property includes a complete description of the length of the rental period, the monthly rent, the various appliances, cupboards, light fixtures, and so on, that are included. Look it over carefully because you often only get the bare bones. Be sure you know what to expect.

You will pay the equivalent of two months' rent as a security deposit, and the first month's rent is payable when you sign a lease. In an apartment building, you'll pay service charges for the concierge fee, heat, hot water, and such, though homes will have separate utilities. A *taxe d'habitation* is based on the apartment's value and is paid each year by whoever inhabits the property on January 1.

Buying a Home

Prices in Paris vary greatly, with location being the prime criterion. The view is also a deciding factor; properties overlooking greenery or the Seine command the highest prices. The most expensive areas in Paris are in the central areas near the Seine, including the 6th, 7th, 16th, and 17th *arrondissements,* which include the Left Bank, Isle St. Louis, and the Champs Élysées. Many nineteenth-century buildings are being converted into loft apartments. The lowest-priced lofts are in the working-class 18th, 19th, and 20th *arrondissements.*

The best deals in housing are in small towns or the countryside. Large cities, particularly Paris, Provence, and those in southern coastal areas, have higher prices. Those lovely stone homes and massive fireplaces are fascinating, but don't be carried away by the romance of living in France. Take your time to review many properties before putting money down on your dream home.

My wife and I looked for a place to retire in Spain, but the property was too high and the real estate dealings were a little too loose for my liking. We ended up building [in France]. Unlike the experiences in *A Year in Provence,* we had a good builder and are very happy with the house.

Mike MacDonald, Sorede

There is no computerized shared listing service in France so you need to review properties at several different agencies or *notaries*. In most parts of France, the seller pays the agent's fee. However, in certain *departements,* including the Dordogne, it's the other way around. In any case, it will cost more for the same property if you use an agent since the seller will raise the price. It's easier to use agents, but it's cheaper to deal directly with the seller so don't forget to check classified ads and ride around areas that interest you and look for *A Vendre* signs.

As with rentals, check out specialty publications, including *De Particulier á Particulier, Le Journal des Particuliers,* and *French Property News,* which is packed with pictures, descriptions, and ads by real estate agencies along with private listings. For information, email info@french-property-news.com.

Look at many properties to compare their value. When you find one that you're interested in, have a builder or architect inspect the property. Roofs and walls are most important. Tile or slate roofs last sixty to seventy years, but replacing the wooden lathe is expensive. When purchasing in the rather arid south of France, make sure you have access to a steady source of good water.

Whatever you buy, keep in mind that the asking price is not the final price. Offer at least 5 or 10 percent less.

Once you have decided on a property, you sign a *promesse d'achat* (promise to buy) and the seller signs a *promesse de vent* (promise of sale). At this point you have an agreement, and you now provide a 10 percent *dépôt de garantie.* This money goes into an escrow account, earning no interest, until the purchase is completed (two to three months on average). The deposit covers the cost of the mortgage application, notary and legal fees, and real estate agent commissions. You can get out of an agreement only by forfeiting the *dépôt de garantie* so be sure before you sign.

The *promesse d'achat* should contain a *clause suspensive de prêt* that renders the *promesse* invalid if you cannot obtain a mortgage. Otherwise, if you can't get financing, you'll lose your deposit.

Buy property individually or with your spouse. Due to the country's complex inheritance laws, avoid other arrangements such as joint purchases with relatives. Even if making the purchase with a spouse, get professional advice and check out inheritance laws *before* you purchase since any changes must be made prior to home purchase.

Apartments are purchased *en copropriété,* which is comparable to condominium sales in the States, in that all owners share the costs of maintaining the outside grounds, the building's exterior, and often the heat or hot water as well. Before you buy, find out what these charges include and how much they will be every month.

If you're planning to renovate an old property, make sure it's worth the time and expense. One real estate company estimates that you should plan to spend one to two times the purchase price on restoration. Before beginning your project, get a free estimate, called a *devis,* from at least two masons or construction firms.

It's possible to obtain a mortgage from a French bank. Your real estate agent and a notary will help you obtain a mortgage as part of the 10 percent fee you pay with your *promesse.* The application process is straightforward. You provide the essential information regarding proof of income that can include tax returns or proof of Social Security or pension.

Mortgage terms in France are limited to a maximum of fifteen years. Rates are based on the term, the amount of down payment, and whether the rate is fixed or variable. A fifteen-year adjustable mortgage is currently under 5.5 percent interest with 10 percent down. Compulsory mortgage insurance is required; it adds about $25 more a month.

The final purchase papers will be signed before a *notaire,* who holds powers from the state that are closer to those of an attorney than an American notary. The *notaire* acts as both a government official and a legal advisor to both parties involved and is responsible for making sure the vendor has full and clear title, that the vendor is paid, and that stamp duties and registration fees are paid. The *notaire* collects the purchase tax and the capital gains tax.

It's the buyer's prerogative to choose the *notaire,* but if the seller does not agree with the buyer's choice two notaries can be used and they will split the fees.

You can find a *notaire* by the official signs they hang outside their offices in almost any good-size town, or look in the yellow pages. However, you may want one who speaks a little English or has experience with foreign owners in order to advise you on matters related to taxes and inheritance. For recommendations ask the local consulate, the bank, or other expats in the area.

Your property is taxed based on its value. A discount is made on taxes for properties built within the last five years and sold by the builder or first buyer, in which case the tax is 2.5 percent of the purchase price. Otherwise the tax is between 6.5 and 11.5 percent of the purchase price, depending on the region.

After the real estate transaction, the buyer makes three payments (in addition to the property's purchase price): the fees of the *notaire,* the stamp duty, and the land registration fees, though the *notaire* usually collects all the sums at closing and parcels the fees out. The *notaire's* fees for preparing the *acte de vente* (including the TVA, France's value-added tax) are charged on a sliding scale according to the property's purchase price. The stamp duty *(enregistrement)* includes several taxes, which are recovered by the central, regional, and local governments. In general, the total fees for purchasing a home will range from 10 to 20 percent of the purchase price.

LA VIAGÈRE LIVES!

Occasionally you'll see a home listed as *rente viagère.* This is a rather archaic system by which the buyer can purchase property for a low down payment and promises to make a regular monthly payment to an elderly owner who can continue to live in the house. The trick is that you pay as long as that person lives. They get an income for life while you're betting they'll kick off and leave you with a good deal. Possibly. But the most famous case concerned a *rente viagère* in which the seller lived to be the oldest woman in France. The buyer never did get to live in the home. He died and his estate continued to pay . . . and pay . . . and pay.

Utilities and Infrastructure

Water: Tap water is drinkable though most people enjoy mineral water, either *gazeuse* (bubbly) or *nongazeuse* (flat).

Electricity: The system in France is 220 volts, 50 hertz, not the U.S. 110 volts, 60 hertz. You'll need adapters for electrical plugs and converters or transformers for any U.S. appliances you bring. Be aware that converters and transformers change only the current, not the hertz, so many electronic devices, including computer printers, will not run properly.

Communications: The postal service is so good that a letter goes anywhere in France within a day. It even delivers *The International Herald Tribune* throughout France on the day of publication. Telephone service is excellent and offers a range of convenient options. The monthly fee is low, but all calls, even local ones, are billed. However, the people at France Telecom are well trained and friendly. Visit your local office, and they'll help you choose a plan that is most economical for the type of calls you make.

Time Zone: France is an hour ahead of Greenwich Mean Time—six hours ahead of Eastern Standard Time in the United States.

Weights and Measures: France uses the metric system.

MOVING PLANS

You can import your personal and household belongings to France without paying import duty as long as you have owned them for six months before moving. Don't bother moving television sets, which use the NTSC system and won't work on the French PAL/SECAM system. You'll need a French version. North American VCRs will not play French tapes, but you can still play your U.S. tapes (with the proper adapter and transformer, of course.)

Review all the paperwork your moving company prepares and make sure it's accurate. You won't want your belongings held up at customs longer than necessary.

PAPERWORK AND RESIDENCE RULES

You can stay in France for up to three months on your U.S. passport. If you plan to stay longer, you must apply for a long-stay visa at your nearest French Embassy or Consulate while still in the United States. You'll fill out an application form and seven copies, plus provide passport photos for each, copies of your passport title page, and proof of sufficient financial resources to not work in France, such as proof of pensions, dividends, savings, or Social Security benefits.

You will also have to provide proof of medical insurance, proof of French residence, and a statement from the local police that you do not have a criminal record.

Once you get to France, you will take the approved paperwork to the local *prefecture de police* or *la mairie,* the mayor's office, where you will apply for a residence permit, *la carte de visite.* The prefecture will review your information and let you know whether it's acceptable. If it is, they will send you a form that you must send back with 1,000 French francs for an official physical exam. Always carry your papers with you when traveling in France—or anywhere outside the United States, for that matter.

Pets

The French are a nation of dog lovers so it's relatively easy to enter the country with your pet. Your cat, too, is welcome. However, pets must be over three months old, and you must have the proper paperwork showing that they are healthy. This includes a vaccination certificate for rabies and the usual diseases, such as feline distemper and leukemia. Some shots are time-specific, meaning they must have been given more than thirty days but less than a year before travel so check the regulations with the French Consulate and follow them exactly.

Once you're living in France, a veterinarian will provide a Livret International de Santé to list all your pet's health information. Dogs are required to be tattooed with a number so they can be tracked if lost. You can have this done, but it's not always required of visiting pets.

GETTING THERE AND GETTING AROUND

Countless direct and connecting flights from cities in the United States enter France at the airports in Paris and Nice. Carriers include Air France, American, Delta, Northwest, and United.

The French railroad system, Société Nationales des Chemins de Fer, or SNCF for short, is superb. The hub is Paris, where six stations serve different regions: Gare de l'Est goes to eastern France, Switzerland, and Germany; Gare de Lyon goes south toward the Riviera and Marseille; Gare d'Austerlitz goes to central France and Spain; Gare Montparnasse serves Brittany and the outskirts, such as Chartres; Gare Saint Lazare serves Normandy and St. Germaine en Laye; and Gare du Nord trains head for the north coast, Denmark, Holland, and boats traveling to Great Britain.

The French railroad offers several economy-priced options for seniors, couples, children, or anyone purchasing eight, or for bigger discount, thirty, days in advance. The special TGV trains are the fast trains that offer smooth rides and cut travel time; they require reservations and charge a reservation fee. Men over sixty-two and women over sixty can buy a Carte Senior (senior citizen pass), which provides 25 to 50 percent off train travel on most trains. It costs FF285 (about $45) and is valid for a year from the date of purchase.

The Paris Métro is fast and efficient. You can buy individual tickets or the more economical ten-ticket *carnet* or a pass called the *carte orange*.

Driving

A U.S. driver's license is valid in France, but if you reside there you'll need a French driver's license. If you're lucky, you already have a license from one of the U.S. states that have reciprocal privileges with France. In that case you can trade your U.S. license for a French one. (If not, you'll need to take costly driver's lessons and a driver's test.) The states include Florida, Illinois, Kansas, Kentucky, Michigan, New Hampshire, Pennsylvania, and South Carolina and more are being added. The U.S. Embassy in Paris offers the "Blue Book" Guide to U.S. Citizens Resident in France. View it online at www.amb-usa.fr.

Despite being in a country that offers wines by the barrel, drunk driving is not tolerated. The French breathalyzer, *alcooltest de dépistage,* is much stricter than the U.S. versions. For the full list of driving regulations, look for the *Livret de Conduire* at driving schools or some bookstores.

MANAGING YOUR MONEY

The cost of living in France can vary wildly from the high-flying life in Paris and the Côte d'Azur to the simple lifestyle of a country farmhouse. On the low side, basic costs enable you to live in France for as little as $25,000 to $35,000 a year, though you'll want more if you plan extensive travel.

> My basic philosophy is that most people in the world are poor, and yet people are everywhere. Well, if poor people can live anywhere, so can I!
>
> Selwyn Berg, Aix-en-Provence

The franc is the traditional unit of currency in France and is divided into one hundred centimes. As of January 2002, the euro will replace the franc, which will gradually be withdrawn.

An ATM is the cheapest way to handle infusions of cash for daily expenses. You'll get the wholesale exchange rate, with no commission fees other than service fees for ATM use. Simply withdraw cash from your U.S. bank account, it will come out in francs, or euros in the future. To transfer large amounts, your U.S. bank can wire money to your French account. You can even write a U.S. dollar check to your bank; it will take several days to clear but is simple to do, and the cost is about the same as having the money wired.

French banks offer an array of banking products. You'll probably want a checking account to pay local bills and provide for your various *prélèvements.* A *prélèvement* is an automatic direct debit, and the system is highly popular in France. You can pay most recurring bills—including utilities, mortgage, taxes and insurance—automatically. Your bank can provide you with a bank card *(carte bleu)* for about $37. Savings accounts are available and are paying about 4 percent interest.

If you become a resident, your account becomes subject to foreign exchange control laws. This means that you must have permission from the Bank of France to transfer funds in excess of FF10,000 out of France.

If your visits in France are irregular or you don't need a resident permit, you can probably keep a non-resident bank account indefinitely. The following large French banks maintain correspondents or representatives in the United States: Sociéte Genérale (known as the European American Bank in the United States), Crédit Lyonnais, Banque Nationale de Paris, Crédit Industriel et Commercial, and Crédit Agricole. U.S. banks maintaining branches or subsidiaries in France include American Express, Bank of America, Bankers Trust Company, Chase Manhattan Bank, First National Bank of Chicago, Citibank, and Morgan Guaranty Trust Company of New York.

Gasoline, at about $4.75 a gallon, is a real shock for Americans. Electricity tends to be expensive too, which explains all the gizmos the French have to turn off lights automatically and start appliances at night when electrical costs are less.

Senior discounts are available in France on everything from movies to trains to museum entrance fees. Special groups for *le troisième age* (the third age) provide opportunities for entertainment and travel at reduced prices.

Taxes

France is notorious for its high income taxes so plan accordingly. You may decide to stay in France less than full-time. But if you live in France more than half the year, with no extenuating circumstances, France will be considered your residence and you'll pay tax on worldwide income. A double-taxation treaty exists between the United States and France so you avoid paying twice. If you are required to pay taxes, you'll file your *déclaration de revenu* (tax return) with the local *inspecteur*. The declaration includes income, capital gains, and VAT. French tax returns are simple; the government works out your tax for you, but yours will be complicated if you're an American living in France. Find an accountant who knows the regulations thoroughly.

Property tax is low by U.S. standards. You do not have to pay this tax the first two years following the completion of a new building or the restoration of an old building. One tax Americans aren't familiar with is on TVs. The tax is about $100 a year for a color set. When you buy a TV, you fill in a form and receive a bill every year; this helps support the TV system.

STAYING HEALTHY AND SAFE

Health care in France is good and extremely reasonable in price. In fact, the World Health Organization rated the French health-care system the best in the world. A general doctor's visit costs under $25, a visit to a specialist costs under $60. Hospital care is a third the cost of that in the United States.

Most physicians in large cities speak a little English, but if you don't speak any French at all you'll be more comfortable with someone who speaks English well. Ask the American Embassy for their list of recommendations or talk to other expatriates for referrals. If you need a regular supply of a prescription, have your U.S. doctor write a prescription with the generic name and the dosage given in the metric system. You cannot fill this prescription directly; a French physician must issue it in France.

Medicare will not cover Americans in France. You'll need private health insurance coverage such as is offered by one of the numerous expatriate health insurance companies. (For some listings, see Chapter 25.)

You won't need any special immunizations though a tetanus vaccination is highly recommended if you'll be working in a garden. The tetanus virus is in the soil.

Security

France is a safe country for the most part. You'll feel safe in most areas, even major cities late at night as long as you stick to the populated areas and traveled streets. The major problems are property crime and pickpocketing in tourist locations. Use common sense to keep your belongings safe. Don't flash money or jewelry. Keep your passport and credit cards where your pocket can't be picked.

FOR MORE DETAILS

Below are some resources to help you further investigate a long-term stay in France.

Official Sources

French Government Tourist Offices

Chicago
676 N. Michigan Avenue
Chicago, IL 60611-2819
Phone: (312) 751-7800
Fax: (312) 337-6339

Los Angeles
9454 Wilshire Blvd., Suite 715
Beverly Hills, CA 90212-2967
Phone: (310) 271-6665
Fax: (310) 276-2835

New York
444 Madison Avenue, 16th Floor
New York, NY 10022-6903
Phone: (212) 838-7800
Fax: (212) 838-7855

French Embassy

4101 Reservoir Road, NW
Washington DC 20007-2185
Phone: (202) 944-6000
Fax: (202) 944-6212 (visa section)

United States Embassy in Paris

2 avenue Gabriel
Paris
Phone: (33) (01) 43 12 22 22

Internet Connections

Bonjour Paris
www.bparis.com

French language information
www.pratique.fr

French regions, history, culture, activities, classifieds
www.france.com

France search engine
www.searchenginecolossus.com/
   France.html

Living in France
www.parisfranceguide.com/
   France/living/index_living.html

Paris Tourism Office
www.paris-promotion.fr/

Background Reading

Buying a Home in France
by David Hampshire
Survival Books, 1999

Culture Shock! France
by Sally Adamson Taylor
Graphic Arts Center Publishing,
  1991

**The Grown-Up's Guide to
Living in France**
by Rosanne Knorr
Ten Speed Press, 2000

Travelers' Tales: France
edited by James O'Reilly, Larry Habegger,
  and Sean O'Reilly
Travelers' Tales, Inc, 1995

16

Germany

I mentioned to a German friend that I was doing a book on countries that Americans would enjoy in retirement. He immediately asked whether Germany was included. Oops. I was sitting in that country at the time, and yet I hadn't even considered it. For one thing, the weather isn't exactly warm, and also Germany's history has precluded many people from considering it a haven.

But when Erhard asked the question, I began thinking about the country's many lovely attributes and decided that *his* modern Germany does belong in this book. The scenic countryside encompasses regions covered with great vineyards, lovely lush forests, and charming country towns with centuries of history. The largest cities are cosmopolitan, and many of the small

Highlights

- **Medieval castles and other cultural treasures**
- **Scenic forests and river valleys**
- **Central European location**
- **Placid vineyards and their delicious product**
- **Sauerbraten, sauerkraut, *und bier!***

villages are peaceful retreats complete with half-timbered homes and cobblestone streets. You certainly can't fault the wine or the beer, nor the desserts that are a sweet-lover's dream come true. The active retiree can work them off, as the Germans do, hiking in the Black Forest or biking along the Rhine River. Germany's central location in Europe enables the resident here to explore in several directions throughout Central, Western, and Eastern Europe.

THE BASICS

The Federal Republic of Germany, as it's officially named, is centrally located in north-central Europe. It's bordered by France, the Netherlands, Belgium, Luxembourg, Denmark, Switzerland, Austria, the Czech Republic, and Poland. Its boundaries are on the North and Baltic Seas to the north while the Alps make up the border on the south, the Rhine River on the west, and the Oder River on the east.

The country consists of rolling hills, mountains, and the Rhineland plateau. Major cities include the capital of Berlin, Hamburg, Munich, and Frankfurt. For pastoral beauty, you can't beat the Rhineland's vine-yards, Bavaria's charming villages and the Black Forest, the Bavarian Alps, and the lake areas.

Politically, Germany is divided into sixteen states called *Bundesländer.* The country was reunified after being split between West and East Germany at the end of World War II. It's still dealing with the problems of combining thriving West Germany with former Communist East Germany. The economic disparities and right-wing groups that grew out of them cause some local problems, but overall the country's politics steer a moderate course and national politicians take a strong leadership role in European politics.

Most Germans are Protestant, but there is no state-sponsored reli-gion. In major German cities some churches serve the English-speaking community or at least offer some services in English. Synagogues exist for the Jewish community.

Climate

You won't retire to Germany for beach weather, but it's not necessarily frigid. The northwest has a maritime climate with warm summers and mild winters. Frankfurt's average high temperature is 66°F in August and 34°F in January. Farther south and east, the climate becomes more continental, with warmer summers and cold, damp winters. Munich's average daytime temperature is 73°F in August and 33°F in January. In winters many Germans head to Florida or southern Portugal for a sunny holiday.

Language

The official language is German, but English is commonly taught in the schools and most people, especially the young, understand and speak it at least a little. Of course, if you intend to stay here for any length of time, learning some of the language will be polite and will enhance your understanding and enjoyment of the experience. Though many German words may seem long and ungainly at first, the language is not as difficult as it sounds. In fact, many German words are related so closely to English that you'll recognize them, helping you achieve basic communication fairly quickly.

Adult education classes, tapes, and self-teaching books will help you get a grounding in the language. One of the best sources for language training is the Goethe-Institut, which promotes German language and culture. Classes are held in various cities in Germany and in many major U.S. cities, where you can get a head start.

> I love the European way of life, especially the sense of community one gets from a culture that doesn't revolve around the automobile. I love taking trains or walking down the pedestrian streets on Sunday afternoons or most evenings. The thing I dislike the most is the acceptance of tobacco use everywhere!
>
> Robert Starkey, Berlin

YOUR NEW LIFESTYLE

How will you fill your days? Here's an overview of activities and interests that are part of daily life in Germany.

Food and Drink

Germany is nirvana for hearty meat-and-potato types. Food tends to be basic roast meats, with huge portions of everything. *Weisswurst* (veal sausages) are popular as is roasted pork knuckle. *Spatzle* are tiny dumplings served with almost every traditional dish. What goes with those hearty meals? Beer, of course. Beer is brewed throughout the country, resulting in over six thousand varieties. Don't forget German wines, of which the Rhine and Mosel whites are famous. Schnapps are liqueurs that are high in alcohol.

Desserts are often piled high with whipped cream, and Germans don't always wait until dinner to enjoy them. Pastry and coffee shops present an array of calorie-filled goodies for patrons taking a late afternoon break.

Arts and Entertainment

Germany has a long history of excellence in the performing arts—think Bach to Beethoven, Handel, Mendelssohn, Schumann, and Wagner. That's just for starters. Munich and Berlin are particularly rich in culture, but you'll discover concerts, theater, opera, and cabaret performances in all manner of cities and towns.

U.S. movies are popular in Germany but are usually dubbed in German. Larger cities, however, often have a theater that shows original-language films that are listed as *OV* or *OmU,* which stands for *original mit Untertiteln.* Major cities such as Munich and Berlin with large groups of English-speaking expatriates have English language social clubs and offer many cultural events, including theater, in English.

GRANDPARENTS CAN'T BEAR TO MISS THIS

German dolls are popular and charming examples of the country's art. But nothing beats the array of bears. Bavarian bears in lederhosen and peaked green caps. Lovable floppy bears with shaggy fur. Eyelashed girl bears in frilly aprons. And collectible bears that cost an arm and a leg. In fact, bears by the dozens can be found attracting crowds in animated toy store displays. Such delights are a constant temptation so make sure your grandchild has plenty of shelf space to display your gifts.

Outdoor Life and Sports

Germans are a hearty lot, active and extremely sports minded, which may explain how they can eat all those desserts and drink all that beer. Among the favorite activities are biking, hiking, and skiing. Swimming pools, saunas, and fitness facilities get a good workout as well. In team sports, football (called soccer in the States) is easily the most popular. Other sports include horse racing and tennis.

Shopping

All the products you need for a comfortable life are available in Germany. Prices tend to be high though the exchange rate has turned around recently, bringing prices down for Americans. Supermarkets are common and similar to those in the United States. Specialty shops and outdoor farmers' markets provide an interesting shopping experience.

Shopping hours are limited compared to the United States. Most stores are open weekdays from 8:00 A.M. to 6:30 P.M. and Saturdays from 8:00 A.M. to 2:00 P.M. Some stores are permitted to stay open until 8:00 P.M. on weekdays and close at 4:00 P.M. on Saturdays. In small towns where shops are family owned, the proprietors close for their lunch from about 12:30 to 2:00 or 3:00 P.M.

Shopping is another favorite sport to be enjoyed, but unfortunately only until the comparatively early closing hours of shops due to rather rigid German law. The concept of capitalism differs somewhat here from that which Americans understand.

Bernadette Engelhardt-Hoegerle, Hamburg

Social Life

Large numbers of Americans live in Germany so you'll have many opportunities to make new friends who speak your language. The embassy can provide you with a list of expatriate groups such as the American Women's Clubs, the German-American Club, Democrats or Republicans Abroad, and many others. Many Germans speak English well and may welcome the chance to meet you; be sure and try out your German.

WHERE TO LIVE IN GERMANY

Your choice of places to live ranges from cosmopolitan cities to charming Old-World style villages. Of the amazing number of possibilities, here's a sampling.

Munich

Munich is arguably the most beautiful large city in Germany, with its parks, woods, and lake incorporated into city life. It doesn't hurt that Munich is well situated within Bavaria, one of the loveliest regions of all Germany. The city has drawn a cultured populace and is lively and entertaining, with superb restaurants, shopping, theater, and opera.

The city center features a pedestrian area with upscale shopping. Encircled by broad avenues, the city has expanded far beyond the original city walls. The public transportation system is among the most extensive of all German cities, enabling you to travel throughout the city quickly and efficiently on subway, bus, and tram.

Pleasant residential areas, such as Bogenhausen, combine the convenience of city life with quality of life, thanks to parks and lovely older homes and apartments. However, housing is hard to find in the central area of the city, and furnished apartments are expensive, ranging from about $850 to $2,500 a month for a one- or two-bedroom. One Internet site to check out is http://mrlodge.de.

You'll find a greater choice of housing in the suburbs. Thanks to the excellent transportation system, most of these are within easy reach of the city via streetcar or trains. The rolling hills of the Isar River Valley and the Wurm River Valley are both within forty minutes of Berlin and offer parks, lakes, and a variety of homes and apartments.

Berlin

The largest city in Germany, Berlin is also the capital of the reunited country. (Bonn was the capital of West Germany when the governments were split.) The city is completing the transition of government offices and is busy undergoing a revival. Combining the former Communist east with the more prosperous western sectors of the city is not without its problems. However, the city has much to recommend it. It's a sophisticated city with impressive buildings, which are often set beside elegant, wide boulevards. The city's many lakes, parks, and forests create an excellent ambiance. Berlin is a cultural hub, with countless art galleries and museums and not just one, but three opera houses. The main shopping and entertainment area is the Kurfurstendamm, in what was formerly West Berlin.

The former East Berlin has less expensive housing than West Berlin, but that's primarily because the area's amenities are not yet up to Western standards. You may want to pay the higher price and live in the former West Berlin.

Many expatriates live in the south and southwestern sections, where you can find individual homes with gardens and apartment buildings. Among the neighborhoods, Charlottenburg, Schöneberg, and Wilmersdorf near the town's center, have more affordable lodgings. Grunewald is an especially nice area while Neu-Westend is more luxurious and expensive.

Wine Country

Rhine rhymes with wine and no wonder. The Rhineland is one of the best-known areas for excellent German wines. It's also known for the array of medieval castles, adding a fairy tale flavor. The Rhine River itself is a massive industrial artery where barges lumber down the dark gray water, but the stretch of the Rhine from Wiesbaden to Koblenz has some lovely towns. I should note that the major city of Frankfurt is nearby. It has charming sections, but it is a commercial city, without much to recommend it for tranquil retirement. Go west, young retirees, go west, where you'll find more charming areas, most of which are still within easy train ride of Frankfurt if you feel the need for big-city hustle and bustle.

Wiesbaden is a favorite town of mine, with its lovely tree-lined streets and green spaces. The well-maintained pedestrian center is a delight with small shops, art galleries, and cafés. Nearby, Mainz is the home of the Gutenberg Museum, with its famous native son's *Gutenberg Bible* on display. Though the city could make more of its location on the river, it does have a lovely old center that's often used for fresh-air markets. The town of Heidelberg is strung along the River Neckar. Its castle commands the high ground above, overlooking half-timbered buildings on the shopping streets and squares. The town's known for its university, the oldest in Germany, but today's young people help give the area a lively aspect.

If you want a larger city, Cologne is famous as one of Germany's oldest cities. Roman ruins have been found in the middle of town near the cathedral, and a Roman-German Museum includes remnants of the city's past. Though it was heavily bombed in World War II, the famous Gothic cathedral survived. Most expatriates live in the southern section of the city. Neighborhoods such as Lindenthal and Marienburg are particularly nice; Marienburg is known for beautiful mansions and its location beside the Rhine River. Lindenthal is close to the town center but the Stadtwald woods give it a residential tranquility. Other areas to check out include Surth, Sulz, Frankenforst, Raderthal, and Rodenkirchen.

Near Cologne on the Rhine River, Düsseldorf was originally a small fishing village but is now a sophisticated and contemporary city. It's a major industrial center, especially for the fashion industry, but it's a pleasant city. The Königsallee is the main boulevard for shopping, restaurants, and art galleries, which border the city's old moat on both sides. The oldest section of the city, the Alstadt, is composed of quaint homes and churches, situated on charming pedestrian streets. You'll find many of the city's restaurants and clubs here. As with most commercial centers, housing is difficult to find in the city and can be costly, especially if you're looking for a large apartment or an individual home. Residential areas cover both sides of the river, and expatriates have settled in Alt-Stockum, Kaiserswerth, Ratingen, Wittlaer, and nearby areas.

The Mosel Valley is quieter than the Rhine area, with steep vineyards and romantic villages, and even a few castles of its own. Kues, in the heart of the Moselle wine region, is famous for its half-timbered houses and charming market square. But I go on and on. Charming towns and villages dot the Rhine and Mosel regions but are too numerous to enumerate. Many are located near the area's larger cities, providing both access to shopping and entertainment and a more tranquil, small-town German lifestyle. If you're interested in wine country, it's best to arrange for a car, take your time, and explore.

SETTING UP HOUSE

Most Germans rent apartments, even in the smaller towns. Expatriates who live here do the same—especially if they're unsure about how long they'll be staying. As far as prices are concerned, generally the closer you are to the center of a city, the more expensive the housing will be.

Properties can be listed according to size in square meters or by number of rooms, not including kitchen, halls, or bathrooms. For example, a one-bedroom apartment with living and dining room would be a three-*Zimmer* apartment. Most apartments are impeccably cleaned before a new tenant moves in, and you're expected to return it to that condition before you leave.

Finding a Rental

Look for accommodations in local classified ads, ask other expatriates for suggestions, check the Internet, or use a real estate agent, *der Grundstücksmakler.* If you go the latter route, you'll usually pay a fee equivalent to two months' rent plus the tax.

Rentals may include heat, electricity, hot water, cleaning services, or other property services. The term *Exklusive* means that the tenant pays for heating, utilities, and maintenance separately from the monthly rent; this is more common with unfurnished houses. *Inklusive* means that the heat is included in the rent; this is more common with furnished accommodations. Be sure to ask which option you are getting for the rent and have it noted in your rental contract.

Unfurnished rentals are bare bones, meaning the apartment or home will usually lack all appliances, light fixtures, even towel racks and cupboards. It's essential to pin down exactly what comes with an apartment other than four walls. If you want the landlord to include some items, you can negotiate for them at a higher rent. Or you can install them yourself and keep them for your next property or try to sell them to the next tenant.

You'll pay a security deposit of two or three months' rent, which is returned with interest if you meet the lease requirements. That's a good reason to go through the property with the owner and make a detailed description of its condition before you move in. Since Germans tend to rent rather than buy, lease contracts run long-term. They range from two to five years, with a six-month notice required before moving out. If you're unsure about staying that long, request a shorter lease period. Your rent is usually paid automatically by automatic withdrawal from your checking account. Have an attorney review the lease before you sign it.

Buying a Home

Housing in Germany has been relatively flat in terms of inflation so this is not a place to buy with the intention of reaping the rewards of increased prices. Most Germans tend to wait until their early forties before purchasing a first home. If you want to settle in a house or apartment and find one that you like, a notary public will handle the sale contract. Have the contract translated into English for you. The notary will also transfer the real estate into the *Grundbuch,* which is the official record of all real estate holdings in Germany. Transaction costs in Germany are about 5 to 6 percent of the purchase price. Mortgage loans can be arranged through mortgage companies for about 5.75 percent.

Utilities and Infrastructure

Water: Sanitation in the former West Germany is excellent. Drinking water quality is well controlled. Conditions in the former East Germany are not as good though major cities are usually OK.

Electricity: Electric service is 220 volts, 50 hertz; North American appliances of 110 volts, 60 hertz will not operate in Germany without converters or transformers and adapter plugs.

Communications: Deutsche Telekom is the number one phone company in Europe. Services are efficient and modern, with high-speed transmission lines through most of the country. Internet providers are easy to come by. Postal services are efficient and provide the full array of services.

Time Zone: Germany is on Central European Time, which is an hour ahead of Greenwich Mean Time. It observes daylight savings time from late spring through fall.

Weights and Measures: Germany uses the metric system.

MOVING PLANS

Remember that the electricity is different in Germany; electrical appliances will need converters or transformers plus adapter plugs. North American televisions will not function at all there since the transmission system is completely different. If you need a car, consider buying a new or used one in Germany. It will be easier than importing a car from the States that would have to meet European standards before it could be registered.

PAPERWORK AND RESIDENCE RULES

We went into the restaurant. Our dog took his place under the table. The waitress came and we ordered coffee and cake. My wife then asked the waitress if she would bring a bowl of water for our dog. The waitress returned with the water, which the dog enjoyed to the last drop. By the way, there were several other dogs there, all very well behaved. Why is it that dogs always bark and try to attack other dogs, yet in a German restaurant, they remain so quiet? Could this happen in America?

Norm Burgo, Bitburg

U.S. citizens can stay in Germany up to three months on a valid passport. If you plan to stay longer, you should apply for a residence permit at the German Embassy or Consulate nearest you. You'll need to submit a valid passport, two application forms with passport photos for each, and proof that you will be self-supporting. Start the procedure early; the residence permit can take up to three months to be processed.

Pets

Dogs and cats can be brought into Germany provided they meet the health requirements. All animals must prove they've had their rabies vaccination at least 30 days, but not more than 180 days, prior to entry. A health certificate written in English and German must be issued within 10 days prior to your pet's flight to Germany. The local German authorities must also issue an import permit. Consult the closest German Embassy or Consulate for current requirements when you plan your move.

Dogs must be licensed by the local town hall every year. Keep your pet on his leash in public and clean up after him; owners can be fined if they omit the last step. The Germans love dogs and they're permitted most places, except food stores.

GETTING THERE AND GETTING AROUND

Germany's national airline is Lufthansa, which provides international and domestic service. Other international carriers, such as American, Continental, Delta, Northwest, TWA, United, and USAir also service Germany.

Public train and bus transportation is efficient and extensive in all German cities. The rail system, Deutsche Bundesbahn, is among the best in the world, serving every area of the country with frequent connections as well as points throughout Europe.

Subway systems serve the largest cities, among them Berlin, Munich, Frankfurt/Main, Bonn, and Cologne. The underground systems are called U-Bahn; a suburban surface rail service is called S-Bahn. Ferries operate in port cities and along the Rhine River.

Driving

Driving in Germany can be enjoyable, and it can be dangerous. It helps to have nerves of steel on the Autobahn, which has no speed limit. Remember, though, that other highways are limited to 100 km/h or 50 km/h in cities unless otherwise marked. Seat belts must be used in front and rear seats. In winter, be wary of snow and black ice, which is difficult to see on the asphalt.

Your Driver's License

If you intend to stay a year or less in Germany, you can drive on your U.S. driver's license. The law is a bit peculiar in that if you intend to stay longer than a year, you must have your German license within six months after entering the country. The licensing procedure is complicated, and you should start planning for it before you move.

German driving schools provide the paperwork and register you for testing, but driving lessons are costly. You can get around taking them if you have a driver's license from a state with a reciprocal agreement with Germany. In that case you can simply submit an application for your driver's license to the local administrative center, *Stadtverwaltung,* along with the required documentation, including your passport, residency registration, original U.S. license with your statement of its validity, photograph, and sometimes proof of a recent eye test.

At this date, the states that have reciprocal agreements with Germany include Alabama, Arizona, Arkansas, Colorado, Delaware, Illinois, Kansas, Kentucky, Louisiana, Massachusetts, Michigan, New Mexico, Pennsylvania, South Carolina, South Dakota, Utah, Virginia, Wisconsin, Wyoming, and Puerto Rico.

Some states have partial agreements with Germany. If you have a driver's license from Connecticut, Florida, Idaho, Mississippi, Missouri, Nebraska, North Carolina, Oregon, Tennessee, or the District of Columbia, you can skip the road test, but you'll still need to pass the written test. Contact the local *Stadtverwaltung*. You can take the test in English, but it includes driving-related German terms. Since the various agreements and regulations are in a state of flux, check with the German Embassy or Consulate or the German Ministry of Transport at the time of your move for current regulations.

Car Registration

All cars must be registered in Germany. You must register your vehicle and keep the title *(Fahrzeugschein)* with you when driving, but don't leave it in the car. Automobiles must carry a triangle caution sign and a first aid kit at all times. If you bring a car into Germany, it must pass a technical inspection within ninety days of its arrival before it can be registered. All cars must have an inspection every two years, and you must display the inspection decal on the rear license plate. Non-diesel cars must also pass an exhaust emissions test every year though some newer American cars need only do this every two years.

All cars must be insured for liability. Mark your calendar for these various tests since there are fines if you forget and are late with the testing.

MANAGING YOUR MONEY

Though the cost of living in Germany does not reach the stratospheric levels of countries such as Monaco or Switzerland, it's high. Generally, prices will be about 15 percent higher than comparable costs in the United States, though your cost of living will depend on where you settle. As a rough estimate, you might live modestly in a small town on $30,000 a year, but you'd do better to allot more. If you live in a high-cost city like Munich, you'll pay for the privilege.

The current German currency is the deutsche mark, called the "mark" for short or written as DM. There are one hundred pfennigs in a mark. The euro is also an official currency, and those bills and coins will be available starting January 2002. Deutsche marks will gradually be withdrawn from circulation during a six-month period and will no longer be accepted after June 30, 2002.

Credit cards are accepted in most large shops, restaurants, and hotels. If you need cash, ATMs are found throughout Germany. Check for the insignia of your bank network, such as CIRRUS. Using an ATM provides local currency direct from your U.S. bank account at an excellent rate of exchange, though you'll be charged a fee for transactions at an ATM where you do not have an account. You can also change money at banks for good exchange rates; street front exchange facilities, hotels, and such will apply a less favorable rate.

A check in Germany can be cashed by whoever holds it, not necessarily the person to whom it's written. If you want some degree of protection, mark it *"Nur zur Verrechnung"* (for deposit only). You can open a German checking account in deutsche marks or dollars. If you deposit dollars, you can only withdraw them as marks. A direct debit system enables you to have regular expenses such as utility bills paid from your checking account each month.

Taxes

German residents are liable for taxes on worldwide income; non-residents pay tax only on income from German sources. You're considered a resident if you have your domicile in Germany or have lived there for six consecutive months. The six months can fall between two calendar years.

Taxes must be paid on employment, business, and real estate income, less personal deductions for things such as home mortgage interest. A retiree who does not have earnings in Germany won't be affected by these income taxes. However, other taxes apply. Even non-residents pay a net worth tax on German property. Everyone pays a value-added tax (VAT) of 15 percent on most products and services, except food, which is taxed at 7 percent.

For specific information on your personal tax liability, consult a specialist. Several U.S. accounting firms have international branches or are affiliated with firms in Germany.

NUMBERING SYSTEMS

In Germany, as in many other European countries, numbers are written differently. They slightly top the one, which makes it look like a U.S. seven; the seven has a short slash through its vertical line.

When writing large figures, Germans use commas and periods the opposite of the way North Americans do; that is, $1,200.34 would be written as $1.200,34.

STAYING HEALTHY AND SAFE

German health care services are superb. Hospitals are of very high standard, though they often don't provide personal items such as towels or toilet articles. Many large hospitals have staff who speak English, especially in the major cities. For names of recommended physicians and dentists who speak English, contact the U.S. Embassy.

Medicare does not cover Americans overseas. A few U.S. policies may cover you for a brief period of time, but you'll pay for the services yourself and then apply to be reimbursed. You should carry other health care insurance, such as an expatriate health insurance policy. (See Chapter 25 for some options.) In the Frankfurt area U.S. citizens, including tourists and military personnel, may join a new patient-care system. In Germany, contact American Medical Support Services at 06224-78985.

Security
Violent crime is not high in Germany, but property crimes are increasing, especially burglary and pickpocketing in tourist areas. Guard your passport and personal belongings, and use common sense when walking in large cities, especially Berlin, and most especially at night.

A few extremist groups have surfaced in Germany, with attacks against some foreigners and ethnic minorities. Stay alert and informed via the U.S. Embassy hotline at (49) 228-3391 or call the hotline toll-free in Germany at 0130-826-364.

FOR MORE DETAILS

Below are some resources to help you further investigate a long-term stay in Germany.

Official Sources

German Consulates
Located in Atlanta, Boston,
   Chicago, Houston, Los Angeles,
   Miami, New York, and
   San Francisco.

German Embassy
4645 Reservoir Road, NW
Washington, DC 20007-1998
Phone: (202) 298-4393
Fax: (202) 471-5558

U.S. Consulate General
Koniginstrasse 5
80539 Munich
Phone: (49) (089) 2888-0

U.S. Embassy
Neustädtische Kirchstr, 4-5
10117 Berlin
Phone (49) (030) 8305-0

Internet Connections

About German language and culture
http://german.about.com

Berlin
http://oas.berlin.de

German Embassy Information Center
www.germany-info.org

Munich
www.munich-tourist.de

Background Reading

Culture Shock! Germany
by Richard Lord
Graphic Arts Center Publishing, 1996

The German Way: Aspects of Behavior, Attitudes and Customs
by Hyde Flippo
NTC Publishing, 1996

Living and Working in Germany
by Nick Daws
Survival Books Ltd., 2000

17

Italy

Italia! Ah, here's a country that needs those exclamation marks, a country where bountiful fresh food, plentiful wine, centuries of artistic heritage, and a scenic countryside all contribute to the joy of living. Let's not forget the people who personify the country. The Italians grab every day with gusto,

Highlights

- **Cultural and artistic centers**
- **Tranquil countryside**
- **Cosmopolitan cities**
- **Wine, cheese, and** *scaloppini al Marsala*

and their attitude charms many visitors into wanting to share the joy with them for longer than a short vacation.

On the other side of the coin, many Italian systems run slowly, and you'll need patience to maneuver around the bureaucracy. One couple enjoyed living in Italy for two years but eventually moved next door to France "so we could get something done."

THE BASICS

Italy is a long, narrow boot that's kicking up its heels in west-central Europe. At the top, its closest neighbors are France to the northwest,

Switzerland and Austria to the north, and Slovenia on the east. The toe and heel stretch into the Adriatic, Tyrrhenian, Ionian, and Mediterranean Seas. Greece is a close neighbor to the south, with regular ferries connecting Brindisi to the Greek isles. Italy is hilly and sections are mountainous since the Alps and the Apennines run through it.

The country is governed as a republic. Two areas within Italy are not controlled by the Italian government: Vatican City and San Marino. Vatican City was created in 1929 when Pope Pius XI and Benito Mussolini agreed to set apart this special area. San Marino is so small it's completely surrounded by Italy, but it remains a republic all its own.

Though it's the third largest economy in Europe, Italy is not known for its economic power nor for its efficiency. The country has sophisticated business centers, but there are also impoverished areas with high unemployment, especially in the southern regions. The Mafia and political corruption are deeply ingrained in the culture, despite periodic efforts to minimize, if not eliminate, the problems.

Most Italians are Roman Catholic, and the church, though not a part of the secular government, holds some sway in popular discussions since it's the center of Italian social life. The Italian constitution guarantees freedom of worship and other religions are practiced in Italy, especially in the main cities. Small towns are often focused on the local Catholic church.

Climate

As a long country that runs approximately northwest to southeast, the weather in Italy varies greatly depending on longitude and altitude. While usually mild, the northern and central regions have chilly winters, while the southern island of Sicily stays warm under the winter sun. The average temperatures in Florence range from a high of 88°F in July to 51°F in January; the lows average 63°F in July to 35°F in January. In Palermo, Sicily, the hot August highs average 84°F; lows average 75°F. In January the highs average 59°F with lows averaging 51°F. Of course, these are averages; summer can be blazing hot, sometimes reaching up to 100°F and higher in some areas. Most rain falls in the winter months.

Language

Italian is a beautiful language; unfortunately it's not commonly spoken many places other than in Italy. You'd do well to learn it, though, if you intend to live here for any length of time. For a short visit, you only need to learn the basics, most people speak some English in the large cities and tourist areas.

How to learn? Take lessons or use some good language tapes before you go to Italy. Learn the introductory phrases at home, then take classes when you arrive. It's easy to find language schools in the major cities and large towns in Italy. A few of them are:

Bologna
Centro Cultura Italiana
Via Castiglione 4
40124 Bologna
Phone: (39) 51 228003
Fax: (39) 51 227675
The Centro also has branches in
  Manciano and Arezzo.

Florence
Scuola Leonardo da Vinci
Via Brunelleschi 4
50123 Florence
Phone: (39) 055 290 305
Fax: (39) 055 290 396

Rome
Dante Alighieri
Bologna 1
00162 Rome
Phone: (39) (06) 4423 1400
Fax: (39) (06) 4423 1007

Scuola Leonardo da Vinci
Piazza dell' Orologio 7
00186 Rome
Phone: (39) (06) 6889 2513
Fax: (39) (06) 6821 9084

Siena

Scuola Leonardo da Vinci
Via del Paradiso 16
53100 Siena
Phone: (39) (05) 7724 9097
Fax: (39) (05) 7724 9096

Università per Stranieri
Via Pantaneto 45
53100 Siena
Phone: (39) (05) 7724 0347
Fax: (39) (05) 7728 3163
Email: info@unistrasi.it

YOUR NEW LIFESTYLE

How will you fill your days? Here's an overview of activities and interests that are part of daily life in Italy.

Food and Drink

Dieting and Italy can't be said in the same sentence. An Italian meal is an extravaganza. Though you can find a version of fast food here, save time for a true Italian meal. *Antipasto* "comes before" the pasta or rice. The spaghetti that we Americans eat as a main dish becomes a side dish or the first course *(il primo)* of gastronomic pleasures. The main course of meat or fish comes after that. Cheeses *(formaggi)* are every bit as wonderful as those in France, though in less variety. Try pecorino, fresh mozzarella, and Parmigiano. Ice cream shops are around every corner, and Italian gelato is up there with the world's best frozen wonders. For a more solid dessert, *pasticcerias* serve sweets.

Wine is popular, and a carafe of the local vintage is very inexpensive. Mineral water and beer are also sometimes drunk at meals.

Arts and Entertainment

Italy has a long history of artistic riches. You will discover a bounty of great art from early Roman remains to Renaissance art and architecture and sculpture to today's array of opera, music, film, and art festivals. The Biennale art festival takes place every two years in Venice and attracts artists from around the world. Milan is the place for opera, but music is a part of life in Italy with concerts of all types in cities and small towns.

Artists flock to Tuscany to paint the sturdy hill towns, and galleries are filled with the results. Retirees may be tempted to seek their own creative muse.

Outdoor Life and Sports

Soccer *(calico)* is the overwhelming passion of sports fans in Italy. Rome has two teams, and matches are held in the Stadio Olimpico. Florence also has a professional team, which plays at Stadio Comunale. Leisure matches are played all over the country.

Skiing is extremely popular in the Dolomites, snowy peaks that are part of the eastern Alps near Austria. Italy's most famous ski resort is Cortina, which offers a range of runs from novice to advanced. Cross-country skiing and ice skating are also available there.

Swimming is popular at the seaside resorts—and there are countless numbers of them thanks to Italy's long coastline. Hiking is also popular, especially in the Dolomites.

Shopping

Most Italians shop daily for their fresh ingredients. Supermarkets and major shopping complexes abound in large cities and towns, but mom-and-pop shops are still valued for their personal service. Outdoor markets are often held one day a week in each locale, and that's where you'll find the freshest local produce.

You can decorate your new lodgings with beautiful glazed ceramics in hand-painted designs. Lace and engravings are also popular home décor. Italian fashions are renowned. You'll have no problem finding high-quality leather goods, including shoes and boots, bags, and luggage. The best handcrafted products aren't cheap, but they are a good value when you consider their quality and the work that goes into them. Just make sure you're getting the real thing and a fair price, especially in the tourist areas.

Social Life

Rome and Florence are cosmopolitan cities, with American clubs, but many retirees prefer a quieter existence. You'll find peace in the countryside, especially in Tuscany, which has become to Italy what Provence has become to France.

If you want to associate with Italians, learn the language and start a conversation. The people are effusive, and you won't be alone long. That said, if you're an attractive woman, be careful of attracting the blatant attentions of Italian men. It does wonders for the spirit but if you don't want their company, ignore them or glare pointedly and go on your way.

WHERE TO LIVE IN ITALY

Whether large city or rural village, Italy maintains its effusive character and charm. Where will your dream lead? Here are just a few ideas to start you on your quest.

Rome

The capital and largest city of Italy, Rome is a city of contrasts. The classical antiquities, including the Colosseum, are juxtaposed with the contemporary life of fine restaurants, shops, and buzzing Vespas. Rome is one of those places that people feel strongly about. They either love it or hate it. If you love it and want to stay in Rome, be aware that housing, as in any major European capital, is expensive. Most of the available housing is apartments. There are many beautiful areas, but a large proportion of Americans and other English-speaking residents live in the northwest, southwest, and center. In the center are myriad restaurants, shops, and entertainment. Traffic is a problem everywhere.

Outside Rome, about nine miles north, is Cassia, an area of new buildings, shopping centers, and open spaces. Many of the international schools are located here, making it popular with expatriate families. Upscale residential communities have their own pools and tennis courts.

Esposizione Universale di Roma is an elite area just four miles south of the city's center. The area is popular with embassy and government personnel so it is the place to find more prestigious apartments.

Suburbs abound near Rome, and outside the city you can find villas with gardens plus green spaces—even golf clubs, sports centers, and riding stables. For the most part, the farther the suburb is from the city's center, the less costly it is.

Florence

Florence is a bustling, large city, but it gives the impression of being smaller and more placid. Small parks and plazas dot the city, and it's enjoyable to walk in—unless you're behind the tourist hordes near one of the extraordinary Renaissance sites. If you live in Florence, you will have the time to take it all in at your own pace. Stroll past the Ponte Veccio, packed with its jewelry boutiques; visit the extraordinary Uffizi Gallery; the massive Santa Maria del Fiore cathedral; and more architectural, artistic, and sculptural delights. When you're sated with the big city, you can always enjoy the peaceful hill towns nearby.

Housing in the city is expensive, especially for furnished apartments since these cater to tourists and can easily run $3,000 a month. Renting an unfurnished apartment and finding secondhand furniture or downsizing considerably will lower your costs.

Siena and Tuscan Hill Towns

The Tuscan mystique has captured the American imagination with dreams of charming villages, vineyards marching up gentle hills, and the distinctive punctuation of cypresses pointing toward sunny skies. Though Florence is in Tuscany, I think of Siena as the entry point to the hill towns. When you enter the walled city of Siena, you feel as though you've entered a quieter era, which is not to say that the city is quiet. Siena has attracted its share of tourists who pack the cafés surrounding the main square or *campo*. It's a lovely place for wandering, especially outside the main squares.

Beyond Siena the Tuscan hill towns have a mystique all their own, and have been covered extensively in popular travel books. (Actually there are hill towns galore in Italy, these just happen to be in Tuscany.)

They do have a special attraction, with homes and churches built of old stones that have lasted for centuries. One of the more well-known towns is Montalcino, featuring a castle and local wine. The wine, Brunello di Montalcino, really puts it on the map. Monteriggioni is a walled hill town that's still beautifully preserved. Not all of the hill towns are inhabitable, but their appeal has attracted more development to the countryside. In many cases the area's popularity means higher prices than most countryside living in Italy would warrant. Certainly it's a wonderful area; however, if you're on a strict budget, other areas in Italy are equally beautiful, but less popular and less expensive.

Umbria

Tuscany's neighboring region to the southeast is Umbria. The tour books cover it, but it hasn't captured the popular acclaim that Tuscany has; ergo Umbria has much of the charm, with less of the expense and tourism, than Tuscany. If you're dreaming of country living with lovely landscapes of hillside vineyards, you may want to look into this region. Villages dot the area, and if you're really into rural living, you may find an available farmhouse. The Italian government is encouraging people to buy and renovate farmhouses to save the country way of life.

The Riviera

The Italian Riviera is less well known than its French neighbor, which means it offers many of the seaside charms associated with the Mediterranean, with a lower price tag. In fact, if your idea of charm does not include high-rise hotels and traffic jams, you'd be better off here. The villages reflect a more peaceful Italian life, and you can still find beaches and palm trees without driving bumper to bumper.

Tiny beaches and fishing ports fill the valleys running north to south between the mountains and the sea. They are sheltered from the east and west winds and open to the sun from the south. One of the most scenic areas is called the Cinque Terre, where five villages perch on the rocky coastline. The five towns are Monterosso, Vernazza, Corniglia, Manarola, and Riomaggiore.

SETTING UP HOUSE

If you live in a city or large town in Italy, you'll most likely live in an apartment since rental apartments outnumber individual houses by a wide margin. All housing tends to be in short supply in major cities. Rental agents, called *immobiliari,* can help you find property to rent or purchase in Italy. Be aware that unfurnished houses are often completely empty so you'll need to spring for kitchen cupboards, light fixtures, and appliances. Furnished housing will include all the basics, but will often not include linens. In some heavily industrialized regions, the need for telephones has outstripped the available supply. If you want one where you live, you might have to find a residence that already has one or check into getting a cell phone.

Finding a Rental

A number of residences and *pensiones* rent attractive apartments and rooms for extended periods of time. Check listings in the Yellow Pages under *Case albergo e appartamenti ammobiliati, Pensione,* and *Camere ammobiliati.* Newspapers list rentals for short- and long-term stays; among them are *La Nazione* (Sunday, Tuesday, Wednesday, and Thursday advertising sections); *La Pulce* (Monday, Wednesday, and Friday); *Panorama Casa* (weekly); and *La Vedetta* (Siena).

Monthly rents are paid in advance. When you sign your lease, you'll be expected to also pay a security deposit of one or two months' rent. Do a complete inventory before moving in and have the landlord sign it. It may not completely protect your security deposit, but it will help.

Buying a Home

In large cities the options for purchase are generally apartments. The countryside will offer a range of housing from new homes to piles of stone with potential, which you can renovate to your liking. Keep in mind, however, what such an undertaking will cost in time and money. If you want to renovate a charming farmhouse, have it inspected first, then get an estimate of the cost to improve it to the standard you'd like.

Immobiliari will help you search for a property. You can also check the classified ads in local papers. When you make an offer on a property, you'll pay the seller a deposit. A notary, who is an official of the government, will do the paperwork and hold the meeting at which the buyer and seller close the sale. At that time you'll pay the notary and real estate agent's fees and taxes. The notary fees will range from $1,200 to $3,000. Legal fees will be a few hundred dollars. You're taxed at a rate of 10 percent on the assessed value of a residence or 17 percent for land alone.

Utilities and Infrastructure

Water: Tap water is safe to drink in most areas; however, many people order mineral water with meals.

Electricity: Voltage in Italy is 220 volts. You'll need plug adapters and converters or transformers for North American appliances.

Communication: Mail and telephone services are below the standards of those in other industrialized nations. As mentioned earlier, make sure you can get phone service when you rent accommodations.

Time Zone: Italy is one hour ahead of Greenwich Mean Time, which is six hours ahead of Eastern Standard Time in the United States. Daylight savings time operates from the end of March until the end of September.

Weights and Measures: Italy uses the metric system.

MOVING PLANS

Personal and household belongings can enter Italy duty-free for your own use. You can import a car, but the process isn't worth the trouble. You'll have to register it and pay import duty plus a value-added tax. It's better to buy a new or used vehicle in Italy, where service and parts will be readily available.

When planning what to bring, keep in mind that electrical service in Italy is different than in North America. Your appliances will need adapters and transformers, and some things such as North American televisions won't work at all due to the different broadcast systems.

PAPERWORK AND RESIDENCE RULES

You can stay in Italy for up to three months with a valid passport. Don't be surprised if you stop in a hotel and they ask to keep your passport. The police require that all tourists be registered so the hotel must copy the required information. Just be sure to get your passport back.

To stay longer than three months, you can apply for a ninety-day extension at the local police station. It will usually be granted if you don't intend to work and can prove that you have a means of support. Thus, you can remain in Italy for up to six months.

If you want to reside in Italy longer than the extension will allow, you'll need to request a visa before leaving the United States. Consult the nearest Italian Embassy or Consulate. You'll need to show your passport and provide supporting documents on your health and fitness and your ability to support yourself.

If your grandfather was born in Italy, you can apply for citizenship for yourself. (You can keep your American citizenship as well.) For more details, contact the Italian Embassy or Consulate near you.

Pets

Your dog and cat can enter Italy provided they meet the health requirements. These include an International Health Certificate and a Certificate of Origin issued within 6 days before the time of entry. All routine immunizations must be current, and the records must accompany your animal. A rabies vaccine must have been given more than 30 days but fewer 180 days prior to entering Italy. For information and forms, contact the Italian Embassy or Consulate or an official Italian Government Travel Office.

GETTING THERE AND GETTING AROUND

Italy is well served by national and international flights. Alitalia is the state airline for domestic and international service. Numerous other airlines fly from main cities in the United States.

The train system covers the country though the schedules can be a tad loose at times. If you plan a lot of travel, the Italy Rail Card passes provide discounts. In large cities, such as Rome or Florence, the public transportation, including the Rome Metro and bus service, is inexpensive. Taxis are expensive, though, and beware of tricky surcharges.

Driving

You'd be better off without a vehicle in the big cities. The traffic and boisterous Italian drivers would scare any sane person. If you must have mobility, you could try a Vespa scooter. They're economical and can zip in and out of traffic more efficiently than a car. You still have to have the bravery of Evel Knievel, however.

Outside the major cities, you'll need a car to wander the small towns, vineyards, and countryside. You can use your stateside driver's license at first, but residents must obtain an Italian driver's license within a year. Or you can use an International Driving Permit, provided you get it updated once a year. Liability insurance is mandatory. Road taxes vary from about $75 to $250 a year.

I do love Italy so. Of course, there are difficulties as in any country, but there is so much to be thrilled by. By the way, the driving there is pretty wild. Everyone tailgates; you simply have to adjust. Speed limits, forget it.

Wendy James, Cennina

IT'S JUST A TOY CAR ANYWAY

Italians have a devil-may-care attitude, but it's a can-do one too. This became clear one day when the bus I was on couldn't quite make a sharp turn due to a badly parked Volkswagen. We were stuck. So was all the traffic behind us. Then we watched the curly dark heads of four youthful Italians below the windows as they headed gleefully toward the car and hoisted it onto the sidewalk. The bus continued on its way.

MANAGING YOUR MONEY

The Italian currency is the *lira,* which is in the process of changing to the euro. The latter is already the official currency, but the actual bills and coins will not be issued until January 2002, after which the lira will gradually be withdrawn.

Italy does not restrict the amount of foreign currency brought into the country, but it does restrict the amount of lire taken out. Therefore, be sure to declare the amount of money you bring in, especially for big purchases such as property, so you can take it out with you later.

Your best bet for changing money is to use an ATM, which will draw lire automatically from your U.S. bank account. You can also change dollars to lire (or euros) through banks. Be wary of street-side exchange services that often have higher fees.

Credit cards are popular and most major shops, hotels, and restaurants accept them, but small, independently owned businesses may not. Personal checks are not readily accepted in Italy.

To open a bank account in Italy, be prepared with your passport and your *Permesso di soggiorno* (permit to stay in the country), a declaration of residence from the public population registry, a fiscal code (*codice fiscale* obtained from your provincial tax office), and your deposit. Your account can be held in lire or in dollars or another foreign currency. With a lire account you'll be able to make utility, rent, and other bill payments by automatic deduction. As a bank customer you are eligible for a Bancomat ATM card, which enables you to withdraw funds from your Italian account.

If you'd prefer a bank with international connections, some of Italy's big banks with branches in New York include:

Banca Nazionale del Lavoro
25 W. 51st Street
New York, NY 10019
Phone: (212) 581-0710

Banco di Napoli
277 Park Avenue
New York, NY 10172
Phone: (212) 644-8400

Banco di Roma
100 Wall Street, 24th Floor
New York, NY 10005
Phone: (212) 952-9300

CARIPLO
10 East 53rd Street
New York, NY 10022
Phone: (212) 832-6622

Credito Italiano
375 Park Avenue
New York, NY 10152
Phone: (212) 546-9600

U.S. banks with branches in Italy include: American Express International Banking Corporation; Bankers Trust Company, New York; Chase Manhattan Bank, N.A., New York; Chemical Bank, New York; Citibank, N.A., New York; First National Bank, Chicago; Morgan Guaranty Trust Company, New York; and Bank of America NT & SA, San Francisco.

Taxes

Non-residents in Italy, that is, those who have not taken up official residence, are taxed only on income received in Italy. For tax purposes, a resident is considered to be anyone who lives in Italy more than six months a year or who has principal interests in Italy. Italian residents are taxed on their worldwide income, with rates progressing from 10 percent on taxable income of 7.2 million lire (about $3,800) or less to 51 percent for the portion of income in excess of 300 million lire (about $160,000), with assorted credits, including local taxes paid. A tax treaty between the United States and Italy helps avoid double taxation.

There are two income taxes charged to individuals in Italy: *imposte dirette* (direct tax) and a local income tax. In addition, indirect taxes can include a value-added tax, registration tax, inheritance and gift tax, stamp duty, taxes on buildings, and other minor taxes. Real estate gains are taxed at 3 to 30 percent, depending on time held. Price Waterhouse provides financial and tax information for American investors overseas; they have offices in fifteen Italian cities.

STAYING HEALTHY AND SAFE

Health care in Italy is generally good, and it's very affordable compared to North American prices. Public facilities are the least expensive, though they're less likely to be well staffed or to have English-speaking personnel. Some private facilities provide care specifically for English-speaking patients. These include the American Hospital and the Salvator Mundi International Hospital in Rome.

Medicare doesn't cover Americans beyond U.S. borders. Medical facilities will expect immediate payment for services and do not accept credit cards or your foreign insurance so you will have to pay first and seek reimbursement from your insurance company later. You may wish to find an expatriate health insurance policy that will cover you in Italy. (For some expatriate insurance providers, see Chapter 25.)

First-aid service *(pronto soccorso)* with a doctor on hand can be found at airports, marine ports, railway stations, and all hospitals. In case of emergency, telephone 113 or 112 for the state police or the Immediate Action Service. These numbers are *only* for emergencies. Every drugstore *(farmacia)* posts a list in the window of the pharmacies that are open at night and on Sundays.

Use common sense to safeguard your health. Sanitary standards are high in the major cities. If you're in a very rural area and feel unsure about the water, you may want to choose bottled water to be on the safe side.

Security

The amount and type of crime depends on where you are in Italy. Large cities and tourist areas are packed with pickpockets, and there are tales of trains heading south that are filled with thieves-to-go. Be especially wary on overnight train trips. Watch your belongings and if you have a compartment, lock the door. The most crime-ridden cities, according to a study in 1999 by *Panorama* magazine, were Rome, followed by Milan and Bologna. The farther south you go, the higher the figures for violent crimes. Naples reported the highest number of murders; however, small provincial towns such as Potenza, Sondrio, and Matera tend to be peaceful and relatively crime free.

FOR MORE DETAILS

Below are some resources to help you further investigate a long-term stay in Italy.

Official Sources

American Club of Rome
c/o Marymount International School
Via di Villa Lauchli 180
00191 Rome
Phone: (39) (06) 329-5843

American Women's Association of Rome
c/o Hotel Savoy, Via Ludovisi 15
00187 Rome
Phone: (39) (06) 482-5268

The Italian Embassy
1601 Fuller Street, NW
Washington, DC 20009
Phone: (202) 328-5500

**Italian Government
Tourist Office**
630 Fifth Avenue, Suite 1565
New York, NY 10111
Phone: (212) 245-4822
Fax: (212) 586-9249

U.S. Consulate
Lungarno Amerigo Vespucci 46
50123 Florence
Phone: (39) (55) 239-8276

U.S. Consulate in Milan
Phone: (39) (02) 290-351

U.S. Consulate in Naples
Phone: (39) (81) 583-8111

U.S. Embassy
Via Vittorio Veneto d121
00187 Rome
Phone: (39) (06) 46741

Internet Connections

**Embassy of Italy in the
United States**
www.italyemb.org

Tuscan Dream
www.tuscandream.com

Background Reading

Culture Shock! Italy
by Raymond Flower and
Alessandro Falassi
Graphic Arts Center Publishing, 1994

Live and Work in Italy
by Victoria Pybus
Vacation-Work, 1999

*Living, Studying and Working
in Italy*
by Travis Neighbor and Monica Larner
Henry Holt, 1998

Travelers' Tales: Italy
edited by Ann Calcagno
Travelers' Tales, Inc, 1998

18

Spain

Spain's flag fits the country's personality: sunny orange and yellow stripes reflecting the people's warmth and vibrant energy. For retirees Spain offers cosmopolitan cities filled with pedestrian centers and great museums, charming small villages, and scenic splendors. The landscapes rival each other for drama, from the snow-capped peaks of the Pyrenees to the deep El Greco-esque sky of the broad central plateau, from the undulating hills of endless olive groves in Andalucia to the sizzling beaches and high-rise-topped coastlines of the south and southeast.

Sociability is a big part of the Spanish culture. It's exercised daily in the traditional Spanish *paseo*, the early evening stroll where families push baby carriages, young people flirt, and elders chat and catch up on the day's news. It's a habit that retirees here have learned to share with pleasure.

Highlights

- Temperate climate
- Long coastlines
- Cultural treasures
- Moorish architecture
- Sophisticated cities
- Moderate cost

THE BASICS

Spain is the second-largest country in Europe and makes up the largest portion of the Iberian peninsula. France borders Spain on the northeast, and Portugal is tucked in to the west. Spanish coastal areas follow the Mediterranean Sea on the east and southeast and the Atlantic Ocean on the southwest and north. Spanish territory includes the Balearic Islands in the Mediterranean Sea, the Canary Islands in the Atlantic, and two cities on the coast of Morocco.

Mountains, great plains, and the sea define the country. The dramatic Pyrenees mountains dominate the northern border with France, and the Sierra Nevada overlook the south. A great plateau covers the central portion with Madrid as its anchor. Andalucia spreads along the southwest, with Seville as its main city. The east, southeast, and southern Costa del Sol are well known for their coastal resorts.

> I've been here twenty years and continue, as I have not apparently learned the lessons I came here to learn. And they are very simply patience, understanding, and acceptance. Spain is the perfect place to learn these concepts.
>
> Jim Dodson, Madrid

Spain's archaeological and artistic heritage includes Greek and Roman influences, but it's the impressive Moorish design that distinguishes much of its architecture. The Moors arrived in Spain from North Africa and brought their Muslim religion and architecture with them. More contemporary contributions include those of great artists, architects, and writers such as the painters El Greco, Goya, and Picasso, the architect Gaudí, and Don Quixote's creator, Cervantes.

Spain's government is a constitutional monarchy. The king, Juan Carlos, is head of state, but a prime minister presides over the congress of deputies and the senate. Municipalities are run by elected officials. The country is generally peaceful, with the violent exception of sporadic attacks on government representatives by Basque separatists who are seeking a separate state.

The religion is primarily Roman Catholic, though it's not a state religion. Protestants make up the next largest religious group. There are small Jewish and Muslim communities.

Climate

Spain's climate is one of the warmest in Europe due to its southern location. Exactly how warm? That depends on whether you're in the coastal south, the vast inland plateau, or the Pyrenees mountains. Andalucia, in the south, is temperate except for summer temperatures that can be extremely hot, sometimes exceeding 100°F; the benefit is that winters are lovely, mild and dry. There's a good reason for calling this area the Costa del Sol, the Sun Coast.

Summers in Madrid, and the whole area on the dry central plain, can be unspeakably hot. In July the average temperature is 89°F, and it often boils up to over a 100°F. Winter can be cold but generally dry; temperatures average highs in the 50s, lows about 34°F. Northern areas are more moderate in temperature; Bilbao, for example, averages 50°F in winter and 66°F in summer.

Language

Spain's official language is Castillian Spanish; however, regional languages are common, including Catalàn (spoken in Barcelona), Galician (in the northwest), and Basque (in the north central area of Spain, bordering France). In the larger cities and coastal tourist areas, people often speak English, but don't count on it in rural areas. If you intend to live in this country, learn some Spanish. Fortunately, Spanish is a relatively easy language to learn, especially if you want to communicate with your neighbors, become part of the community, or simply know how to order the best cut of meat at the butcher's.

Spanish is a popular language so you'll easily find adult education courses in the States, and you can take classes in Spain. You'll find schools in all the main cities and in many smaller communities that have study abroad programs. The Pimsleur language tapes are excellent; ask about them at major bookstores. In addition many Web sites provide Spanish lessons via the Internet.

YOUR NEW LIFESTYLE

How will you fill your days? Here's an overview of activities and interests that are part of daily life in Spain.

Food and Drink

Be prepared for big changes in your dining habits; Spanish meals start later and last longer than Americans are accustomed to. Lunch takes place during a long break of two to three hours during which most businesses close up tight from about 2:00 to 4:30 P.M.

Tapas bars are common and are a unique specialty of Spain. Look for counters spread with a multitude of finger foods making it easy to pick and choose your favorites. The best are a true feast for the eyes as well as the stomach. They vary from the simplest olives or fried mushrooms to elaborate combinations of fresh tuna, snails, or omelettes. A small helping is call a *porción,* a larger serving is a *ración.*

The tapas help you make it through to dinner, which, according to Spanish custom, is served at what most Americans consider bedtime. Ten o'clock or later is not unknown for dinner, though some restaurants may open at eight for early diners—mostly tourists.

Spanish meals can be delicious, but it's helpful to learn ingredient and cooking terms so you know what you're ordering. Seafood predominates as a main dish. Meats, including tender pig and lamb, are often roasted or grilled. *Paella,* the saffron rice dish that includes shrimp, mussels, chicken, sausage, peppers, and other vegetables, is a well-known specialty.

Arts and Entertainment

Madrid and Barcelona are cultural capitals worthy of several visits to see their impressive museums and architecture. Don't stop there, though. Spain has countless sites, large and small, that are worth visiting, from the Moorish Alhambra (unfortunately, always jammed) to the world-famous Seville cathedral to charming chapels and tiled squares in towns and villages throughout the country.

Fiestas, celebrating religious and political holidays, are popular in Spain. Flamenco is the national dance and it fits the emotional tenor of Spain, with ecstatic stamping of the feet accompanied by the metronomic clacking of castanets.

You can find English-language magazines and newspapers in Madrid and various sections of the country with large expatriate populations, especially Andalucia.

Outdoor Life and Sports

Most people associate Spain with bullfighting. Though animal rights activists complain about the sport, it maintains its popularity.

Soccer *(el fútbol)* is the more generally accepted sport these days, whether it's played by professional teams or amateurs who take advantage of countless soccer fields throughout the country. *Jai alai,* which goes by several other names, including *pelota,* depending on its method of play, is popular in Basque country. Each town has its *frontón,* or playing wall. The fast-moving ball is played off the wall with a basket-like racket or, in one version, bare hands (definitely the most difficult!).

With large coastal areas and a typically nice climate, swimming, snorkeling, boating, windsurfing, and fishing are all popular. Golf courses are found near the main cities and tourist areas. Although Spain is generally warm, skiing is possible in the Sierra Nevada and the Pyrenees.

Shopping

Stock up on leather products while you're in Spain. Shoes, coats, luggage, and small leather goods are of fine quality and are reasonably priced. Pottery is a real find here, with colorful enameled pots for sale at a fraction of what they'd be across the border in France or in the

United States. For more mundane purchases such as household items, try El Corte Inglés, a chain found throughout Spain.

When shopping, allow time for the midday rest. You might as well: Shops in most areas of the country close at lunchtime, and the streets are deserted except near restaurants. With recent increases in tourism, more big-city shops stay open in the afternoon. But in small towns or small shops, the lunch hours—notice the plural—are sacred. Most business doors close from 1:30 to 4:00 or 4:30 P.M.

Social Life

The Spanish are extremely sociable, effusive, and family oriented. The *paseo,* the early evening promenade where friends and family chat as they stroll, is common in cities and towns. Other Americans and the British have already discovered Spain so you won't lack English-speaking companions. American clubs exist in Madrid, Barcelona, and popular expatriate areas such as Estepona, Malaga, Marbella, Fuengirola, Torremolinos, and Nerja. For lists of American groups contact the U.S. Embassy.

NAME GAMES

Don't expect to be on a first-name basis immediately in Spain. The Spanish are traditionalists and use titles such as *señor, señora,* or *señorita.* That's easy to understand. The tough part is understanding *which* last name to use. The Spanish have two last names; the first is the father's family name, the second is the mother's family name. Address the person with the first part of the last name. For example, Carlos Rodriquez Garcia would be Señor Rodriquez.

WHERE TO LIVE IN SPAIN

Whether in the city or country, Spain has more areas to enjoy than can possibly be listed. These are just a small sampling to help you start dreaming.

Andalucia

France has Provence. Italy has Tuscany. Spain has Andalucia. The name of this area in southern Spain rolls off the tongue with romantic abandon. As well it should. After all, its main city is Seville, the fourth largest city in Spain and easily one of the loveliest. Seville combines modern conveniences with the charms of yesteryear, including the largest cathedral in Europe. (If you need exercise, tackle the steps up the Giralda tower for fabulous views of the city.)

Charming old towns can be found by the score here in Andalucia, among them Córdoba, which is both a tourist site and lovely town with modern suburbs. Granada is the old Moorish capital and home of the Alhambra. It's a maze of narrow streets, packed with tourists; it is fun to visit but may not be the best place to choose for a tranquil retirement spot.

The International San Pablo Airport in Seville provides access to Andalucia. You can rent a furnished one-bedroom apartment for $2,000 a month in high season (summer), but you'll find better deals out of season or for year-round, unfurnished apartments. A variety of properties are available, from established expatriate-planned communities to old farmhouses ready for renovation. Prices in one listing ranged from $29,600 for a secluded cottage with five rooms and three outbuildings to $177,631 for an old mill with a four-bedroom house and its own swimming pool.

Costa del Sol

The Costa del Sol is technically part of southern Spain, but its ambiance is so different from inland areas that it is a different beast entirely. It's a massive tourist draw, especially for snowbirds flocking here from northern Europe in the winter. You can pretty much count on the sun shining more days than not, and some people return year after year. The bad news is that the influx of tourists and retirees has resulted in shoulder-to-shoulder high-rise developments that have denuded the coastal areas of their original charm. (The surplus of rentals, however, is one reason that you can occasionally find a good deal on a long-term rental off season.)

Málaga is the largest town on the Costa del Sol and its transportation hub. Nearby Marbella is considered the most exclusive spot on the Costa del Sol. Located on the sea, its beaches are crowded in season, and the roads leading to them are packed as well. Thankfully, the old town, with its walking streets, is an island of tranquility compared to the crowded high-rise-packed coast just beyond. The pedestrian-only center features upscale boutiques in whitewashed buildings.

Property prices in exquisite Marbella are steep. You can find better deals in or just outside Málaga. A one-bedroom furnished apartment might rent for $700 off season, but the price rises to $2,000 and up in peak season. Naturally, unfurnished, year-round rentals offer better pricing. Heading toward the mountains, remote villages are more tranquil and less costly, and many are within easy reach of the coast.

Islands in the Sun

Part of the Balearic Islands, Mallorca and Menorca share a warm climate and exotic ambiance. Mallorca is the largest island and the main commercial center. The main airport is in Palma, the capital. Menorca is the second-largest island and is the more scenic of the two; it's less developed and has not yet enticed as many jet-setters as Mallorca has. Both share the high costs of islands that attract tourists and need to import most products. But where there's a will there's a way; one retired couple maintained their budget while living there for several months as house sitters for other Americans.

The Canary Islands are Spanish but have their own personality. It's not surprising when you consider that this tropical paradise is off the coast of Africa, hundreds of miles from mainland Spain. The Canaries consist of seven islands of which Tenerife is the largest. Its geography ranges from vivid green scenery to dramatic mountains formed from volcanic activity. The Canaries are lovely but are expensive for daily living since most of the products for daily life must be imported.

Madrid

Madrid is the capital of Spain, located in the middle of the central plain at 2,120 feet above sea level, making it the highest capital in Europe. It's a thriving center for the arts and finance. Due to its big-city commercial dealings, thousands of expatriates, largely government and business people, call Madrid home. Housing in the central area is found in apartments, but you can find more green spaces and larger, independent houses further out.

The west area is slightly less costly than the northern section, but it's still convenient to the city via a commuter train that connects it to central Madrid. One area in the western suburbs popular with Americans is Somosaguas. The American School is located here, along with shopping malls, restaurants, and recreation areas. Housing includes a variety of detached homes and smaller terrace houses.

Northern areas of Madrid with large expatriate communities include Ciudalcampo, Fuente del Fresno, and La Moraleja—all situated along the Burgos Highway. Ciudalcampo is eighteen miles from Madrid and offers individual homes at reasonable prices. Fuente del Fresno is less crowded, yet within ten miles of the city, with hourly bus service. The area has a range of apartments and houses. La Moraleja, just seven miles from Madrid, offers a wide variety of housing from apartments to condominiums to independent houses. The area includes shops, sports clubs, and foreign schools.

Barcelona

Barcelona is Spain's second-largest city and the capital of the Catalonia region. Residents are particularly proud of their Catalàn heritage so you'll hear Catalàn—a mixture of Spanish and French—widely spoken. In fact, be careful not to refer to the city's residents as Spanish. They'll quickly tell you they're Catalàn.

Barcelona is vibrant and sophisticated, a leading seaport and business center. The old town surrounds the cathedral area, but Barcelona has expanded well beyond its original boundaries and now encompasses new areas with broad avenues and modern architecture.

Most housing is found in apartments; rarely are individual houses for rent or sale. The central part of the city has some nice apartments, though they're older and the amenities may be dated. The international schools are on Barcelona's western edge; therefore, expatriate families tend to live in those areas, among them Bonanova, Pedralbes, Sarriá, and

Tres Torres. Pedralbes has more modern apartments with amenities such as gardens and swimming pools.

If you want to live closer to the Mediterranean and enjoy more spacious surroundings, check out the residential neighborhoods that extend north and south of Barcelona. These areas include beach communities as well as towns slightly inland. These neighborhoods offer individual homes but are close enough to the city for residents to benefit from entertainment and shopping there. The prices are more reasonable outside the city.

Basque Country

One of the least settled areas by expatriates is the Basque country of northern Spain, near the French border. The countryside and small towns are lovely, and I can't resist mentioning the region. It should be added, however, that the Basque separatist group, ETA, has been active with terrorist attempts to establish an independent homeland here. They target government officials (even as far as Madrid) so the general public in Basque country isn't necessarily at risk unless ETA changes tactics and seeks new targets. However, check carefully on the current situation before you visit or settle there.

Coastal towns such as San Sebastion offer a relaxed lifestyle with beaches and charming pedestrian-only areas. Bilbao is the largest city in the region and a major industrial center, but apart from the acclaimed Guggenheim Museum, it does not offer a great deal of culture nor charm—yet. The museum has sparked a renaissance along the riverfront, and the city is in the process of adding parks and walking paths.

Inland, Pamplona is a large city with a small-town feel and a variety of local parks. The people are hospitable and the lifestyle is pleasant and slow. Things speed up during the world-famous festival of San Fermin in July, when young runners dash in front of the bulls running through the city streets. Though the weather is cooler and less sunny than farther south, the area is relatively temperate, surprisingly so considering its proximity to the Pyrenees.

Smaller towns throughout the region offer tranquil living conditions at reasonable prices. The easy access from this area to France, which is a mere half hour drive from San Sebastion, permits you to enjoy two cultures from one residence. Heck, if you're interested in the area but the Spanish Basque problems continue, you could always settle in the French Basque region across the border and visit Spain whenever you want.

SETTING UP HOUSE

Except for tourist accommodations, most rented lodgings in Spain are completely unfurnished, often without even cupboards or light fixtures. However, some short-term apartment facilities are available in major cities.

Individual central heating and air conditioning are not common in older properties; newer buildings or upscale homes will have them.

Finding a Rental

Rental agents can help you find a place to live; the fee will range from a month's rent to 10 percent of the annual rent. You can also check the local classified ads, look on the Internet, or ask other expatriates for acceptable places. Numerous English-language publications in Andalucia include classified ads, among them are *Sur* in English, published free on Fridays, and *The Entertainer,* free on Thursdays.

Local rentals will cost less than tourist accommodations. Most leases are made for five years though it's possible to find leases for a year. You'll pay a month's rent in advance plus a security deposit equal to a month's rent. Be sure to inspect the property before you move in and note any damage; have the landlord sign your inventory so you have a record; any damage would be deducted from your security deposit. It's also a good idea to hire a lawyer to check the legalities of your rental agreement.

Most apartments include a fee for community charges, such as garden or pool upkeep and exterior maintenance.

Buying a Home

Multiple listing service does not exist in Spain so your search for property should include several real estate agents. If you're looking in Andalucia, check the same English-language publications mentioned above in the rental section. Many real estate agents also publish their own free magazines periodically.

Prices tend to be reasonable in Spain, unless you pick one of the prestigious resort areas. Some restrictions do apply to purchases. Foreigners can't buy land in strategic areas for defense, which includes some areas bordering France and Portugal.

When you find a property you like, verify that it has a clear deed. A notary can do this for you since all property in Spain is registered in the Registro de la Propriedad. You'll pay for that service through Land Registry charges. Be sure to have a lawyer review the sales contract before you sign.

The sale incurs notary fees; these are usually paid by the seller, though in some cases the buyer will pay them. If purchasing from an individual seller, the stamp duty is 6 percent of the purchase price. All told, the transaction costs in Spain are about 8.5 percent of the purchase price.

If you want a mortgage, Spain has some of the lowest rates in Europe, typically about 5.5 percent or less from some of the major institutions.

Utilities and Infrastructure

Water: Water in all the main areas of Spain is safe to drink, though bottled mineral water is popular.

Electricity: Power in Spain is provided at 220 volts, 50 hertz. North Americans will need transformers or converters and plug adapters.

Communications: Telephone and postal services are good in Spain, though the Internet has not yet made great inroads. Internet cafés exist but are not common yet. Main post offices provide fax and telegram services as well as the usual postal products.

Time Zone: Spain follows Central European Time, which is six hours ahead of Eastern Standard Time in the United States. The exception is the Canary Islands, which are an hour behind the rest of Spain. Daylight savings time operates from the last Sunday in March to the last Sunday of September.

Weights and Measures: Spain uses the metric system.

OUCH! BEWARE THE "HIGH C"

When you turn on that water tap in Spain, remember that "C" doesn't mean "cold." It stands for *caldo* or hot, hot, hot. Otherwise one scalding will teach you the hard way. *Frio* or "F" is cold.

MOVING PLANS

Due to the different electrical system (220 volts, 50 hertz), your small electrical appliances will need transformers or converters as well as plug adapters. Even if you put your TV on a transformer, it won't work; the broadcast system is different in Europe. You'll need to buy a television in Spain.

You can ship your car to Spain (see the Driving section), but between the technical requirements and the bureaucracy you may find it easier to sell your car in the States and purchase one overseas. Used cars tend to be a good value in Spain. Car purchases are subject to an import tariff and a VAT of 16 percent.

As for household items, bring pillows if you like to snuggle into one. Spanish pillows are long bolsters that don't provide the cuddly support American heads are accustomed to.

PAPERWORK AND RESIDENCE RULES

As an American you can visit Spain for ninety days with just a passport. To stay longer, you'll need a residence visa, which you must obtain from the Spanish Consulate in the United States *before* entering Spain to live permanently. The visa is stamped in your passport, which must be valid for at least six months afterward. Various types of visas are offered, including one for retirees. The specific documentation needed varies, but basically you'll need a valid passport, photographs, proof of health insurance, and proof of financial self-sufficiency.

Always carry your passport in Spain; the Spanish police are permitted to request to see it, and you can be fined if you don't have it.

Pets

Pets can enter Spain provided they're prepared with the proper paperwork. This includes a veterinarian's certificate, issued within ten days prior to arriving in Spain, stating that your animal is in good health. The certificate must be endorsed by your nearest USDA office and certified by your nearest Spanish Consulate. Supply proof that all routine vaccinations are current, including rabies. Vaccinations must have been given more than thirty days but less than a year before your pet's arrival in Spain.

GETTING THERE AND GETTING AROUND

Iberia Airlines and international carriers such as Delta and American serve Spain, many with direct flights from main cities in the United States. Ferry services connect Spain with Great Britain, the Canary Islands, the Balearic Islands, and various coastal cities within Spain.

RENFE, the state-run train system, is comfortable and efficient though not particularly fast. Avoid local trains, which seem to stop every two feet; choose the express trains when you can. High-speed *AVE* trains connect Madrid with Seville (two-and-a-half hours) and Madrid and Córdoba (two hours). Local commuter trains serve the area around Madrid.

Madrid and Barcelona have subways in the downtown areas; service is efficient and inexpensive. Bus service in the city costs the same as the subways. Taxis are available in cities at reasonable rates.

Driving

Like the rest of continental Europe, cars drive on the right-hand side of the road in Spain. Roads are generally good, unless you're high in some mountain wilderness. Major highways are of two types: *autopistas,* which charge tolls, and *autovias,* which don't charge tolls. Gasoline is easy to find on main routes but, as in most of Europe, is expensive.

You must have a current U.S. driver's license and liability insurance coverage from a registered Spanish company. It's recommended that you bring an International Driving Permit. You can use it for up to six months in Spain until you receive your resident permit. You then have a year to get a Spanish license. Apply at the Jefatura Provincial de Tráfico office.

You can ship your car to Spain without duty or VAT provided that you can prove you've owned it for at least six months before your departure, that the car was legally registered, and that you paid tax on it originally. You must register your car, and the fee is based on the depreciated value of the purchase price. Your car must undergo a technical inspection before it can be registered and certain adjustments may be required before it comes up to Spanish requirements. In addition, car repairs could be more expensive if you bring a car that's not common in Spain. Sell your car in the States and find a good used one in Spain.

FILL-UP TIPS

When driving through Spain, don't assume you'll find a gas station or handy rest stop on every corner. Even traveling from one population center to another, some sections of the country become rural quickly. Don't wait until the tank's close to empty to fill it up. Diesel is the same word in Spanish, though it's pronounced dee-eh-sel. Unleaded gas is *sin plomo*.

MANAGING YOUR MONEY

The dollar goes farther in Spain lately, thanks to a propitious exchange rate. Your actual living costs will depend on whether you choose a big city or a small town, whether you live in the countryside or want to have a high-priced sea view. Living on the local economy without buying a lot of expensive imported foods, for example, you could have a comfortable life on $25,000 to $35,000 a year. Allot more for large cities, luxuries, or lots of travel.

The euro shares the status of the official currency of Spain with the peseta. Euro bills and coins to be issued in January 2002 will gradually replace the peseta, which will be withdrawn from circulation over the following six-month period.

Spanish banks operate comparably to those in North America, and you'll want a checking account to pay local bills if you live there. A system of automatic debiting of accounts applies for many of your recurring bills, including rent and utilities. Though some American banks have offices in Spain, including Citibank and American Express, their branches are located in Madrid and other large cities. You'd be just as happy with a Spanish bank.

ATMs are common, and they're the easiest and most economical means of changing your dollars into pesetas (or euros when the time comes).

Taxes

If you choose to live in Spain more than 183 days a year, you are considered a resident and will pay income tax on worldwide income. Non-residents pay on Spanish-source income only. Spain has a tax treaty with the United States that allows dual residents to avoid double taxation.

A net worth tax on worldwide assets applies above 17 million pesetas (about $105,000) for residents; non-residents only pay the tax on property in Spain. Property taxes are just 0.7 percent of the appraised property value. Capital gains taxes from a home sale are exempt provided the amount is reinvested in another home within two years. Estate and gift taxes apply to residents; non-residents are taxed only on assets in Spain.

Spain's value-added tax (VAT) is charged on all goods and services. Basic necessities such as milk and medicines are taxed at 4 percent, but regular goods are taxed at 16 percent.

STAYING HEALTHY AND SAFE

Spain has a modern public health system. Some hospitals are not up to North American standards but are acceptable. Ask at the consulate or other expats. If in doubt, choose a university hospital where possible. The Clínica Quirón in Barcelona has a large English-speaking staff as does the Clínica Cuzco and several others in Madrid. For lists of English-speaking doctors or dentists, check with the U.S. Embassy or ask other expatriates for recommendations.

Costs for health care are extremely reasonable compared to those in the United States. However, Medicare does not cover retired Americans living in Spain. If you live in Spain full-time, you'll want to find overseas health insurance from one of the many European providers. (For some options, see Chapter 25.)

Expatriate health insurance coverage offers a choice of worldwide coverage excluding or including the United States. Choosing to include the United States will raise your rates about three times higher so if you're already covered by Medicare you might choose the lower-priced European coverage, then rely on Medicare when you visit the States.

Security

Spain is not particularly dangerous despite the headlines every time the ETA Basque terrorist group targets a Spanish official. For the most part, visitors have no need to worry. Throughout Basque country, they've even posted signs welcoming tourists—but reminding them they're in Basque country, not Spain. That said, terrorists don't always use logic. Take normal precautions as you would anywhere to avoid confrontations or large gatherings.

The main concern in Spain is not bodily safety, but the safety of your belongings. Major cities such as Barcelona and Madrid are well known for expert pickpockets. Get into the habit of stowing your valuables out of reach and leave nothing in your vehicle. If you must leave something, keep it out of sight in the trunk.

FOR MORE DETAILS

Below are some resources to help you further investigate a long-term stay in Spain.

Official Sources

Embassy of Spain
2375 Pennsylvania Avenue, NW
Washington, DC 20037-1736
Phone: (202) 728-2335
Fax: (202) 728-2313

Tourist Office of Spain in Beverly Hills
San Vicente Plaza Building
8383 Wilshire Blvd., Suite 956
Beverly Hills, CA 90211
Phone: (323) 658-7188
Fax: (323) 658-1061
Email: oetla@tourspain.es

Tourist Office of Spain in Chicago

845 N. Michigan Avenue, Suite 915E
Chicago, IL 60611
Phone: (312) 642-1992
Fax: (312) 642-9817
Email: oetchi@tourspain.es

Tourist Office of Spain in Miami

1221 Brickell Avenue, Suite 1850
Miami, FL 33131
Phone: (305) 358-1992
Fax: (305) 358-8223
Email: oetmiami@tourspain.es

Tourist Office of Spain in New York

666 Fifth Avenue, 35th Floor
New York, NY 10103
Phone: (212) 265-8822
Email: oetny@tourspain.es

U.S. Consulate in Barcelona

P.O. Reine Elisenda de Montcada, 23
08034 Barcelona
Phone: (34) (93) 280-2227
Fax: (34) (93) 205-5206

U.S. Consulate in Seville

Paseo de las Delicias, 7
41012 Sevilla
Phone: (34) (95) 423-1885
Fax: (34) (95) 423-2040

U.S. Consulate in Valencia

Calle de la Paz, 6-5° local 5
46003 Valencia
Phone: (34) (96) 351-6973
Fax: (34) (96) 352-9565

U.S. Embassy

Serrano 75
28006 Madrid
Phone: (34) (91) 587-2200
Fax: (34) (91) 587-2303

Internet Connections

American Club of Madrid
www.go-spain.com/acm

Official Board of Spanish Tourism
www.tourspain.es

Real estate
www.casa2000.com

Sí Spain with search engine
www.SiSpain.org

Tourist Office
www.okspain.org

U.S. Embassy in Spain
www.embusa.es

Yahoo Groups
http://groups.yahoo.com/group/
   costablancaexpats

Your Spain
www.tuspain.com

Background Reading

Buying a Home in Spain
by David Hampshire
Survival Books, 2000

Culture Shock! Spain
by Marie Louise Graff
Graphic Arts Center Publishing, 1992

Driving over Lemons
by Chris Stewart
Pantheon Books, 2000

Living and Working in Spain
by David Hampshire
Survival Books, 2000

Spanish Lessons
by Derek Lambert
Broadway Books, 2000

Travelers' Tales: Spain
edited by Lucy McCauley
Travelers' Tales, Inc., 1995

ISLAND HOPPING

What cures the burn-out blues? Discovering your own brand of paradise, of course. And nothing symbolizes paradise more than palm trees waving under a bright yellow orb while gentle waves lap on a beach of the softest sand.

Most people content themselves with a short vacation to their island paradise, but some have gone so far as to move there. Easygoing personalities are best suited to this style of life, filled with quiet days and somewhat constraining circumstances. When living on an island, you can't just get in the car and drive toward new adventures.

You can sail toward them though. The sea and boating draw many American retirees to island life. Some take that much-vaunted year to sail around the Caribbean. Others have a base on the islands and dive, fish, or swim to their heart's content. Not every island is a truly feasible place to retire, even for a year's sojourn. Some, such as Bermuda, are far too expensive or exclusive to accept newcomers. Others lack the infrastructure, such as convenient and quality health care, that most retirees put high on their list of requirements. However, if an island paradise tempts you, following are a few of the more viable possibilities.

19

The Bahamas

Sunny skies, aqua-blue seas, and soft sand beaches. What more could you ask for in the way of a tranquil retirement? In The Bahamas, even the names of the various islands have a relaxing ring to them: Eleuthera, Abaco, Bimini, Spanish Wells . . . seven hundred islands for you to choose from. Well, OK, a few of them might be a tad small—only about forty of the islands are actually populated—but there are still enough for everyone. Coral reefs are a big draw for snorkeling and fishing, and there's plenty of warm weather to enjoy them both in the subtropical climate that is relatively consistent year-round. You can enjoy the lively entertainment of the main cities such as Freeport, the activities offered tourists including golf, tennis, and country club amenities, or simply settle in a secluded spot near a beach and

Highlights

- Sandy beaches and azure seas

- Shorts and T-shirt weather year-round

- English-speaking paradise

- Less than an hour flight from Florida

- Eight-month stays possible without a visa

- Tax-free residency

listen to the surf. Best of all, you can enjoy all this easily, retiring away from cold winter weather for up to eight months a year without the bureaucratic hassles of a visa.

THE BASICS

The Bahamas is one country of seven hundred islands, give or take a few islets here and there. They stretch for almost five hundred miles over the Atlantic Ocean, starting just fifty-five miles southeast of Palm Beach, Florida, and finishing at a point near Haiti. Some of the islands are large and well populated—Grand Bahama, Eleuthera, New Providence, Abaco, and Cat Island, for example. Others are a mere point in the sea.

Much of the land consists of flat coral reefs, though some sections include a few rounded hills. The very highest point is Cat Island's Mount Alvernia, but it's still only two hundred feet above sea level. The islands include pine forests, sandy beaches, limestone caves, and the world's third-largest barrier reef.

The government is stable, with a British-style legal system. The Commonwealth of the Bahamas became independent in 1973. The majority of the people are of African descent; many of their ancestors were brought here as slaves in the early 1800s. About 12 percent of the population is European; about 3 percent is Asian or Hispanic. The predominant religion is Baptist, but Anglicans, Roman Catholics, Methodists, and other religions are represented.

> ### THAT'S NOT KITSCH; THAT'S PATRIOTISM
> Go ahead and put fluorescent pink flamingos all over your yard if you want. The flamingo is the national bird of The Bahamas.

Climate

The Bahamas has an idyllic semitropical climate year-round. Temperatures rarely go below 60°F or higher than 90°F. The averages are about 84°F in summer and about 72°F in winter. The most pleasant time of year is December to May; the rest of the year can be humid. Most rain occurs in brief summer showers, but tropical storms sweep through occasionally; they're most common between June and November.

Language

The language spoken in The Bahamas is English, with a lilting Bahamian dialect. Remember that the English is British in origin so expect spellings like *colour* and *cheque* and *centre*.

YOUR NEW LIFESTYLE

How will you fill your days? Here's an overview of activities and interests that are part of daily life in The Bahamas.

Food and Drink

Seafood is an island staple. Enjoy conch chowder, conch fritters, or conch salad—just say it "conk." Grouper fingers are small fried pieces of the fish. Turtles are bred for food, and you'll see turtle steak or stew on the menu. Try it. It can be delicious and tastes a bit like . . . no, not chicken. But not bad. If you order the side dish called peas and rice, don't expect green peas; these are more like lentils. Wash it all down with a tropical concoction, something with rum perhaps. Liquor is amazingly cheap here, but beer isn't.

Arts and Entertainment

Nassau is the center of arts and entertainment with performances at the Dundas Centre for the Performing Arts. In Freeport, the Regency Theatre sponsors performances. If you like music, the Port Lucaya Marketplace includes Count Basie Square. (The jazz pianist had a home on Freeport.) Entertainment includes jazz and rhythm and blues. For late-night entertainment, casinos and cabarets add excitement to Nassau, Paradise Island, and Freeport.

The government owns The Bahamas Broadcasting Corporation and runs Radio Bahamas and ZNSTV. Additional international programming can be captured by satellite. Movies are mostly from the United States, and video rentals are common.

IS SANTA CLAUS BEHIND THAT JUNKANOO MASK?

Christmas in The Bahamas has a British flavor. Bahamians celebrate the traditional Boxing Day, December 26. Christmas celebrations in Nassau and other island locations begin that day and last through New Year's with colorful Junkanoo parades featuring costumed marchers, music, and dancing. Junkanoo? That's the name but no one seems to know exactly how it derived. One possibility, based on the disguises worn, is *gens inconnus*, which is French for "unknown people."

Outdoor Life and Sports

The sun, shore, and sparkling sea are prime draws here and, thanks to the coral reefs, snorkeling and diving are especially fulfilling. The Underwater Explorers Society (UNEXSO) is based at Lucaya. Baseball is one of the most popular team sports, along with soccer, rugby, cricket, and volleyball. Other active sports include kayaking, hiking, fishing, and horseback riding. Jeep trips through remote areas provide a view of the birds and mangroves.

Shopping

Freeport's International Bazaar has eighty shops and restaurants that imitate France, Spain, Greece, and other exotic locales. In Lucaya, the Port Lucaya Marketplace is a waterfront shopping, dining, and entertainment complex. Local markets offer produce and seafood in season. Stick with them to cut costs since imported specialties are pricey.

Social Life

You'll have no trouble meeting people in The Bahamas, though many may be tourists passing through. For a more consistent social life, you'll meet more people in residential areas than in hotel areas. A variety of service groups meet in The Bahamas, including Rotary and Kiwanis Clubs. Winter (February and March in particular) can be inundated with college students on spring break.

NECESSITY IS THE MOTHER OF RELAXATION

What would anyone who lived in a sunny, subtropical paradise need? Just something to enjoy their leisure more thoroughly. Perhaps that's why the Arawaks, natives of The Bahamas, invented the hammock.

WHERE TO LIVE IN THE BAHAMAS

It's a tropical life wherever you are, but some places are placid, others more active. Here are a few areas to investigate.

New Providence/Nassau

The bustling hub of The Bahamas, its largest population center and the capital city, is Nassau, which is located on New Providence Island. The city is active and crowded but, thankfully, the powers-that-be were smart enough to preserve the sheltered harbor, Victorian mansions, cathedrals, and eighteenth-century forts. Parliament Square in the city center consists of nineteenth-century buildings, painted in cream and pink—a delightfully different take on the usual staid government offices.

Paradise is literally found just across the bridge from Nassau on Paradise Island, known for its resorts, casinos, and nightlife. No, you probably won't live here, though the former Shah of Iran and millionaire Howard Hughes did.

The East End is a more pleasant residential area with large homes whose relaxing verandas face the sea. Exclusive communities abound, including the Coral Harbour development and Lyford Cay.

Grand Bahama/Freeport

Freeport is the major city on Grand Bahama Island and the second-largest city in The Bahamas. The city has a buccaneer history, but it was pirates of another sort who built it. Freeport was expressly developed for tourism, started from virtually nothing in the 1960s. Today, Freeport is one of the best-developed communities in the Caribbean, with an excellent infrastructure that includes all the services necessary for a comfortable lifestyle. City power, city water, paved roads, and cable television systems are fully operational.

The entire island is settled, though some areas are rustic. The towns of the West End are reminiscent of yesteryear.

Out Islands

Eleuthera, Exuma, Abaco, Bimini, Spanish Wells . . . the list goes on. The Out Islands range in size from the largest, Andros, to the miniscule. The third-largest town in The Bahamas is Marsh Harbour on Great Abaco. Its main commerce is sea related. The Abacos are the sailing capital of The Bahamas, and it's here that a sailor and his or her boat can find happiness. You won't find the full list of amenities on the Out Islands, though the larger ones include tourist facilities.

SETTING UP HOUSE

Arrange for temporary accommodations, then do a lot of digging to find a long-term rental that fits your needs. As with most places, renting first will help you get the lay of the land so you can determine the best location, size, convenience, and price for you.

Finding a Rental

Can't you just imagine yourself sitting on the front porch of a pastel pink home—or blue or yellow or glistening white one—while listening to the gentle hush of ocean waves? Dream as much as you like. Just realize that the oceanfront properties, though common in this land of islands, do not rent cheaply. The prime locations will have high-priced units that are furnished for the tourist who stays a week. If you're planning long term, the easiest way to find something affordable is to find an unfurnished—ergo, nontourist—apartment. You may also want to consider an inland location, which will bring your costs down considerably.

Buying a Home

Foreigners can buy a home, townhouse, apartment, or up to five acres of land without a permit. You can even buy your own island. More than a third of the seven hundred or so islands in The Bahamas are privately owned. They don't come cheap though. Very little does. The top properties near water are the most expensive. On Grand Bahama near Freeport, you can find a furnished two- or three-bedroom townhouse in a gated community with pool and tennis courts for $150,000 to $200,000. On the oceanfront, comparable two- and three-bedroom townhouses start at $595,000. Prices go up from there. These are the top-quality units; you can find lower prices though you certainly won't find anything cheap.

Be aware that properties in The Bahamas are sold "as is." You will purchase the house or apartment with its full inventory of appliances and furniture except for the seller's personal possessions. However, make sure you know where the line is drawn. Get the inventory in writing.

The buyer and the seller each pays their own attorney 2.5 percent of the property price. Government stamp duty equals 1 percent to almost 10 percent depending on the property's value. The seller pays the real estate commission. An international buyer must register the real estate for a fee, usually under $100. A Homeowner Residence Card costs $500, renewable annually for a small fee.

Utilities and Infrastructure

Water: Water and sanitation quality are safe in urban areas but can't be counted on anywhere else.

Electricity: The Bahamas uses 120 volts, 60 hertz power—the same as in North America.

Communications: The Bahamas has an advanced telephone system. Services are run by The Bahamas Telecommunications Corporation and include direct dialing to North America, to Europe, and throughout The Bahamas. Cellular service is available in the northern most islands only, but there are plans to extend the service.

Time Zone: The Bahamas is on Eastern Standard Time, which is five hours behind Greenwich Mean Time. Daylight savings time occurs April to October.

Weights and Measures: The standard is metric.

HAVING A GREAT TIME, WISH YOU WERE . . . GLUB, GLUB, GLUB

Across from Nassau, Coral Island's underwater observatory is designed to let visitors meet sea beasts at their own level. The observatory's mailbox is the only one in the world that's known to be underwater. But how do you lick the stamp?

MOVING PLANS

Since the electrical system is the same in The Bahamas as in North America, electrical appliances will function here as in the United States. However, household belongings, such as small and large appliances and furniture, are subject to duty assessed by customs officers, and the duty can be up to 45 percent of the item's value! Firearms cannot be brought into The Bahamas without specific permission; tourists who do not follow this rule are liable to be heavily fined and/or subject to prison terms.

PAPERWORK AND RESIDENCE RULES

U.S. citizens can stay in The Bahamas for up to eight months without a visa. You can request a long stay prior to arrival, or on arrival you can request an initial two to three months, then apply for extensions. Be prepared to show proof of U.S. citizenship such as a valid (or even an expired) passport or U.S. birth certificate and photo identification. You must also have a valid return ticket and be able to prove that you have a place to stay, such as confirmed hotel reservations.

The Bahamian government offers a permanent residency certificate to people who purchase a residence worth over $500,000. The certificate enables the owner, spouse, and minor children to live in The Bahamas. Those who purchase less expensive properties will pay $500 for a Home Owners Residence Card, which can be renewed for a small fee annually.

Pets

Your dog or cat can enter The Bahamas provided you follow certain regulations regarding health and have an import permit. Basically, your pet must be over six months old and have a valid rabies certificate proving your pet was vaccinated more than one month but not more than ten months prior to entry. You must present a Veterinary Health Certificate within forty-eight hours of your pet's arrival to a licensed veterinarian for examination.

To get an import permit, send your request in writing with $10 to Director of Agriculture, Ministry of Agriculture, Trade and Industry, P.O. Box N-3704, Nassau, Bahamas. You can download the proper form on the Internet at www.bahamas.com. Under Travel Info, look at the Documents/Forms section. Or call the offices at (242) 325-7502 or (242) 325-7509.

Dogs must be licensed yearly. A male or spayed female is $2; an unspayed female is $6.

GETTING THERE AND GETTING AROUND

Nassau/Paradise Island and Grand Bahama Island are served by international airlines, among them Delta, American Eagle, and USAir. Countless charter flights also arrive from all over the world, most frequently from North America. The national carrier, BahamasAir, connects Nassau to the major Out Islands with scheduled flights, as do various charter airlines. Private planes are also for hire. Inter-island mail boats connect the islands every week and accept passengers for a modest one-way fee of $35. It's slow but relaxing.

Most major islands have public transportation in the form of buses and taxis. The bus fare in Nassau is 75 cents for adults. In Nassau you can even get romantic and ride the horse-drawn surreys.

Driving

Remember The Bahamas has a British heritage. You'll drive on the left side of the road. Roads in The Bahamas are generally good in the cities and tourist areas, though back roads in other areas are only fair to poor. Riding a moped or bicycle can be a fun means of transportation, but be especially careful. Remember to stay on the left and wear a helmet.

MANAGING YOUR MONEY

The currency in The Bahamas is the Bahamian dollar, which equals the U.S. dollar and is used interchangeably throughout the islands. The country is the leading offshore financial center, with more than 350 financial institutions handling banking and financial trusts. Banking secrecy is part of the environment, and the country welcomes foreign investment. Real estate and tourism are both big draws here.

Taxes

The Bahamas is a tax haven since residents do not pay taxes—not capital gains, income taxes, sales, corporate, inheritance, or dividend taxes. Residency here can also avoid U.S. taxation in some cases. See an expert before you commit to making the move for this reason.

STAYING HEALTHY AND SAFE

Medical services are usually good in Nassau and Freeport, with full hospital services there, but health care services are more limited the farther you get from main centers. You'll be expected to pay immediately for health services. Most physicians were trained in the United States, Canada, or Great Britain, and they all speak English. People with extremely serious conditions are normally airlifted to hospitals in the United States for treatment.

Medicare does not cover you in The Bahamas. If you have private health insurance, ask whether it covers you outside the United States and for how long. Chances are it won't cover you for longer than a month or two, and then only for emergencies. You may need to purchase travel health insurance or an expatriate health insurance policy. (For some options, see Chapter 25.)

Security

Hurricanes are a recurring weather threat, with most of them occurring in the summer and fall. When one hits, it can cause major flood and wind damage, not to mention danger to human life. Monitor weather reports and learn the precautions you should take when a storm is predicted.

Most crime occurs in the rougher areas of Nassau or Freeport so learn which areas to avoid. Use common sense and avoid traveling alone on lonely beaches or empty streets at night.

FOR MORE DETAILS

Below are some resources to help you further investigate a long-term stay in The Bahamas.

Official Sources

The Bahamas Consulate in Miami
Phone: (305) 373-6295

The Bahamas Consulate in New York
Phone: (212) 421-6925

The Bahamas Ministry of Tourism in Los Angeles
3450 Wilshire Blvd., Suite 208
Los Angeles, CA 90010
Phone: (213) 385-0033
Fax: (213) 383-3966

The Bahamas Ministry of Tourism in Miami
One Turnberry Place
19495 Biscayne Blvd., Suite 242
Aventura, FL 33180
Phone: (305) 932-005
Fax: (303) 682-8758

The Bahamas Ministry of Tourism in New York
150 East 52nd Street, 28th Floor North
New York, NY 10022
Phone (212) 758-2777
Fax: (212) 753-6531

The Bahamas Ministry of Tourism, Main Office
P.O. Box N 3701, Nassau
Phone: (242) 322-7500
Fax: 242-328-0945

Embassy of the Commonwealth of the Bahamas
2220 Massachusetts Avenue, NW
Washington, DC 20008
Phone: (202) 319-2660
Fax: (202) 319-2668

U.S. Embassy
Queen Street, Nassau
Phone: (242) 322-1181

Internet Connections

The Bahamas Ministry of Tourism
www.bahamas.com

Background Reading

Frommer's 2001 Bahamas
by Darwin Porter and Danforth Prince
Frommer, 2000

Islands in the Stream
by Ernest Hemingway
Scribner, 1997

20

Cayman Islands

It took just one week in the Cayman Islands years ago to hook me on the possibility of living there. The trip took place during our prere-tirement era, when we were stressed with fifty-hour workweeks. The idea of a place where the most important meeting of the day was held on the beach to rate the sunsets was immensely appealing.

Highlights

- Laid-back lifestyle
- Sun and powdery sand beaches
- English speaking
- Convenient to southern United States
- Financial center

We even liked the relaxing fact that, unlike many tourist-oriented resorts, the Cayman Islands pro-hibits vendors from selling their wares on the beach or streets, ensuring more calm while you soak up the rays. Of course, many North Americans come here for the scuba diving, which ranks among the best in the world. My husband still raves about swimming through schools of tarpon over the edge of a wall five thousand feet deep.

I settled for snorkeling in the clear waters; that was enough. Soon the puttering motor scooters we'd rented began turning in at For Sale signs, and we strolled through the new condos being developed on Grand Cayman. We dreamed of going home, telling our respective bosses where to go (not the Caymans!), and coming back to zone out on sea and sand. OK, so practicality got the best of us, and we headed home. But many people don't leave. Scuba divers and sailors who want the quiet life have found their retirement dream for a few months or even years in the Cayman Islands.

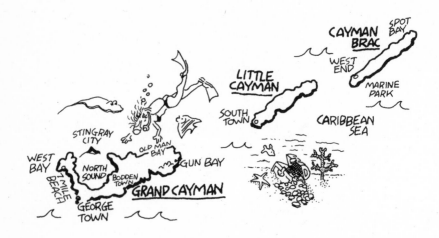

THE BASICS

The Cayman Islands is a group of three islands in the Caribbean Sea, halfway between Cuba and Honduras. The largest island is Grand Cayman, next is Cayman Brac, and the smallest is Little Cayman. All are flat limestone platters set on the sea, with little arable land; the coral reefs surrounding them have made the country a thriving tourist destination famous for its scuba diving. Underwater visibility is enhanced by the fact that there is no runoff from the islands, which consist of porous limestone rock and have no rivers or streams.

Great Britain colonized the Cayman Islands in the eighteenth and nineteenth centuries. In fact, the islands are still a British crown colony and are part of the overseas territories called the British West Indies. Of all the British West Indies, the Cayman Islands has the best living standards and modern amenities. The islands are politically stable and reap the benefits of being a British territory. Queen

Elizabeth II is the chief of state though day-to-day government is run by elected and appointed officials. The capital is George Town on the large island of Grand Cayman.

The country is secular, but the main religions are Christian. Various congregations serve Roman Catholics, Anglicans, Seventh Day Adventists, and Presbyterians.

Climate

Don't worry about bringing woolies to the Caymans, though a sweater or two and rain gear are a good idea. The Cayman Islands is truly a tropical paradise, with temperatures averaging about 80°F year-round. Summers average about 84°F, but they can be rainy and tropical storms are most likely to occur then. Winters are cooler but certainly not cold, with an average high of 78°F. Winters are relatively dry compared to summer; the driest months are March and April.

Language

The language is English, with a British flavor.

LONG WAVE THE TURTLE

The coat of arms for the Cayman Islands includes a pineapple, which symbolizes hospitality, and a turtle with a shield and three stars, one for each island. The motto is "He hath founded it upon the seas."

YOUR NEW LIFESTYLE

How will you fill your days? Here's an overview of activities and interests that are part of daily life in the Cayman Islands.

Food and Drink

Seafood is popular, and even turtle is served occasionally. But you'll find food to fit all tastes in Grand Cayman. The Taste of Cayman food fair is held every year in July, when you can sample hundreds of local culinary delights. Rum still packs a punch as a staple for mixed drinks.

Arts and Entertainment

Learn about early plantation life in the Caymans at the Pedro St. James historic site. Enjoy jazz and steel band concerts, local theater, comedy clubs, and seasonal festivals.

Four local television stations and four local radio stations serve the Cayman Islands. The programming is limited so if you want greater choice, you'll need to order cable TV service, which costs about $55 a month, not including special movie channels. Or you can always rent videos. Blockbuster Video outlets serve Grand Cayman and Cayman Brac.

Outdoor Life and Sports

Diving is central to the Cayman Islands' lifestyle, but if that's a bit overboard for you, snorkeling also lets you enjoy the multicolored tropical fish and coral. You can even swim with stingrays at Stingray City on Grand Cayman's North Sound. Sailing, fishing, cricket, bicycling, horseback riding, golf, and other participation and spectator sports are available at various locations in the islands.

You can visit the National Museum and the Queen Elizabeth II Botanic Park and Gardens. Discover historic buildings, bird sanctuaries, wetlands, and nature trails on all three islands.

Shopping

George Town is the center for shopping with elegant boutiques, art galleries, and small restaurants. This is tourist country so many of the shops are dedicated to the ubiquitous T-shirt. Dive shops galore cater to the hordes of visitors who enjoy the sport and want to take home dive-related souvenirs.

Social Life

The Cayman Islands is populated by tourists and employees of the countless financial organizations that call this port home. To meet people who aren't leaving after two weeks of sun and sand, choose a residential area rather than hotel row and get involved in the local community.

THIS NAME'S A CROC

Christopher Columbus discovered the Cayman Islands in 1503. The country's name comes from the Caribe Indian word for crocodile.

WHERE TO LIVE IN THE CAYMAN ISLANDS

Of the three islands, Grand Cayman is the most suitable for a retiree, with restaurants, shopping, and good medical facilities. Grand Cayman attracts most of the country's tourists to the hotels that line its Seven Mile Beach area. For more tranquil living you'll want to live in some of the more residential areas. Governors Harbour, Parkway, Snug Harbour, and South Sound have nice apartments and homes that are close to town, beach, and amenities. The Prospect is a growing new area just ten minutes from town with a shopping center, supermarket, and plans for a five-screen movie theater. For more reasonable housing, check out West Bay and Bodden Town, which have traditional homes; they're just twenty minutes from George Town.

Cayman Brac has a modern airport and a hotel, but other options are limited unless you've got a one-track mind dedicated to the extremely basic pleasures of beach, coral, and clear blue seas. Little Cayman is the most paradisiacal in some ways, with secluded beaches and spectacular diving—but there's little to provide for a resident's daily life.

The tight-knit group of expats become your substitute family. The closeness cannot be described. Everyone has left their home country and formed a true bond. My close friends are from Cayman, New Zealand, Canada, Ireland, England, and Jamaica.

Pamela Skibinski, Grand Cayman

SETTING UP HOUSE

Whether renting or buying, the cost of accommodations depends on how close you are to the beach. Of course, nothing's that far from the beach in the Cayman Islands so if you're willing to bike or walk a bit, you will find that the rates become more reasonable.

Finding a Rental

A variety of homes, condominiums, and apartments are available for rent, but for the best choices, time your search for May or June. That way you'll avoid the winter high-season when you would be competing with tourists, employees, and other new residents. By December, good and reasonably priced rentals can be hard to come by.

Reflecting the island's tourist base, most rentals come furnished. Real estate agents differentiate between the terms "furnished" and "fully furnished." Furnished includes major appliances, beds, window treatments, and such; fully furnished includes everything needed to start living there, such as kitchen equipment and linens. Unfurnished apartments include appliances but nothing else. You'll pay a security deposit of one month's rent plus the monthly rent paid in advance. Deposits are required for utility, cable, and phone.

Rents are not cheap, though you can find better deals off the beach. A one-bedroom apartment within walking distance of the sea will be about $1,200 a month. A three-bedroom, two-bath villa with a large yard, completely furnished was advertised for $2,250 a month.

Buying a Home

The Cayman Islands does not limit foreign ownership of property, and real estate agencies compete against each other to sell their piece of paradise to the large numbers of North Americans looking for a second home or investment property.

The country maintains strict building code standards so much of the worry is taken out of your home search; however, it doesn't hurt to be wary. Have a property professionally inspected before you make an offer or finalize the contract. When you find a property that interests you, you won't need a title search; the British government insures the title on homes and land. At closing you'll pay a stamp duty of 7.5 percent of the sales price or of the appraised value if that's higher. After that, you'll pay no property taxes—ever.

Housing prices vary based on location and amenities. For example, a furnished two-bedroom, two-bath condominium with a garden view might go for $100,000. But an oceanfront unit with just one bedroom and one bath including new furniture and all appliances, with pool and tennis on site, may cost $150,000 and prices go up from there. If money's no object, go for the three-bedroom, two bath, oceanfront villa complete with private pool. But expect to pay $600,000 and up.

Utilities and Infrastructure

Water: The water is safe from the tap though most people prefer bottled water. Water is conserved in the Cayman Islands since there is no natural freshwater resource; drinking water is supplied by rainwater.

Electricity: Service is supplied at 110 volts, 60 hertz, the same as in the United States. Electricity costs more here though, and your bill can be massive if you're addicted to air conditioning.

Communications: Modern telephone service covers all three islands with international direct dialing service. Internet service is available.

Time Zone: The Cayman Islands is on Eastern Standard Time all year round.

Weights and Measures: The metric system is used here.

THE MAIL FROM HELL

Jagged black limestone rock seemed like someone's idea of the netherworld. Thus was the village of Hell named. Send your mail home from the original Hell Post Office, and give the recipient pause for thought.

MOVING PLANS

You can ship household items to the Cayman Islands duty-free if you've owned the items for more than six months. You must import your belongings during the first six months of your residency. If you wait longer than the six months, you'll pay a 20 percent duty.

Since electricity is supplied at the same voltage as in the United States, you can safely bring North American small appliances with you to the Cayman Islands. Many of the properties here are already furnished, so you may not need to ship any large appliances or major furnishings.

The British West Indies are strict about drug possession so don't even think of bringing in illegal drugs. To avoid delays at customs, bring medications in their original containers, with a copy of your doctor's prescription.

PAPERWORK AND RESIDENCE RULES

You can stay in the Cayman Islands for up to three months based on your U.S. passport, a naturalization certificate, or an original certified birth certificate plus photo identification. (A driver's license or voter's registration card is not accepted.) You must also have sufficient funds for your stay and the ticket to leave. You'll receive a pink immigration slip that acts as a tourist ID card; keep it with your other important papers since you'll need it when you leave.

To arrange a longer stay after you arrive, you must visit the Department of Immigration of the Cayman Islands, Phone: (345) 949-8344, for an extension. Or you can request a visa before you arrive, permitting you to stay for up to six months. (You cannot work without a work permit.)

The British Embassy and Consulates handle information on entry and customs requests. Contact the British Embassy in the United States at 3100 Massachusetts Avenue, NW, Washington, DC 20008; Phone: (202) 462-1340. British Consulates are also located in Atlanta, Boston, Chicago, Dallas, Los Angeles, New York, and San Francisco.

There is no U.S. consul in the Cayman Islands; the Cayman Islands falls within the consular district of the U.S. Embassy in Jamaica.

Pets

The Cayman Islands is free of rabies so regulations are strict for entering pets. Your pet must have had its rabies vaccination less than a year but at least thirty days prior to entry. An International Health

Certificate must be issued within fourteen days of your animal's arrival, and the Department of Agriculture must issue your animal an Import Permit. For details and forms see the Internet site http://cayman.com.ky/visiting/catsdogs.htm. Or contact Veterinary Services, Department of Agriculture, P.O. Box 459 GT, Grand Cayman, Cayman Islands; Phone: (345) 947-3090; Fax: (345) 947-2634.

Think twice before bringing a pet. Most rental accommodations don't accept them, though some will allow a pet with an increased security deposit.

GETTING THERE AND GETTING AROUND

Major airlines, including Delta, American, US Airways, and Cayman Airways, and charters serve the Cayman Islands regularly via Owen Robers International Airport on Grand Cayman Island. The flight takes just an hour from Miami.

Most internal transportation takes place by motor scooter, small car, and boat. Minibuses make runs to each of the main areas of Grand Cayman, and the service is convenient. Even if you don't see a bus stop, you can often just flag down a bus, and it will leave you where you request on the route.

Many people bike to the beach and to run errands since the island is flat and easy to get around. Bikes must be licensed at the Vehicular Licensing Department for a small fee.

> It [the lifestyle] is not for everyone. I have found "dreamers" that cannot turn their ideals into reality. But on the other hand, I have seen "bankers" get into the reggae and fit right in. Somewhere in the middle is key.
>
> Pamela Skibinski, Grand Cayman

Driving

The most important thing to remember about driving in the Cayman Islands is that driving is British-style—on the left side of the road. City and rural road conditions are good; roads are well maintained and monitored.

You can bring your own car, but the duty will add 25 to 40 percent to the cost depending on the vehicle's value. You'd be better off finding a new or used vehicle on the island. Remember that using the bus, taxis, or biking will lessen your need for a car so you can cut costs by choosing an auto that meets your most basic transportation needs.

MANAGING YOUR MONEY

The standard of living in the Cayman Islands is the highest in the Caribbean, and one of the highest in the world. Your cost of living will also be very high. Most products are imported and housing prices reflect the exclusive nature of the islands.

The basic unit of currency is the Cayman Islands dollar, which has a fixed exchange rate with the U.S. dollar. If you don't want to bother exchanging U.S. dollars for Cayman dollars, you can use your U.S. currency anywhere in the islands, but at the exchange rate of one U.S. dollar buys CI $.80. This rate is used throughout the islands, and the Caymans are one place where banks do not give a better rate of exchange. Major credit cards and traveler's checks are widely accepted. Automatic teller machines accept cards with Cirrus affiliation and can be found at several banks and at the Owen Roberts International Airport.

As an international finance center, Grand Cayman is wall-to-wall banks, with almost seven hundred of them. Many are strictly corporate or offshore centers that won't handle your checking account. You'll want a full-service bank that offers customer services. These include Barclays Bank, Scotiabank, Bank of Butterfied, Royal Bank of Canada, Cayman National Bank, Canadian Imperial Bank of Commerce, and British American Bank. Banking hours are normally Monday through Thursday from 9:00 A.M. to 4:00 P.M., and until 4:30 P.M. on Friday.

Taxes

Taxes are a big no-no in the Cayman Islands: no property tax, no income tax, no gift, sales, or value-added tax. No capital gains, inheritance, or estate tax.

STAYING HEALTHY AND SAFE

In most of the British West Indies, medical care is limited. Fortunately, the Cayman Islands is an exception; its medical care is comparable to that of the United States. Government-operated hospitals and other modern medical services are available on Grand Cayman and Cayman Brac. Grand Cayman has two modern hospitals. The George Town Hospital on Grand Cayman includes emergency, maternity, surgery, medical, and pediatric units, dental and eye clinics, and a pharmacy. The hospital is affiliated with Baptist Hospital of Miami, and patients needing advanced or critical care may be evacuated to the United States. Since the Cayman Islands is known for its diving, the George Town Hospital is one of the few places with a recompression chamber and an expert on call twenty-four hours in case of emergency.

The Chrissie Tomlinson Memorial Hospital is privately owned and operated with modern facilities for maternity, surgeries, and intensive care. Various clinics are staffed by resident medical practitioners and a variety of specialists. Cayman Brac's Faith Hospital has eighteen beds and an emergency room.

Hospitals and health providers usually expect cash payment immediately. Medicare, Medicaid, and most U.S. private health insurance do not cover you abroad. Depending on how long you intend to stay in the Cayman Islands, you'll need an expatriate health insurance policy or traveler's insurance. (For some options, see Chapter 25.) Make sure your insurance covers medical evacuation in case you need to be airlifted back to the United States.

Security

You'll generally feel very safe in the Cayman Islands. Just use common sense in keeping your belongings safe. Petty thefts do occur so don't leave money, credit cards, or your passport laying around on the beach. No U.S. Embassy or Consulate exists in the Cayman Islands, but if you're living there you may want to register with the consular section of the U.S. Embassy in Kingston, Jamaica, which has jurisdiction over the Cayman Islands.

As with all Caribbean countries, the Cayman Islands can be in the path of hurricanes, especially summer through late fall. Be aware of weather conditions and know the steps to take if a storm is approaching.

FOR MORE DETAILS

Below are some resources to help you further investigate a long-term stay in more the Cayman Islands.

Official Sources

British Consulates
Located in Atlanta, Boston,
  Chicago, Dallas, Los Angeles,
  New York, and San Francisco

British Embassy
3100 Massachusetts Avenue, NW
Washington, DC 20008
Phone: (202) 462-1340

Internet Connections

Cayman Islands Tourist Site
www.caymanislands.ky

Consular Information Sheet
http://travel.state.gov./british_windies.html

Background Reading

The Cayman Islands:
The Beach and Beyond
by Martha K. Smith
Cuchipanda Inc., 1996

Diving Cayman Islands
by Jesse Cancelmo
Aqua Quest, 1997

21

Greece

When I think of Greece, I think of liquid pleasures—the blue-green waters of the Aegean Sea shimmering below cubist white villas, the local wines and strong-flavored retsina, and the mellow green-gold of fresh olive oil. But one can't ogle the sea and eat all day. No problem. Greece offers centuries of history to explore, whether it's the Acropolis in the middle of bustling Athens or the island of Delos, completely dedicated to its impressive archaeological treasures.

Highlights

- Temperate climate
- Mainland and island lifestyles
- Beaches and water sports
- Rich in antiquities
- Moderate prices

The sea is an incredible azure shade, seeming to go on forever as it blends with the blue skies. And the sea dictates the pace of life here—literally. The Greeks have accustomed themselves to living by boat schedules, a fact poorly understood until the first strong wind cancels the regular ferries, stranding you until the ferry services restart. But the Greek islands are magic places with incredible scenery, a temperate climate, and a relaxed ambiance.

THE BASICS

The Hellenic Republic, as Greece is officially named, is located in southeastern Europe. Its mainland is connected to Europe, and more than two thousand islands are scattered around it. Italy lies to the northwest, Albania, Macedonia, and Bulgaria to the north, and Turkey to the east. The topography is astounding since the Greek islands consist mostly of submerged land. Some are fertile, some craggy and bare.

The country is democratic—and was long before the United States came into being. The framers of the U.S. constitution based it in part on Greece's democratic ideals. The Greek constitution guarantees civil, political, and human rights. The Greek government is headed by a president and a prime minister. Legislative powers are held by Parliament.

Greeks are warm, hospitable people who value their families, friends, and life. The country is one of the most homogenous in the world, with 98 percent of the population being ethnic Greek. They have the Greek Orthodox Church in common, which influences social life and the culture with feast days and celebrations.

The country is proud of its sports history. Greece founded the ancient and modern Olympic games and has been chosen to host the 2004 Olympics.

Climate

With idyllic postcard images depicting beaches and sun-drenched bungalows, it's easy to think of Greece as a tropical paradise year-round.
The truth is, you'll shiver if you wear a bathing suit in winter. The climate is moderate, but hardly warm. However, the farther south you go,
the warmer the winters will be. Crete gets the earliest spring. Greek
summers can be extremely hot and dry though refreshing sea breezes
keep the islands more comfortable than the mainland. Athens swelters
in the summer with temperatures that average 102°F. January's highs
are 64°F with lows in the 40s. Throughout Greece, spring and fall are
the best seasons.

NAY-SAYING

In Greece, if you shake your head and say "nay" you could be saying the
opposite of what you mean. The Greek word *né* means "yes."

Language

Although Greek is the official language, many people speak English in
Athens and tourist areas. It's handy to understand the basics of Greek
if you intend to be here longer than a few weeks. You won't have to say,
"It's all Greek to me" if you take a beginning Greek course or teach
yourself the rudiments with a book and cassettes. Two suggestions are
Breakthrough Greek (Pan Macmillan book and cassettes) or *Greek in
Three Months* (Hugo, Dorling Kindersley book and four cassettes). At
the very least get a phrasebook and learn a few polite words like hello,
please, and thank-you. Also learn the Greek alphabet; it's a tremendous
help for reading and pronouncing directional signs. The good news is,
the Greek alphabet has only twenty-four letters, not twenty-six.

Don't be surprised to discover that most names for Greek towns
and sites are translated several different ways. For example, the island
of Santorini is also known as Thira. Dilos can be spelled Delos, and
so on. At first it's confusing, but you'll eventually learn the various
treatments.

BLAZING CHEESE

Opa! That's what they yell when they flame the saganaki cheese in a Greek restaurant. It sounds like a cry of joy or exuberance. Well, it is that. But the word's meaning is actually closer to "Whoops" or "Watch it!"

YOUR NEW LIFESTYLE

How will you fill your days? Here's an overview of activities and interests that are part of daily life in Greece.

Food and Drink

Greek meals are based on roasted meats such as pork and lamb, seafood including shrimp and squid, and various pasta and eggplant dishes. Honey, olives, and olive oil serve as delicious compliments. One common lunch is souvlaki, meat served with a yogurt sauce and flat grilled pita bread. If you have a sweet tooth, pastry shops are common, and they offer a wider array than most restaurants. Be sure to try Greek yogurt served with honey and walnuts as dessert. Yogurt is special here, milder and more flavorful than most natural yogurts. For something richer, try one of the flaky pastry and honey desserts such as baklava. Wash it down with Greek wine. Retsina is white wine with resin added. Yes, it takes some getting used to.

Arts and Entertainment

Traditional Greek folk music is not common these days, but it's still played at festivals, concerts, and various cultural programs. The distinctive sound derives from its instruments, especially the lyra, a type of fiddle with three strings. Contemporary sounds such as rock and jazz are taking over. Museums, art galleries, and numerous archaeological sites are waiting to be discovered in Athens, on the mainland, and on countless islands. Opera takes place at the Greek National Opera in Athens. Greek theater will be a bit of a loss unless you suddenly acquire an amazing knowledge of the language.

U.S. movies are popular in Greece. They're usually shown in their original language, with Greek subtitles, so you'll be able to understand them. English-language newspapers, magazines, and paperbacks can be found in specialty bookstores in Athens and on racks at some newsstands in popular tourist areas.

Outdoor Life and Sports

Water is the word for sports. Beautiful swimming beaches are found throughout the islands and even around Athens. Other popular water sports include scuba diving, snorkeling, sailing, and yachting.

Hiking is popular. After all, in Greece the scenery is just too good to miss. I'll personally attest to the fact that the world-famous Samaria Gorge on Crete, with its eighteen kilometers of rocky terrain, is one of the most incredible hikes for scenic splendor. But wear comfortable hiking boots. I dared it with sneakers, and my toes will never be the same. More civilized sports are popular, including tennis and golf. Even skiing is possible if you head to the Italian Alps.

Shopping

As the largest city, Athens offers the greatest selection for inveterate shoppers. The main shopping in Athens is found on Ermou Street and near Syntagma Square. Plaka's narrow cobblestone streets, ranged with handicraft and tourist stores, is more charming. The Kolanaki area showcases luxurious goods in designer boutiques. If you want gold jewelry, Greece is the place to buy it since prices are amazingly inexpensive. Silver, embroidery, and icons (many of which are replicas) are also popular.

THE BIRTH OF A NAME DAY

The Greek Orthodox religion is strong and evident in everyday life. Most people are usually named after a saint, who has a special day in the calendar. Greeks often celebrate their name day, the day of the saint for whom they were named, rather than their birthday.

Social Life

Greek people are friendly and some speak English, but if your language skills are limited you'll want English-speaking friends. A large English-speaking population lives in Athens, and various English-language newspapers can be found that provide information on clubs and social activities. You can broaden your friendships with visiting Germans and Dutch who often speak English well.

Some groups to investigate include the American Women's Organization of Greece—6 Sinopsis and 11 Evinou Streets; Phone: (30) 778-0329 or (30) 779-2247 ext. 7—and the Hellenic American Union—22 Massalias; Phone: (30) 362-9886—which arrange cultural activities.

WHERE TO LIVE IN GREECE

How do you find your own special place in Greece? When I dream of Greece I imagine a laid-back island lifestyle, but not everyone has the same picture in mind. Some people find their dream spot on the mainland where there's more activity and cultural events—and life is not subject to the whims of ferry schedules. Do you want to be smack-dab in the middle of the big-city hustle and bustle of Athens? Would you prefer a smaller city or a suburb on the mainland?

Or perhaps you'd be charmed by one of the countless islands ranging in size from large to tiny.

With over 1,400 islands you can choose from pastoral green countryside to dramatic, dry, and volcanic scenes. But you don't have to research all 1,400 of these dots in the sea. Many of them are uninhabited, which narrows the choices down to manageable proportions. Consider various factors, such as your desire to be near international airports, efficient mass transit, good medical facilities, and other retirees and expatriates. Read on to discover which locations suit your dreams.

Athens

Athens is the capital and the largest city of Greece. Nearly half the population lives in Athens, along with a large number of foreigners. A large contingent of Americans, there for business or through the government, have prepared the way with American social groups. The problem is that Athens is crowded, noisy, and polluted and living costs are higher than anywhere else in Greece. Ordinarily I wouldn't dream of recommending such a place, but then I'm not a big-city person. One American woman retired in Athens, but she admits that "you either love it or hate it."

Athens is certainly where the action is in Greece. The city is modernizing, bolstered by the 2004 Olympic Games. A host of special projects are breathing new life, if not fresh air, into the city's attitude, infrastructure, facilities, and cultural offerings. To cut pollution, a new metropolitan subway system will hopefully encourage people to leave their cars at home. An odd/even license plate system is regulating who can drive and when. Walking routes are being designed to connect historical monuments, making the city more pedestrian friendly.

For midtown accommodations, the most elegant area is Kolonaki, which is close to foreign embassies, restaurants, cinemas, and shops. You'll find apartments, but no individual houses, and the area is as expensive as it is elegant. Northern suburbs such as Paleo Psychico and Philothei offer newer housing, high standards of living, and international schools that draw expatriates. These towns offer proximity to big-city amenities but don't suffer from Athens's air and noise pollution. Many executives live here so, again, it's pricey.

South of downtown is Vouliagmeni, with a well-reputed spa. Rafina, a fishing and port city on the Aegean about an hour from Athens, is a charming seaside town with ferry connections to all Greek ports.

Thessaloniki

Situated on the Aegean Sea, three hundred miles north of Athens, Thessaloniki offers city living that's more manageable than bustling Athens. This doesn't mean that Thessaloniki is a backwoods. It's known for its magnificent Byzantine churches, and many Americans have chosen to live there.

The city offers a high quality of life and was named the 1997 Cultural Capital of Europe. It offers a full range of shopping and restaurants as well as museums that showcase the area's rich archaeological and artistic heritage. An added benefit for people who want city living on the mainland but not Athens's stifling summer heat: The weather is cooler in Thessaloniki.

Crete

Crete is the southernmost of Greece's large islands. The remnants of its Minoan civilization are fascinating. Great palaces, the most famous of which is Knosos, have been found throughout the island from thousands of years B.C. Today the development is along the coasts, where the cities and towns tend to be located along with resorts and beautiful beaches. Iraklio is the main city and port, but Chania has a more picturesque historic center, packed with harborside cafés and charming homes on narrow, winding streets. Crete's interior is dramatically mountainous, and some of the switchback roads require nerves of steel. It includes the scenic Samaria Gorge that I mentioned earlier. (It's beautiful but if you're not a masochist, consider taking the hike from the southern end; it's shorter and less strenuous.)

Corfu

Odysseus praised Corfu for its hospitality three thousand years ago, and the island still welcomes visitors with pleasure. It's already been discovered by the British who have a long history in the area (cricket is even played here!) so you'll hear English spoken. The land is scenic, with beautiful beaches, wooded hills, and clear blue seas.

Corfu Town reflects its Venetian influence with historic churches and fortifications. For scuba divers, Corfu is one of the few islands where diving is permitted nearby. Albania is just one nautical mile from Corfu, for an interesting day trip.

As with most popular areas, Corfu attracts tourists so it's crowded in summer and, of course, it's more expensive then. Look for housing in local classifieds, not in tourist publications. One classified ad in a local paper included a second-floor apartment in Corfu Town with two bedrooms, bath, kitchen, and balcony renting for $625 per month.

Santorini (aka Thira)

Whichever way you turn, Santorini offers idyllic postcard views from the famous caldera—which resulted when part of the volcanic island collapsed into a C-shaped basin—to the dramatic cliffs, to the narrow cobblestone alleys leading through the town of Fira, also called Thira. Yes, the name of this town and island are the same, though each has other names too.

The town of Oia, on the northern tip of Santorini has preserved its sense of place despite the tourists, meaning it's more peaceful than Thira with its regular infusion of tourists and cruise boats. Oia is the spot to watch the sunset at harborside cafés. The island is small, with good roads. Despite the beauty and thus its interest to tourism, it's still possible to get on your motor scooter and ride away on roads with relatively little traffic except near Fira/Thira. Houses here are made of stone, many of them built into the cliff sides that provide natural cooling in the summer. Beaches are beautiful here. You may enjoy your own stretch of privacy off-season, but during July and August it's a full house.

SETTING UP HOUSE

For classified listings to rent or purchase, check English-language papers such as *The Athens News, Athens Today, The Hellenic Star,* and *Kathimerini* (English edition). Also check the *Bulletin* of the American Women's Organization of Greece. You may find good offers via word-of-mouth or the Internet too.

Finding a Rental

Many people rent through real estate agents in Greece though contacts in the expatriate community may find you a better deal. Leases are usually for one to two years. A security deposit of one to two months' rent may be required. You may be requested to prepay the rent in advance by two months to a year. If you do, bargain for a reduction in the monthly rent. It takes a while to get phone service installed in Greece, so find out whether the property already has a phone line. Verify that the building meets safety standards, especially for earthquakes. Most housing is rented without appliances, except in furnished units.

Some international rental organizations deal in fully furnished apartments for short- or long-term stays. They're often for executive transfers so they may be pricier than local offerings, but if you're interested, two such services are Global Home Network, Inc. (703) 318-7081 or (800) 528-3549, and Oakwood Corporate Housing (800) 888-0808.

Buying a Home

Greece restricts property ownership by foreigners in some border areas. Consult a knowledgeable and reputable attorney before you make an offer. You can get names of approved attorneys from the U.S. Embassy in Athens.

Mortgage rates in Greece are among the highest in the world— above 10 percent, according to the European Mortgage Federation. Keep this in mind when deciding how much house you can afford.

Utilities and Infrastructure

Water: Greece's water is generally safe but heavily chlorinated so most people prefer bottled water.

Electricity: The electricity is 220 volts, 50 hertz, though some islands have 110 DC power. The Greek electric company is known by the initials D.E.H. Cut-off is quick if bills go unpaid so handle utility bills promptly.

Communications: The Greek national phone company is OTE. Service is good, with direct lines to all major countries, but rates are among the highest in Europe. Mail is acceptably reliable in the cities and major resort areas. Look for sunny yellow signs and mailboxes.

Time Zone: Greece is seven hours ahead of Eastern Standard Time in the United States. Daylight savings time occurs from the last Sunday in March to the last Sunday in October.

Weights and Measures: Greece uses the metric system.

MOVING PLANS

Small electrical appliances brought from the United States will need a transformer and adapter to work in Greece. Since the European broadcasting system is incompatible with American television sets, don't bother bringing yours unless it's just to play videos. You may want a furnished apartment or house that will eliminate the cost and long wait of shipping your furniture here. Buy a good used or new car in Greece.

PAPERWORK AND RESIDENCE RULES

U.S. citizens can stay in Greece with just their passport, no visa, for up to three months. To stay longer, ask for a residence permit more than twenty days before the three months are over. You should apply in person at the Aliens Bureau, 173 Alexándras, 11522 Athens; Phone: (30) (1) 770-5711. If you cannot get to Athens easily, call them for other sites in Greece.

Pets

Your dog or cat must have specific documentation including an International Health Certificate signed by an accredited veterinarian. The certificate must be signed no fewer than 10 days before departure, endorsed by the USDA, and approved by the Greek Consulate. You must also supply an original certificate showing that your pet is current on rabies and all routine immunizations; these must have been given more than 30 days but fewer than 180 days before departure. Before arriving, make arrangements for a required sanitary inspection in Greece.

GETTING THERE AND GETTING AROUND

The public infrastructure in Greece has undergone a major revival for the 2004 Olympic Games. Projects include a new airport plus road, port, and subway improvements. The new Eleftherious Venizelos International Airport at Spata is just thirteen miles east of Athens. It was greatly needed since the old Hellinikon Airport, though just under seven miles south of downtown, was decidedly inefficient for an international gateway. Other airports are scattered throughout the mainland and the larger islands. International airlines, including Olympic Airways, Delta, British Airways, KLM, and TWA, have scheduled flights.

Trains are run by the state-owned Hellenic State Railway and run to major European cities from mainland Greece. Buses, trolleys, and now the new subway system provide transportation in Athens. Long-distance buses serve other locations. Taxis are relatively inexpensive in

Athens. Ferry service links the mainland with the islands. You can find schedules at any local travel agency or the Greek Tourist Office.

Driving

Greece has won the dubious distinction of having the worst drivers and the highest accident rate in Europe. Not only that, the winding Greek roads can be treacherous for drivers unfamiliar with their twists and turns.

An International Driving Permit, available through AAA in the United States, is required to drive in Greece, though generally speaking, your home country license suffices. Be sure to maintain comprehensive travel insurance.

WE'RE GOING *WHERE?*

Ferry service is often disrupted by strong winds, stranding people wherever they may be. It also mixes up the schedules so a ferry awaiting passengers at 8:00 A.M., which is supposed to be going to Pireás, may really be last night's ferry that's late leaving for Crete. Getting on could send you five hours in the wrong direction. Don't assume that if it's the right time and the right place it's also the right ferry. (OK, I'll admit I learned this the hard way.)

MANAGING YOUR MONEY

The International Monetary Fund commented that in Greece "growth is strong . . . fiscal developments are better than forecast, and inflation has dropped markedly." All this points the way toward Greece's entrance into the European Union in 2001, at which time the euro will become its official currency. Meanwhile, the Greek unit of currency is the drachma, which is usually shown in prices as a "D." Watch those commas and periods, since they're used in reverse of the way the United States does. For example, the sum $6,500.12 would be written $6.500,12 in Greece.

The cost of living in Greece is among the lowest in Western Europe. Living on the local economy rather than insisting on imported goods will keep your budget low. Your actual costs will depend on whether you live in downtown Athens or in the countryside, whether you want the four-bedroom, seafront villa or a small village home.

Banks in Greece offer checking and saving accounts, much as in the United States. For daily transactions, you can establish an account in a local Greek bank; however, deposits are not officially guaranteed so you'd be safer to keep money in the United States and access it via ATM, check, or wire transfer as needed.

The price of doctors — everything, in fact—is negotiable and based on relationships. All jobs are done by knowing somebody; the economy often functions without money.

Judy Lawrence, Athens

The largest Greek banks are the National Bank of Greece and Alpha Credit Bank. Some American banks such as American Express, Bank of America, and Citibank have a few branches in Greece.

Major credit cards are usually accepted in Athens and major tourist sites, though some merchants charge an extra fee for using one. In small shops and rural areas, be prepared to use drachmas. ATMs are common, especially Plus and Cirrus systems, and they offer the best rate of exchange.

Taxes

Greece charges an 18 percent value-added tax (VAT) on most goods and services except for basic necessities, which are taxed at 8 percent. Books, newspapers, and periodicals are taxed at 4 percent.

Residents pay income taxes on earnings worldwide. Non-residents are taxed on Greek-source income only. There is a double-tax treaty with the United States. Consult a specialist. Many of the major U.S. accounting firms have offices or affiliates in Greece.

STAYING HEALTHY AND SAFE

The Mediterranean diet is said to contribute to the health of the Greek population. Health care in Athens and Thessaloniki is good, and many doctors are trained in English-speaking countries so you'll manage the language problem. However, standards in areas outside the big cities may be lower and services may be limited on the islands. Consulates have lists of doctors and dentists who treat foreigners.

Medicare does not cover Americans outside the United States. Look for an expatriate health care policy. (For a list of some expatriate health insurers, see Chapter 25.)

Security

There is normally a low crime rate in Greece, but beware of the pickpockets plying their trade in Athens.

Greece is located in an earthquake zone so learn the appropriate safety procedures. (They're listed on the first page in phone books.) You can call the Tourist Police at 171 in Athens or 922-7777 outside of Athens, and you can reach the U.S. Embassy in Athens at (30) (1) 721-2951 during normal business hours. In fact, it's not a bad idea to register with the U.S. Embassy. They'll contact you with any essential information that Americans in Greece may need.

FOR MORE DETAILS

Below are some resources to help you further investigate a long-term stay in Greece.

Official Sources

American Citizen Services Unit in Athens
Phone: (30) (1) 720-2408 or (30) (1) 720-3652 (after hours)

Greek Embassy
2221 Massachusetts Avenue, NW
Washington, DC 20008
Phone: (202) 939-5800

Greek National Tourist Board (EOT / Greece)
2 Amerikis Street
10110 Athens
Phone: (30) (1) 322-3111

Greek National Tourist Board (EOT / U.S.)

Chicago
168 N. Michigan Avenue, Suite 600
Chicago, IL 60601
Phone: (312) 782-1084

Los Angeles
611 W. 6th Street, Suite 2198
Los Angeles, CA 90017
Phone: (213) 626-6696

New York
Olympic Tower, 5th Floor
645 Fifth Avenue
New York, NY 10022
Phone: (212) 421-5777
Fax: (212) 826-6940

U.S. Consulate General
59 Leoforos Nikis
54622 Thessaloniki
Phone: (30) 31-242-905

U.S. Embassy
91 Vassilisis Sophias Avenue
11521 Athens
Phone: (30) (1) 721-2951

Internet Connections

Greek Embassy
www.greece@greekembassy.org

**Greek National Tourism
Organization**
www.gnto.gr

Greek Realtors
www.greekrealtors.com

Guide to Greece
www.gogreece.com

Live and Work in Greece
www.greekshops.com

Tourist Guide
www.vacation.net.gr

U.S. Embassy in Athens
www.usisathens.gr

Welcome to Corfu
http://corfu.forthnet.gr

Background Reading

Culture Shock! Greece
by Clive L. Rawlins
Graphic Arts Center Publishing, 1997

Travelers' Tales: Greece
by Larry Habegger
Travelers' Tales, Inc., 2000

22

U.S. Virgin Islands

This tropical paradise has it all. Crystal blue seas fringed by glorious coves of white sand. Harbors dotted with sails and elegant cruise ships. Forested hillsides sprinkled with red hibiscus, purple bougainvillea, and winter-blooming frangipani. Find yourself a spot in a charming Old-World village with

Highlights

- Sun, sand, and azure seas
- Caribbean climate year-round
- A sailing paradise
- U.S. territory

pastel villas and wrought iron terraces. The good and bad news is that tourism is the country's main industry. This provides a ready supply of entertainment and a lively atmosphere in the tourist areas. It can also mean that Charlotte Amalie and some beaches are wall-to-wall people when the cruise ships unload their human cargo. Fortunately, the cruise ships have schedules, and you can learn to avoid congestion.

For retirees, one main advantage of the U.S. Virgin Islands is the fact that you're on U.S. soil while enjoying the exotic pleasures of tropical beaches, aqua seas, and pastel-painted villas.

THE BASICS

The U.S. Virgin Islands comprises the islands of St. Croix, St. Thomas, and St. John. At eighty-four square miles, St. Croix is the largest. St. Thomas is next at thirty-two square miles. And St. John is the baby at nineteen square miles. The three U.S. territories, part of a larger chain of islands, are located a thousand miles from the southern tip of the United States mainland in the Caribbean, just east of Puerto Rico.

The terrain is hilly, sometimes extremely so, making for several narrow twisting roads that require concentration and nerves of steel. The vertiginous landscape is the result of the islands' volcanic birth. In the seventeenth century the Virgin Islands were divided into English and Danish ownership, but in 1917, the United States bought the Danish island of St. Croix.

The islands are a hybrid of spicy Caribbean life crossed with Americanization and a multicultural history influenced by Danish, Dutch, Spanish, French, African, Indian, and Caribbean island migrants.

AND THE PREVIOUS OWNER WAS . . .

Seven flags have flown over the island of St. Croix: Spanish, French, English, Knights of Malta, Dutch, Danish, and American.

> **WHAT'S IN A NAME?**
>
> Christopher Columbus discovered the islands in 1493 and named them *Las Islas Virgenes,* not because he was greeted by hordes of nubile young maidens but because the islands were pristine and seemingly endless in beauty. He claimed St. Croix for Spain under the name of Santa Cruz.

Climate

Enjoy tropical living at its finest. Winter temperatures hover between 70° and 85°F, and though summer is hotter at 75° to 90°F, the trade winds manage to cool the air nicely. Winter through spring is relatively dry. The so-called rainy season occurs from late summer through fall (basically July through November), but rain rarely lasts for more than an hour at a time before the sun returns. The exception is that rainy season can also mean hurricane season.

Language

As on the mainland, the official language is English.

YOUR NEW LIFESTYLE

How will you fill your days? Here's an overview of activities and interests that are part of daily life in the Virgin Islands.

Food and Drink

Everything from gourmet cuisine to local seafood, island specialties, and U.S.-style burgers and fries will ensure variety for your meals. Try the conch—especially batter-fried in fritters—or wahoo, grouper, mahi-mahi, or other varieties of fresh fish. International cuisine is not hard to find at restaurants that offer everything from French to Chinese, Italian, and Mexican. West Indian and African-inspired specialties can be found at small local restaurants. Rum punch is a treat for watching the sunset.

Arts and Entertainment

You can go from quietly watching sea turtles and dolphin cavort to watching the high-rollers cavort in the casinos where the nightlife gets lively. The Reichhold Center for the Arts is run by the University of the Virgin Islands. The 1,1960-seat amphitheater on St. Thomas overlooks the Caribbean Sea. The center is home to the Caribbean Repertory Theater Company; it also showcases international talent, such as the Vienna Boys' Choir, Itzhak Perlman, Bill Cosby, and Marcel Marceau. Don't expect to find a wide range of major cultural activities every night, however. If you're an opera fan, bring your CDs.

Outdoor Life and Sports

Sailing is a major occupation in the Virgin Islands. The weather's a delight, the views of sea, beach, and forests are spectacular, and it's easy to wander from one protected cove to another. Viewing the fascinating undersea world through a snorkel mask is better than television anytime. The clear aqua water presents an unimpeded view of tropical fish that show up their northern cousins with vivid hues of yellow, blue, green, and red. For landlubbers, the sports options include tennis, golf, horseback riding, and hiking.

Shopping

Most stores are open from 10:00 A.M. to 6:00 P.M. Monday through Saturday; sometimes they're open later in the evening. Duty-free shops abound in St. Thomas's Charlotte Amalie and Christiansted on St. Croix. U.S. citizens have a duty-free quota of $1,200, which is double what's allowed in other Caribbean islands. Check out bargains on cameras, fine jewelry and watches, china, perfume, liquor, and leather goods. Investigate native crafts too, including artwork, pottery, and jewelry.

Social Life

Politeness is a way of life with residents, who regularly offer a friendly greeting to their island neighbors. Tourist areas are more casual, since vacationers come and go, but residents and snowbirds who return regularly every winter join together in various social events based on activities, much as on the U.S. mainland. Yachting and golf tournaments are among the most popular.

WHERE TO LIVE IN THE VIRGIN ISLANDS

In order of size, here's a description of the three Virgin Islands.

St. Croix

Of the three islands, St. Croix is the largest and offers the most amenities. The island includes rain forest, desert, and beaches. It's the most affordable of the Virgin Islands; it's larger and flatter, which offers more land suitable for building. Early Danish settlers influenced the architecture and language of St. Croix, as is evident in many of the buildings and city names. The two major towns are Christiansted, which is the commercial hub, and Frederiksted. Most retirees settle in Christiansted for its amenities and the charm of its eighteenth-century buildings. Frederiksted is also charming, but it doesn't offer as many modern conveniences as retirees might want.

St. Thomas

St. Thomas is the second largest of the islands and home to the capital of the U.S. Virgin Islands, Charlotte Amalie. The town, named for a Danish queen, is filled with historic buildings and duty-free shops. The port is the most popular in the Caribbean, which makes it a bustling place. When the cruise shops disgorge their passengers for the day, Main Street is jam-packed with bargain hunters. The steep and winding streets leading into the vivid green hills are more peaceful, as is any place on the opposite side of the island from the capital.

St. John

St. John is the closest thing to paradise you'll find, with its miles of white sand beaches, clear azure seas, peaceful lagoons, lush wooded hillsides, and little tourist clutter. Two-thirds of the island is set apart as national park land thanks to Laurence Rockefeller, who first donated over five thousand acres to the U.S. government. The port of Cruz Bay has restaurants, shops, and galleries, mostly for the tourists. The opportunities to live here are much fewer and much more expensive, but don't despair; it's just a short ferry ride from Red Hook on St. Thomas.

SETTING UP HOUSE

If you're lucky, your new accommodations will be designed to capture the cool trade winds and the magnificent views. Open-style floor plans, high vaulted ceilings, and ceiling fans work to cool the indoors while exterior decks extend the living space outdoors. Housing is usually built on rocky steep slopes, and residential buildings have septic tanks.

Finding a Rental

As befits a tourist-oriented destination, most accommodations are available furnished, and bargains are hard to come by. You can choose from apartments, condominiums, and houses, but tourist resorts will be expensive. The spacious homes with views command weekly rents of $2,000 a week and up and up. However, year-round rentals on apartments are available from $350 to $2,500 a month plus utilities depending on size and location.

Buying a Home

Condominiums come fully furnished in most cases. Prices are especially reasonable on St. Croix if you pass up the seaside view. An inland, one-bedroom condominium can go for $60,000 to $80,000. A condominium in a luxury development directly on a sandy beach with pool and excellent views offers one-bedroom, one-bath units with washer and dryer for $120,000. Moving up higher, a three-bedroom villa in a gated Robert Trent Jones golf community ranges from $180,000 to $350,000.

On St. John, prices are double or triple those of St. Croix or St. Thomas. There's so little land not taken by the national park that the demand sends prices sky-high. One two-bedroom home set back in the trees was advertised for $295,000, but the average home costs over $400,000. If you're planning to downsize, some small apartments can be found for $100,000 and up.

Mortgages are available with the usual financial requirements except that interest rates are a bit higher than on the mainland, and the usual down payment is 20 to 30 percent. Financial institutions on the Virgin Islands require earthquake and windstorm insurance with the mortgage.

NOT QUITE A NATIVE

Newcomers to the Virgin Islands are distinguished by their origins. Americans are known as "statesiders" or "continentals." People from other Caribbean islands are called "down-islanders."

Utilities and Infrastructure

Water: Water surrounds the islands, but freshwater is precious so conservation is actively practiced. The main sources of freshwater are desalination plants, rain collection, and potable water from the WAPA (Water and Power Authority). Desalination plants on St. Croix and St. Thomas provide water for urban areas on those islands. Throughout the islands, all residences, hotels, and most public buildings are legally required to have cisterns, which gather water from rooftop precipitation collectors.

Electricity: Electricity is the same as in North America.

Communications: Telephone service is modern and offers all the services you'd expect, including Internet service providers.

Time Zone: The Virgin Islands is on Atlantic Standard Time, which is an hour ahead of Eastern Standard Time.

Weights and Measures: The islands use the metric system.

MOVING PLANS

Most properties are furnished so don't rush to move your belongings until you know exactly what you need to bring. There is no customs duty for Americans; you're technically moving within the United States.

PAPERWORK AND RESIDENCE RULES

United States citizens need no passport or visa to enter the Virgin Islands or to live there. However, you should bring two forms of photo identification with you.

Pets

There is no quarantine requirement for pets coming to the U.S. Virgin Islands though your pets' normal inoculations should be up-to-date. If you intend to take a pet, however, check with the airline on shipping regulations. Some airlines limit pet shipments to temperate weather and curtail them during the summer.

GETTING THERE AND GETTING AROUND

The main entry point for the Virgin Islands, the Cyril E. King Airport on St. Thomas, is about three miles from Charlotte Amalie. Several international airlines, among them American Airlines, Delta, and US Airways, plus tourist charters, serve the area. St. Croix has the Henry E. Rohlsen Airport. LIAT, the largest Caribbean carrier, serves the islands with an island hopper ticket. The office is at the King Airport on St. Thomas.

VITRAN bus service operates on St. Thomas and St. Croix. Most of the major international, as well as local, car rental companies serve the islands.

Driving

Remember to drive on the left, a vestige of the original British rule of the Virgin Islands. Left turn on red is OK; in fact, it's encouraged (after stopping to view oncoming traffic, of course) because not having to idle saves gas. The islands are small so distances are short. They can seem long though, because the narrow, steep roads are often twisty to boot. Small vehicles are easier to maneuver, but get one with enough oomph to make the grades. Though most roads are narrow, St. Croix has a main highway connecting Christiansted and Frederiksted.

Watch your gas gauge. Gas stations are open 6:30 A.M. to 8:00 P.M. Monday through Saturday, but most of them are closed on Sunday; don't be caught short.

You can use your U.S. license; there is no need to have an international version.

MANAGING YOUR MONEY

The U.S. dollar is the currency so you'll avoid cash-exchange problems. In general, your cost of living will be higher than on the mainland since virtually all food and household products must be imported.

Taxes

Taxes are essentially the same as on the U.S. mainland. Property taxes are based on the property's assessed value, which is the same as the actual value. The tax is calculated by multiplying 1.25 percent by 60 percent of the property's value. For questions, contact the Office of Tax Assessor in St. Croix at (340) 773-6449, in St. Thomas at (340) 776-8505, in Frederiksted at (340) 772-3115, or in St. John at (340) 776-6737.

STAYING HEALTHY AND SAFE

One big benefit of retiring in the U.S. Virgin Islands: Medicare covers you. Health care is up-to-date, and services are readily available on the two largest islands, though limited on St. John. St. Thomas has the Roy Lester Schneider Hospital in Charlotte Amalie. St. Croix has the Charles Harwood Complex and the Governor Juan F. Luis Hospital plus a clinic. The small island of St. John has a clinic. For emergency services, call the same number as on the U.S. mainland: 911.

The most common health concern revolves around the sun—namely the potential for sun or heat stroke and sunburns. You'll be getting plenty of sun throughout the day so take it easy, use sunscreen, and drink plenty of fluids. Dengue fever is more serious. The disease causes flu-like symptoms, including high fever and sore joints, so it may be misdiagnosed until the rash appears. See a doctor if you're in doubt. Mosquitoes carry the disease so avoid bites by using a repellent, especially in the evening when mosquitoes are more active.

Some of the flora is more than tropical and pretty; it's also a hazard to your health. Avoid the oleander and the manchineel trees. The oleander wood is toxic when burned so it's not for a beach bonfire and cookout! The manchineel tree is a giant version of poison ivy, and it causes skin blisters. The only insect to beware of is the centipede. It's not usually fatal to a healthy person, but you won't enjoy its poisonous bite.

Security

Crime has escalated in Charlotte Amalie on St. Thomas where even in daylight, locked cars must be empty. Avoid a blatant show of money or expensive belongings. Never wander around the streets and beaches alone at night.

Part of the problem is that drug use has increased, and you may even notice some selling going on. Be aware of your surroundings. You will be safest on the popular public beaches and near the resorts.

FOR MORE DETAILS

Below are some resources to help you further investigate a long-term stay in the Virgin Islands.

Official Sources

**U.S. Virgin Islands
Department of Tourism**
P.O. Box 6400
St. Thomas, U.S. Virgin Islands 00804
Phone (340) 774-8784 or (800) 372-USVI

Internet Connections

Comprehensive guide
www.usviguide.com

Island info
www.usvi-on-line.com

Department of Tourism
www.virginisles.com

U.S. V.I. Department of Tourism
www.usvi.org/tourism

Government site
www.usvi.org

Background Reading

Desiring Paradise
by Karin W. Schlesinger
Conch Publications, 1999

On Island Time
by Hilary Steward
University of Washington Press, 1999

A Trip to the Beach: Living on Island Time in the Caribbean
by Melinda and Robert Blanchard
Clarkson Potter, 2000

EXOTIC AND ENTREPRENEURIAL

Are you retired but not ready to sit on a beach? Are you looking for a new challenge along with a new lifestyle? Then your dream situation may include volunteering or working in a country that's a bit further from the usual retiree's plans. Some countries are begging for Americans to teach English or share their marketing knowledge or entrepreneurial skills. In some cases, you might be paid for your expertise. In fact, for people who couldn't otherwise have an out-of-country adventure, this can be the ideal way to live overseas.

Even if you do not want to "retire" definitively in an exotic location, you may enjoy the dramatic change in lifestyle for a few years of exciting new opportunities in a fascinating culture.

23

Czech Republic

Chosen the European City of Culture for the year 2000, Prague is the Eastern European capital most often compared to Paris for its beauty. In one way the city was fortunate that Germany invaded it so early in World War II. As a result, Prague didn't suffer the devastation that many other European cities did. The buildings are lovely, although they're coated with black remnants of the coal-burning furnaces from the Communist era. Walking the Charles Bridge at dusk is an experience not to be forgotten. The statues loom before you, ghosts of a time long past. Follow the city lights and spend your evening enjoying some of the world's best beer, a hearty meal, and world-class concerts or opera.

Though not up to U.S. standards, the Czech Republic has one of the highest standards of living in Central and Eastern Europe. Meanwhile, the country is dedicated to converting from a state-controlled economy, a remnant of Communist rule, to one based on private enterprise. With little experience in entrepreneurial activities, they've sought partners and

Highlights

- **Cultural center**
- **Eastern European**
- **Historic city life**
- **Entrepreneurial hotspot**

expertise from the West to speed their growth. Retirees who spend time here are often early retirees who are helping the country's economic evolution to a market-based system—and enjoying the culture and chance to travel at the same time.

THE BASICS

The Czech Republic (*Ceská Republika*) is in central Europe. It's bordered by Poland to the north, Slovakia to the east, Austria on the south, and Germany on the west. The capital and largest city is Prague.

Many people think of the country as "Czechoslovakia," as it was called under Communist rule. However, an amazing event occurred in 1989. The citizens rebelled against their Communist leaders with massive, nonviolent protests. The Communists resigned and a new, democratic government took its place. The transition was entirely peaceful, leading to its name, the "Velvet Revolution." But tensions still existed between the Czech and Slovak people. On January 1, 1993, the Czech and Slovak leaders split the country into the Czech Republic and Slovakia.

The Czech Republic has two main regions: Bohemia in the west and Moravia in the east. A small region called Silesia extends north into Poland.

To be part of the redevelopment of the former East Bloc has been a great experience. Of course, Prague is in the heart of Europe so it's a great base from which to see not only Western Europe, but also Central and Eastern Europe.

Bob Jones, Prague

> **WHAT'S IN A NAME?**
>
> The name Czechoslovakia was so ingrained that some people can't remember the new name, even in Europe. Such was the case at a train station in France where the station clerk looked for fifteen minutes and couldn't find the trains listed. He was looking under "T" for Tchècoslovaquie, not under "R" for République Tchèque.

Climate

The Czech Republic is in central Europe, so winters are cold with highs averaging about 23°F. They can be snowy, too, which isn't all bad. A dusting of snow turns Prague's Charles Bridge, the castle, and the surrounding historic buildings into a fantasy landscape. Summers are warm but rarely hot with highs of about 68°F.

Language

Czech is the official language, but Moravians speak a slightly different version from Bohemians. Czech is a Slavic language with Western-style letters. The difficulty comes from the written language having more consonants than English, though some sound like a vowel. Learn them so you can pronounce addresses. Luckily, English is relatively common, especially in Prague where it's the second language taught in the schools.

YOUR NEW LIFESTYLE

How will you fill your days? Here's an overview of activities and interests that are part of daily life in the Czech Republic.

Food and Drink

The normal Czech diet has a lot in common with Germany's. Pub meals are hearty and inexpensive, the staples being roasted meats such as pork served with red cabbage, kraut, and boiled dumplings. The heavy fare is washed down with two of the most celebrated beers in the world: Pilsner Urquell and Budweiser Budvar. Note that the latter is the original, not the U.S. version. These are brewed in the Czech Republic;

in fact, lager was invented here and the local brews are considered national treasures. Taste them and you'll agree!

Arts and Entertainment

It's not difficult to see why Prague was voted a European city of culture. Wandering across the Charles Bridge is a delight of sights and sounds, combining street violinists or jazz combos with views across the city. Prague offers an active calendar of concerts, operas, and entertainment. This is a city of music with concerts, chorales, and operas held nightly—sometimes free. The Rudolfinum Concert Hall hosts the Czech Philharmonic. Tickets for the world-class Prague Spring events go for as low as $6 a ticket.

Films are often shown in the original language. With Hollywood's popularity, there is no lack of English-language movies. English-language books are stocked in several bookstores such as the Globe, Anagram Bookshop, and Kanzelsberger (with several branches). Local English-language newspapers include *The Prague Post* and *The Prague Tribune* (half in Czech, half in English).

Outdoor Life and Sports

Football (otherwise known as soccer to Americans) is the most popular sport for spectators and players. You'll find golf courses near Prague, tennis courts near every major city, and hiking and horseback riding in the countryside. The mountains offer downhill and cross-country skiing.

Shopping

As recently as ten years ago, it was difficult to find a good assortment of fresh fruits and vegetables in Prague, but today you can find most of the things you want in the large supermarkets. Shopping malls, major department stores, and boutiques offer a wide range of fashions including some of the world's top labels. The area around Prague's Old Town Square is packed with small shops that offer typical Czech products, including garnets, glass, porcelain, wood carvings, and handmade toys. Whatever you're looking for, check the Czech Yellow Pages. They're referenced in English as well as in Czech and can help you find what you need.

Social Life

Americans living in Prague are usually involved in helping the country move from its Communist past to a free-enterprise system. The Globe bookstore is a gathering point for people who speak English; you can look for new reading material and enjoy a chat over coffee or lunch. Visit the U.S. Embassy and ask about the various events for Americans and other English-speaking people.

GARNETS, GARNETS EVERYWHERE

I'm sure not every shop in Prague sells garnets. It just seems that way. The deep-red stones are mined northwest of the city, and they're among the finest in the world. Prices are reasonable, and necklaces range from twenty to several hundred dollars or more, depending on the number and size of the stones and the setting. Fake garnets are common so choose a reputable shop when making your purchase.

WHERE TO LIVE IN THE CZECH REPUBLIC

Prague is the place of choice for most expatriates. Other areas are accessible to outsiders, but Prague is where the action is.

Prague

The place to be in the Czech Republic is Prague, which some people compare to Paris. It's a smaller Paris, though, with more hills, fewer bridges, and, unfortunately, more coal residue, which covers most buildings and statues. Most expatriates live near Prague. Many are here for after-retirement work or volunteer activities. Even those who are simply relishing the experience prefer the city for its access to cultural life and expatriate activities.

The River Vlatva courses through the city, above which stands the famous Karluv Most—the Charles Bridge. Watchtowers guard the bridge (ceremonially these days), and historic sculptures cross it on each side. The view of the river and city is unsurpassed at dawn or dusk.

The city is divided into numbered zones. Starting in the center are Prague 1, 2, and 3, which include Stare Mesto (Old Town), Malá Strana (Lesser Town), and Hradcany (Prague Castle). The city's center is convenient, but it's the most crowded area. Many expatriates live in Prague 6, where many of the embassies and international schools are located.

Cities Beyond and the Countryside

You won't find a large group of expatriates in the Czech Republic far beyond Prague. For those who prefer country living, a few expatriates have found properties within range of the capital but distant enough that the property is larger for less money.

> We have fond memories of an extraordinary cultural experience and a beautiful country, rich in heritage and full of natural beauty. We are much richer for our experience here in understanding the amazing, often difficult, and very important history of the Czech lands and Central Europe.
>
> Dian Jones, Prague

If you do want to be away from the crowd, consider Pilsen, a city with strong potential that is not too far distant from Prague for an occasional day in the big city.

Brno is the second-largest city, with lovely historic buildings and a university. It's located in the southeastern section of Moravia.

SETTING UP HOUSE

Most people in the Czech Republic live in towns and cities. Due to a housing shortage, apartments are more common than houses, especially in metropolitan areas. In rural areas, most people live in single-family homes.

Finding a Rental

Finding an apartment or house to rent will be more difficult both for space and cost the closer you get to the center of Prague, where the buildings have more character. On the city's outskirts, block upon block of Communist-era, prefabricated apartment buildings are distinctly ugly, but they're among the few options nearby. Rent-controlled apartments can be found at ridiculously low prices but are usually held within families or by friends.

In Prague a furnished loft studio with a terrace was advertised for a little under $900 a month. A two-bedroom, two-bath apartment in the central area of Old Town (Stare Mesto) with a twenty-four-hour doorman was advertised for about $2,000 a month. Outside the center, in Prague 6, the same price will get you a four-bedroom villa with three bathrooms, a garden, and a garage.

Work with a translator or real estate agent if you don't speak Czech, and have a lawyer review all documents. A Czech notary should notarize the contract or it will not be legally binding. You will generally pay the equivalent of three months' rent as a security deposit plus three months' rent in advance. You will pay utilitiezs separately. Check the ads for housing in the English-language *The Prague Post* or the Czech-language *Announce* newspapers.

If you're single, on a tight budget, and want to experience the culture from up close, you may be able to rent a studio apartment or room with a Czech family. One lucky retiree received his room free in exchange for teaching the family English!

Some real estate agents in Prague specialize in rentals. The commission is usually equal to a month's rent. You can find numerous real estate firms specializing in renting to foreigners listed in *The Prague Post*. They include:

Apt-Rent
www.apartments.cz

**Executive Housing
Specialists**
Phone: (420) 5732 828
Fax: (420) 5732 2032
Email: ehs@ehs.cz

Identity Ltd
Mánesova 83
Prague 2
Phone: (420) 627 3944
Fax: (420) 627 3949
Email: identity@terminal.cz.

Nexus Europe
Phone: (420) (2) 2251 3419
Fax: (420) (2) 2251 4752
Email: Nexus@terminal.cz

Sorent Real Estate Ltd
Phone: (420) 29 84 54
Fax: (420) 24 92 1050
Email: info@sorent.cz

Tide Realty
Phone: (420) 29 77 41
Fax: (420) 29 76 96
Email: tide@terminal.cz

Buying a Home

Property is relatively easy to purchase, though most Americans living here choose to rent. Technically you can't buy real estate in the Czech Republic until your residence visa comes through. However, some buyers establish a "corporation" solely to purchase property. You own the corporation; the corporation owns the house.

Be sure to have the property inspected, and hire a lawyer to review all contracts and ensure that you have clear title to the property. There is no such thing as title insurance.

Many real estate agents speak English. You can ask for recommendations from other Americans living in Prague or look for names in *The Prague Post.* Two are:

Identity Ltd
Mánesova 83
Prague 2
Phone: (420) 627 3944
Fax: (420) 627 3949
Email: identity@terminal.cz

Orion Real Estate
Phone: (420) 2251 6788
Fax: (420) 2251 1649
Email: orion@ms.anet.cz

What are prices like? A five-bedroom villa outside Prague, including garage and garden, was advertised for $78,000. A 2,500-square-foot house just thirty to forty minutes by train outside Prague, semimodernized, and within an eight-minute walk to the train was $75,000.

Utilities and Infrastructure

Water: The water is supposedly safe to drink in Prague, but you may want to stick to bottled water, especially in areas outside the capital.

Electricity: The Czech Republic system is 220 volts, 50 hertz, as opposed to the U.S. 110 volts, 60 hertz. You'll need adapters for plugs and converters or transformers.

Communications: The phone system is poor; bad connections are common. However, the phone system is currently being modernized, and new digital phone systems are being installed. Some pay phones exist in Prague; they require phone cards, not cash, which are sold in the post office and at newsstands. The Internet has reached Prague.

Internet cafés are common, even if home phone service does not make for an easy connection. Expect to pay about $.05 per minute online.

Time Zone: Prague is on Continental Europe Time and is usually six hours ahead of Eastern Standard Time in the United States. Daylight savings time occurs from spring through fall.

Weights and Measures: The Czech Republic uses the metric system.

MOVING PLANS

When choosing which appliances to bring, keep in mind that electricity and wall plugs are different than in North America. You'll need adapters and transformers. You can import a car, provided it meets national safety regulations and is properly registered. You may pay an import tariff as well. With narrow town streets and difficult parking, only bring a car if it's small. In any case, it may be easier to simply purchase a vehicle in the Czech Republic.

PAPERWORK AND RESIDENCE RULES

A valid passport enables you to enter the Czech Republic for less than thirty days. If you're staying longer, you'll need a visa that allows you to stay 180 days. If you leave the country, which many retirees do on a regular basis, you can enter for another 180 days. To apply for residence, you need to show proof that you have a place to live; that should be your first priority.

The Czech Ministry's help line provides residency assistance in several languages, including English, at (420) (2) 6144-1119. However, the application form is in Czech. You'll need to supply your birth certificate, information on your reason for residence, financial independence, a good-conduct form from the police where you resided in the United States, and a doctor's certificate.

Your long-term residency permit is good for one year and must be renewed annually. Permanent residency or Czech citizenship is difficult to obtain. In any case, most retirees, unless they are of Czech ancestry with family in the country, will probably be content with temporary residency.

Pets

To reside here, your pet will need an International Health Certificate endorsed by the USDA. It must be issued within 3 days of your animal's arrival in the Czech Republic. Pets must also have an import license and an original rabies certificate showing the vaccine was given more than 30 days but fewer than 180 days prior to entry. Other normal immunizations must be completed at least 14 days and not more than 180 days prior to entry. Parvovirus is a problem in the Czech Republic so have your dog inoculated against this virus. Pets coming to the Czech Republic are subject to quarantine, but unlike in some countries, this can usually be at the family's residence. Ask about current regulations before arriving.

GETTING THERE AND GETTING AROUND

Prague's Ruzyne Airport is about ten miles from the city's center and can be reached by bus or taxi. The Ceske Aerolinie, Czech Airlines, is the national airline with service to and from North America and Europe. Other major airlines such as American Airlines, Delta, Northwest, TWA, and United also serve Prague.

Trains are inexpensive, but services are not highly rated for efficiency or comfort. Plans are currently underway to revamp the major train stations and improve service. Trams, streetcars, buses, the subway, and taxis will take you anywhere you want to go in Prague for reasonable rates. Tickets are bought in advance from tobacco shops, automated machines, or at metro stations. The cost is about $.23 for fifteen minutes of riding time. When boarding the tram, stamp your ticket to validate it.

Taxis have a bad reputation for gouging in Prague. Try to call for a taxi in advance from a reputable firm such as AAA Radiotaxi. Their dispatchers speak English, and rates are usually fair.

Driving

You can drive in Prague, but the central areas are packed with people, narrow streets, and no parking. Think twice before attempting it. However, to explore elsewhere, driving is not a major problem.

A valid U.S. driver's license enables you to drive legally in the Czech Republic, but an International Driving Permit is required in some neighboring countries. An international license is available from AAA and is valid for a year. You can get a Czech driver's license by paying a small fee and showing your U.S. driver's license. Otherwise, you're required to take driver's training and a full exam. Liability insurance is required.

MANAGING YOUR MONEY

The Czech Republic offers some tasty bargains. You can enjoy a filling traditional pub meal of roast pork, sauerkraut, red cabbage, dumplings, and the world's best beer for $4 or less. The expense comes in accommodations, especially in central Prague, where modest studio apartments can start at $1,000 per month, and lodgings go much higher depending on the size and amenities. If you don't need to live downtown, you can manage on as little as $20,000 a year; but for city living allot more.

The unit of currency in the Czech Republic is the crown *(koruna)*, which is abbreviated as Kc. Each crown is divided into hellers *(haleru)*. At this writing, one U.S. dollar equals approximately thirty-six crowns. Of course, this will float. You are not allowed to bring Czech crowns from outside the country, so you'll need to convert dollars in the Czech Republic. When exchanging money, head straight to an ATM that accepts international Cirrus and Plus networks. It's convenient and you'll get a good exchange rate (though your U.S. bank may charge a fee for the withdrawal). Otherwise, choose a major bank for exchange transactions. You'll get a better rate than those offered by the numerous exchange bureaus in the tourist areas.

People rely more heavily on cash in the Czech Republic than in the United States. Checking accounts do not exist, and most people pay their rent, utilities, and other expenses via cash or by bank transfer.

Some large businesses accept business credit cards, but many do not accept traveler's checks, which is another reason why your ATM card comes in handy here. Most Americans keep their money in the United States, bringing over just enough for living expenses.

Taxes

Tax regulations are based on the amount of time you live in the country. If you live in the Czech Republic less than half the year, you will not pay income taxes unless you earn money there. However, if you stay longer than 183 days, you are required to pay tax on your worldwide income.

The usual taxes include property, gift, and inheritance taxes. Purchases in the country incur a 22 percent value-added tax, which applies mainly to nonessential products. Necessities such as most food items, pharmaceuticals, fuel, and services are charged a lower rate of 5 percent.

For more information on taxes in the Czech Republic, contact:

**American Center for
Culture and Commerce**
Hybernska 7a
117 16 Prague 1
Phone: (420) (2) 421-9844

American Chamber of Commerce
Karlovo nam 24
110 00 Prague 1
Phone: (420) (2) 299-887

STAYING HEALTHY AND SAFE

Health care and medicines cost much less in the Czech Republic than in the United States. A routine appointment with an American-trained physician in private practice costs about $9. Health services are more acceptable in Prague than elsewhere in the country, though even in the capital some services may not be up to U.S. standards due to overcrowding and inefficiencies. The increase in English-speaking expatriates in Prague has given rise to private clinics with better care and the accompanying higher prices.

Be aware that your U.S. Medicare will not cover you in the Czech Republic. You'll need private expatriate health insurance. (For some options, see Chapter 25.) If you become a Czech resident, you'll be eligible for the government-sponsored health insurance.

The greatest health issue of general concern is air pollution from the years of coal-fired furnaces and old automobiles. The situation is particularly severe in Prague and other large cities, which often issue air quality warnings for people with respiratory problems.

Security

Drug abuse and alcoholism are problems, as is the crime that often comes as a result. You won't feel threatened in Prague, even at night, if you stick to the busy streets. But take normal precautions. Don't show off expensive belongings or walk in dark or deserted areas.

FOR MORE DETAILS

Below are some resources to help you further investigate a long-term stay in the Czech Republic.

Official Sources

Canadian Embassy in Prague
Mickiewiczova 6
125 33 Prague 6
Phone: (420) (2) 2431-1108

U.S. Embassy in Prague
Trziste 15
125 Prague 1
Phone: (420) (2) 2451-0847

Czech Embassy
3900 Spring of Freedom St., NW
Washington, DC 20008
Phone: (202) 274-9100
Fax: (202) 966-8540

Internet Connections

Business Journal
English language business and
   financial news
www.pbj.cz

Czech Republic
www.czech.cz

Czech Tourist Authority
www.czech-tourinfo.cz

The Embassy of the Czech Republic in Washington
www.czech.cz/washington/

Official Czech Republic travel guide
www.czechsite.com/index.shtml

Prague Affair
Online magazine and guide
www.pragueaffair.cz

The Prague Post
www.praguepost.cz

Timeout Prague
www.timeout.com/prague/

Radio Praha
International service featuring news
  and live broadcasts, some in English
ww.radio.cz

Background Reading

*Prague: A Traveler's
Literary Companion*
by Paul Wilson, editor
Consortium Book Sales, 1995

Prague Walks
by Ivana Edwards
Henry Holt, 1994

24

Thailand

Thailand was known as Siam until 1939, when a wave of nationalism encouraged the Thais to name their country "land of Thai people." Sad to say, most Americans only know this fascinating country from Hollywood's classic movie, *The King and I,* which was adapted from the book *Anna and the King of Siam.* But don't rave about the movie in Thailand. It's considered

misleading—and often insulting—by Thais themselves who were upset at the image of their beloved leader, King Mongkut, as a barbarian. In fact, he was a learned man who worked diligently to modernize his country, a goal that was carried forward by his son, King Chulalongkorn.

Thais weren't thrilled with Hollywood's more recent movie, *The Beach,* either. It was shot on the sparkling clear Maya Bay in southern

Thailand. Unfortunately, its influence is attracting tourism to this formerly pristine area, with resulting damage to the environment.

A Buddhist country, Thailand is rich in religious architecture and art, including temples, monasteries, and Buddha statues. The attractions are exotic and offer a fascinating glimpse of a culture very different from that found in the United States. The differences mean that living in Thailand full-time is not for everyone. Some aspects are difficult for Americans to adjust to. The language is difficult, toilet and bathing facilities can be primitive outside of the large hotels and resort areas, and the culture is vastly different—much more so than European culture, for example.

Some Americans live in Thailand year-round for business and government reasons, but retirees often live there part-time rather than full-time. They can explore this fascinating culture for several months in the winter while enjoying warm weather and a very inexpensive cost of living.

THE BASICS

Thailand is located on the Indochinese Peninsula in Southeast Asia. The country is roughly the same size as France. It's bordered on the southeast by the Gulf of Thailand and on the southwest by the Andaman Sea. Laos lies to the northeast, Malaysia to the south, Myanmar to the southwest, west, and north, and Cambodia to the southeast.

A lush, tropical country of beaches, jungles, and fertile fields, Thailand has an amazing variety of natural resources. Its lands support orchids, banana plantations, rice paddies, mango and coconut trees, and forests that provide precious teak, rosewood, and rattan. Beneath the beautiful scenery lie gold, tin, coal, and precious stones.

Politically, Thailand is divided into *jangwat,* or provinces, each of which is further divided into districts, subdistricts, village groups, villages, and municipalities. Bangkok's governor and provincial assembly are elected, but the Ministry of the Interior appoints provincial governors for four-year terms.

Tourism is now the largest single business in Thailand with more than six million visitors a year. Most of these go to Bangkok, Chiang

Mai, and the beach resorts. The country's most beautiful beaches and idyllic islands are found on the southern peninsula.

The main religion in Thailand is Buddhism, which strongly influences daily life. It's common for at least one male in a family to study in a monastery. Though 90 percent of the population is Buddhist, the country believes in religious freedom. Other faiths are represented, and services are available (primarily in Bangkok) for Protestants, Roman Catholics, Jews, Muslims, Hindus, and Sikhs.

Climate

Some like it hot, and those people appreciate Thailand's tropical climate. Days can be hot and humid or cool depending on the season and where you live. In summer, temperatures vary from the high 70s to the high 90s. Winter is drier and cooler, with temperatures varying from the high 50s to the low 90s, again depending on the area. The rainy season ranges from May through September, but you won't lack for sunshine. Even during the rainy season, most days have some sun.

Language

The good news is that many schools in Thailand teach English, and English is widely spoken in large businesses and in tourist areas. Most street signs are posted in Thai and English. However, don't expect much understanding from a shopkeeper in an out-of-the-way, small shop. The Thai language is more difficult to learn than most other languages you could pick. For one thing, Thai uses non-Roman characters, as does Japanese, but unlike Japanese, which can be pronounced basically as translated, the meaning of a Thai word depends on the tone in which the word is spoken. Translations of Thai to Roman-style words is difficult, resulting in different spellings for the same word! It is a challenge to become proficient in the language. To survive, learn the Thai alphabet, basic polite phrases, and numbers.

> **LET FREEDOM RING**
>
> The literal translation of Thailand means "Land of the Free." Does that have a familiar ring to Americans, or what?

YOUR NEW LIFESTYLE

How will you fill your days? Here's an overview of activities and interests that are part of daily life in Thailand.

Food and Drink

Rice is a staple and the main crop of Thailand with an almost mystical significance for health and wealth. Meals include rice or noodles with meats, pineapple, peppers, or other vegetables or fruits. Main courses or desserts are often sweetened with coconut cream.

Thai-style food courts are common and offer meals for just twenty to thirty *baht*, or about fifty-five to eighty-five cents. Street-side food carts serve popular snacks, including Thai-style fast food such as banana fritters, noodles, rice, and chunks of fish or meat. Countless other food outlets include storefront operations for take-out food and casual outdoor restaurants. Upscale restaurants are a feast for the eyes as well as the taste buds with their astonishingly intricate carvings of fruits and vegetables, shaping a melon into a lotus blossom or a lemon quarter into a cricket perched on your tea glass.

Menus are often in three languages, including English, Chinese, and Thai. Western-style restaurants and imported food items are available but are more expensive than local dishes. Unless you don't care for Thai food, they're not necessarily better. While food is cheap, beer is expensive at forty-five *baht* for a large bottle in some stores and up to one hundred *baht* (three dollars) in restaurants.

FORGET FUMBLING WITH TWO STICKS

Many Thai restaurants *outside* Thailand provide diners with chopsticks, creating the illusion that Thais use them as commonly as the Japanese do. If you're a butterfingers, don't worry. Thais actually use forks and spoons like Westerners. As for knives, they're virtually never used because Thai food comes in bite-size pieces.

Arts and Entertainment

Thailand is rich in elaborate temples, palaces, and monasteries *(wat)* embellished with soaring multitiered and filigree roofs, Buddha images, and wood carvings. The performing arts include dramatically stylized, angular dances based on centuries-old narrative tales. Musicians play special Thai instruments. If you're in the mood for Western-style entertainment, check out the English-language newspapers such as *The Bangkok Post* and *The Nation*. American movies are popular and, lucky you, they're shown in English with Thai subtitles. Movie tickets cost just $1 to $3. For current entertainment attractions, see the *Bangkok Metro Guide,* which is also online at www.bkkmetro.com.

Outdoor Life and Sports

Kick-boxing is Thailand's national sport. It employs whole-body movements in a dancelike competition that's extremely vigorous and is not for the injury prone. This is not an amateur sport for the common man. For the Thai-on-the-street, the most popular sport is soccer. Other sports include swimming, tennis, biking, basketball, and cricket. Housing complexes often include fitness facilities, a pool, and tennis courts. A membership in a hotel fitness club with sauna, weight machines, and pool will cost under $200 a year.

Thailand's coast has gorgeous beaches, some built-up, others remote. You can take tours or rent boats to find a private picnic spot. To delve deeper into the country's beauty, try scuba diving on spectacular reefs, deep-sea fishing, or jungle tours to view the exotic flora and fauna.

Shopping

Bangkok has modern department stores, malls, and supermarkets that will meet all your needs with a wide range of products. Thailand is known for arts and crafts, especially wood carvings, puppets, lacquerware, fabrics, and silver ornaments. For good quality souvenirs, try the government-sponsored Narayana Phand shops on Rajdamri Road; the profits are returned to the villages that crafted the items. For the joy of the hunt and good deals, visit open-air markets and small shops away from tourist areas. Chantaburi, a four-hour bus ride from Bangkok, is the place to look for rubies and sapphires.

There are great malls, shopping areas, and grocery stores in which you can purchase almost all the foods you would enjoy in America, England, Europe, or Australia. Only the quality of meat and potatoes is still a bit lacking.

Ken Bower,
formerly of Pattaya Beach

Social Life

Thailand has tied itself to the Western world more than many other Asian countries here. This is not to say that Thais have lost their culture, not at all. The country is strongly Buddhist in faith so the holidays are often religious, tied to the lunar calendar. Monks are highly respected and conduct many of the ceremonies, even becoming involved in some secular events such as blessing new corporate offices and other business ventures. People here are very aware of a social hierarchy of finances and family connections. However, they are tolerant and welcome foreigners warmly.

WHERE TO LIVE IN THAILAND

Most American and English-speaking expatriates live in or near Bangkok or Chiang Mai in the north, either of which could be used as bases for further exploration of the country.

Bangkok

The capital, largest city, and main seaport of Thailand is Bangkok. It's the hub for most English-speaking expatriates who come here on business or to retire. However, this isn't the place for a tranquil permanent retirement. The city is known for its traffic congestion, smog, and pollution.

Bangkok is divided in half by the Chao Phraya river. The left bank is the main business area, including the capital buildings, palaces, and major hotels. This is where you'll find the main boulevard, Ratchadamnoen Klang, which was reputedly patterned after the Champs Élysées in Paris. The right bank includes the old district of Thonburi. Many expatriates live in central Bangkok, where they can easily walk or take public transportation to shops, restaurants, and entertainment. Sukhumvit has plentiful housing. Ploenchit/Lumpini is more costly but also more convenient to the center of the city. If you don't care to be in the middle of the city, the suburbs offer more modern housing and amenities with cleaner air and a quieter ambiance.

Furnished apartments are common, and some include hotel-like services for brief stays while you look for a more permanent place. You can find a variety of units for rent, including apartments, condominiums, and individual homes. Newer buildings include amenities such as swimming pools, garden areas, or tennis courts. Even in the central area prices are reasonable, though naturally they're higher than in outlying areas.

Chiang Mai

At least two thousand Americans live in northern Thailand, and they're enthusiastic about the largest city there, Chiang Mai. The city is seven hundred kilometers northwest of Bangkok—a nine-hour drive on an excellent highway. It takes twelve hours on the railway line, or an hour by plane.

Once in Chiang Mai it's easy to see why people enjoy the area. Hundreds of gardens and temples punctuate the city, and talented artisans supply luxurious crafts including gold and lacquer items.

The city is pedestrian-friendly so walking and biking are a relaxing means of transportation. The populace is well educated, and four universities offer many courses in English, but people are always looking for tutors so qualified native English speakers are often able to supplement their income with teaching on the side. Rentals are easy to find and reasonable. Luxurious apartments in an immaculately maintained complex that includes a large swimming pool, a sauna, and satellite dishes are available as two-bedroom units for about $600 a month.

Pattaya

A two-hour drive south of Bangkok is Pattaya and Pattaya Beach, considered by some to be the Riviera of Thailand. It's mainly a tourist resort and it's currently in flux. Pattaya has run the gamut from peaceful fishing village to a place better known for its wild ways, prostitution, and pollution. (Unfortunately, much of this was brought about by American servicemen who discovered the city on leaves during the Vietnam War and began the partying.) Pattaya is now

Thais that live in Pattaya for the most part are partial to Americans and prefer them to the Brits, Europeans, Aussies, and Kiwis that make up the majority of the expat community there. Is Pattaya seedy? Well, yes, as is Bangkok, Manila, and Jakarta. But if you are not into that kind of life, you can avoid most of it. We will never be able to bring Pattaya back to the wonderful place it was in the early 1970s, but if one is set on living in Thailand we would chose Pattaya over Bangkok because it offers less smog, traffic, and pollution and a saner lifestyle.

Ken Bower,
formerly of Pattaya Beach

working to change its image to attract more families, and a new water treatment plant is handling the waste to clean up the sea.

Thanks to tourism, a wide range of accommodations are available from the most luxurious hotels to the most basic bungalows. Gourmet cuisine is served in specialty restaurants that offer ethnic foods from English to Scandinavian, French, Italian, Japanese, and much more. Fast-food and native Thai restaurants provide budget alternatives.

SETTING UP HOUSE

The majority of Thais rent, rather than buy, their accommodations, and a variety of properties—furnished and unfurnished—are available. Furnished housing includes all the basics such as furniture and appliances, excluding small appliances, linens, and such.

Finding a Rental

Look for rental housing through classified ads or signs on houses or apartment gates, or ask other expatriates. Don't hesitate to use a real estate agent. It won't cost you anything since landlords pay the commission.

When deciding on a place, insist on air conditioning. It's essential in this hot, sticky climate. Utilities may or may not be included in the rent, though usually you'll pay electric and water bills based on metering for your unit. Rents are due each month in advance. Furnished properties will often include a maintenance fee, and the price depends on the building services. Leases typically run for one to two years. You'll pay a month's rent in advance plus two to three months' rent as a security deposit.

A modest one-bedroom apartment in Bangkok would rent for about $230 to $350 a month. Chiang Mai is less expensive. A modest two-bedroom apartment or house there would rent for $125 to $250 per month.

Buying a Home

Chances are you'll be renting, not purchasing property, in Thailand. Foreigners are allowed to purchase condominiums but not other property unless they're married to a Thai.

Utilities and Infrastructure

Water: Tap water is not safe to drink in Thailand; it should be boiled or filtered. Bottled water is delivered or can be purchased in stores.

Electricity: Electricity is 220 volts, 50 hertz unlike the U.S. 110 volts, 60 hertz. The plug shape is also different so you'll need plug adapters and transformers or converters. Buy surge protectors for computers, TVs, or other important appliances since the power supply is erratic at times.

Communications: Phone connections are good for internal and international calls. Mobile phones are available that serve customers in Thailand and abroad. Internet connections are slower and less reliable than in the United States. The postal services are reliable. The main post office in Bangkok on New Road is open daily, though with shortened hours on Saturdays, Sundays, and holidays.

Time Zone: Bangkok is seven hours ahead of Greenwich Mean Time, so it's twelve hours ahead of Eastern Standard Time in the United States. Daylight savings time takes place from spring through fall. The standard and twenty-four-hour clocks are used; in addition, Thais divide the day into four six-hour increments.

Weights and Measures: Thailand uses the metric system.

MOVING PLANS

The easiest way to move to Thailand is simply to bring yourself and your personal belongings. You may not need to bring furniture since many properties are already furnished. In any case, most Americans would consider Thailand a warm-weather spot to spend winters or live affordably for several months. It requires a special mind-set to move here permanently.

Don't bring a television or VCR since the broadcasting system is different from the one used in North America. If you buy a VCR in Thailand, look for one that incorporates both the North American and Thai systems—you can rent videos in Thailand and also play American versions from back home. Do not ship your car to Thailand. The cost and taxes are too high to make it worth your while. If you need one, lease or buy a new or used car there.

PAPERWORK AND RESIDENCE RULES

The Thai government is going out of its way to welcome retirees who want to reside in the country. In fact, they've created a special category of residence visas designed specifically for foreign retirees over age fifty-five years. If they bring in foreign currencies worth more than 800,000 *baht* (about $21,000) or a monthly income of 65,000 *baht* (about $1,700), they can apply for non-immigrant visas for a one-year stay in Thailand. The requirements are relatively simple; you'll need a visa application, two passport-size photos, a photocopy of your travel documents, and financial documents. An extension may be granted to this one-year visa as long as you still meet the requirements at that time.

A non-immigrant visa costs $20 and is good for a maximum stay of ninety days. A tourist visa is $15 and permits you to stay for a maximum of sixty days. For stays less than thirty days, no visa is required, just a valid passport.

If you don't meet the retiree status requirements, you can still apply for a residence permit. You'll need the application form, a personal information sheet, a health certificate from a hospital issued within the previous three months, certification of no criminal record in your prior country of residence, official marriage and birth certificates (if applicable), certification of income, a map of your residence, and a copy of your passport. If you decide to reside in Thailand permanently, you can get approval provided you've been permitted to stay in the kingdom for at least three years prior to the date of your application.

Pets

As with many countries, Thailand sets standards of health for dogs and cats entering the country. You'll need to prove that your pet has had its shots, including a current rabies shot, more than 30 days and fewer than 180 days prior to arrival. You'll also need a health certificate issued by an accredited veterinarian, and endorsed by your state's USDA Veterinary Services, within ten days prior to your departure for Thailand.

Pets are not subject to quarantine in Thailand, but an import permit will be required when your pet enters the country with you. If your pet arrives without you as air cargo, then obtain the import permit before your pet arrives. Since regulations change, contact the Thai Consulate for the most up-to-date requirements well in advance of your move.

GETTING THERE AND GETTING AROUND

Air France, Singapore Airlines, and the Thai national airline, Thai Airways, provide international service to Thailand. Thai Airways, Bangkok Airways, and Orient Airlines operate domestic flights.

Train service is comfortable and convenient, using Bangkok as the hub for most destinations. In Bangkok, the recently completed Skytrain elevated rail system is high tech, clean, and fast—and designed to help alleviate some of the city's notorious gridlock. The Skytrain stops at the main business districts and popular tourist attractions, including the weekend market. Buses and taxis are both common and very inexpensive. Air-conditioned buses connect main towns.

Driving

The most important detail to remember about driving in Thailand is to drive on the left-hand side of the road. You can drive in Thailand on a U.S. license for up to three months. If you live there longer, you'll need a Thai license. Major roads are internationally signed, but some carry only Thai signage—a good reason to learn the Thai alphabet! Bangkok traffic is horrendous. Avoid driving there or at least plan to avoid rush hours and holidays.

MANAGING YOUR MONEY

Americans in Thailand boast of the low cost of living, which is one of the country's primary draws. A moderate budget of $15,000 to $20,000 would suffice if you live on the local economy, but imported goods will increase your costs. At a typical Thai vegetarian restaurant you can eat for under $2. An elaborate dinner at a tourist hotel for two with wine could go as high as $80.

The *baht* is Thailand's currency; it's divided into one hundred *satang*. You can exchange dollars for *bahts* at bank ATMs or at the counter inside the bank. Exchange services are open twenty-four hours and will exchange dollars for *baht,* but they don't exchange *baht* for dollars.

The Bank of Thailand is the national bank. Several other banks serve the country, including the branches of some U.S. banks. Checking accounts are not popular and checks are not common so prepare yourself to pay cash for most purchases. You can use major credit cards at large retail stores, hotels, and restaurants, but they charge an additional 3 to 5 percent for the service.

Taxes

If you live in Thailand more than 180 days during the tax year, which runs from January 1 through December 31, you will pay Thai income taxes. However, as a retiree your foreign pension and Social Security are exempt from taxes provided you don't have that money deposited in Thailand.

STAYING HEALTHY AND SAFE

Acclimate yourself gradually to the heat and humidity of Thailand by taking it easy and drinking plenty of fluids. But don't drink the tap water. Watch what you eat, and never accept food or drink from strangers.

Medicare doesn't cover Americans overseas so you'll need an expatriate health insurance policy. (For some options, see Chapter 25.) Due to the distance and high expense of returning to the States in case of a health emergency, you may want to choose a policy that covers medical repatriation to the United States. However, for minor ailments, the services in Thailand are good and amazingly inexpensive. Access to services, and to English-speaking health care providers, will depend on where you live. Services in Bangkok are the best quality in Thailand, and many English-speaking doctors, dentists, clinics, and hospitals are available. The Adventist Hospital, Bangkok Nursing Home, Bumrungrad Hospital, and Samitiveg Hospital all have English-speaking staff.

Many pharmaceuticals are available in Thailand over the counter, and they're reasonably priced. If you purchase without a prescription, stick to brand-name medications.

Security

Generally speaking, Thailand is safe; just take the normal precautions you might anywhere. When you arrive in Thailand, you're advised to register with the U.S. Embassy in Bangkok or the Consulate in Chiang Mai. One recent warning was to use caution near the Myanmar border in Chiang Mai, Chiang Rai, and Mae Hong Son provinces; Myanmar troops were fighting and it occasionally spilled across into Thailand. Drug runners are another problem. Avoid remote roads and stay away from border areas.

For other special exceptions check the State Department's Consular Information Sheets or contact any U.S. Embassy or Consulate. Online you can visit http://travel.state.gov.

FOR MORE DETAILS

Below are some resources to further help you investigate a long-term stay in Thailand.

Official Sources

Royal Thai Consulates General

Chicago
700 North Rush Street
Chicago, IL 60611
Phone: (312) 664-3129

Los Angeles
611 N. Larchmond Blvd.,
  2nd Floor
Los Angeles, CA 90004
Phone: (323) 962-9574
Fax: (323) 962-2128

New York
351 East 52nd Street
New York, NY 10022
Phone: (212) 754-1770

Royal Thai Embassy
1024 Wisconsin Avenue, NW
Washington, DC 20007
Phone: (202) 944-3600
Fax: (202) 944-3611

Tourism Authority of Thailand
611 North Larchmond Blvd.,
  1st Floor
Los Angeles, CA 90004
Phone: (323) 461-9814
Fax: (323) 461-9834
Hotline: (800) THAILAND

Tourism Authority of Thailand
1 World Trade Center, #3729
New York, NY 10048
Phone: (212) 432-0433
Fax: (212) 912-0920
Hotline: (800) THAILAND

Chapter 24

U.S. Consulate General
387 Wichayanond Road
Chiang Mai 50300
Phone: (66) (53) 252-629
Fax: (66) (53) 252-633

U.S. Embassy
120/22 Wireless Road
Bangkok 10330
Phone: (66) (2) 205-4000
Fax: (66) (2) 254-1171

Internet Connections

ASEM Thailand
Web site information
http://asem.inter.net.th/thailand/
thaiweb.html

Bangkok Metro Guide
www.bkkmetro.com

Bangkok Post
www.bangkokpost.net

Chiang Mai News
www.chiangmainews.com

The Nation
www.nationmultimedia.com

Royal Thai Embassy
www.thaiembdc.org

Thailand info
www.thailine.com/bangkok/
index.htm

Thailand server
www.nectec.or.th

Tourism Authority
of Thailand
www.tourismthailand.org

U.S. Embassy in Bangkok
http://usa.or.th/embassy/consul.htm

Background Reading

Culture Shock! Thailand
by Robert Cooper
Graphic Arts Center Publishing, 1991

I Walked Away: An Expatriates'
Guide to Living Cheaply in Thailand
by Michael Ziesing
Breakout Productions, 1996

Travelers' Tales: Thailand
edited by James O'Reilly and
Larry Habegger
Travelers' Tales, Inc., 1994

25

Sources-at-a-Glance

Following are a few sources that will help you continue researching a long-term adventure abroad.

GOVERNMENT SOURCES

Embassy Sites
Links to all embassies in
  Washington, DC
www.embassy.org

U.S. State Department
www.state.gov

U.S. EXPATRIATE ASSOCIATIONS

**American Citizens Abroad
(ACA)**
5 bis, rue Liotard
CH-1202 Geneva, Switzerland
Phone: (41) (22) 3400233
Email: acage@aca.ch

American Citizens Abroad
1051 N. George Mason Drive
Arlington, VA 22205
Fax: (703) 527-3269

**The Association of
Americans Resident Overseas**
B.P. 127
92154 Suresnes Cedex France
Phone: (33) (01) 42 04 09 38
Fax: (33) (01) 42 04 09 12

Federation of American Women's Clubs Overseas (FAWCO)
Network of more than seventy-three international women's clubs in thirty-six countries offering practical advice and social activities.
www.fawco.org

EXPATRIATES ONLINE

Below are just a few of the best Internet sites for contact with expatriates and expatriate groups around the world. Groups for specific countries also exist and some are noted in Part II.

American Citizens Abroad
www.aca.ch

Association of Americans Resident Overseas (AARO)
www.aaro-intl.org

Escape Artist
www.escapeartist.com

Expat Access
Guides for moving abroad from other expatriates.
www.expataccess.com

Expat Boards
Discussion site for expats in a largely European range of countries.
www.expatboards.com

Expat Exchange
One of the largest sites, with members and regular visitors from more than sixty countries who create an expatriate community with information and personal forums.
www.expatexchange.com

Expat Expert
Online help with living abroad.
www.expatexpert.com

Expat World
www.expatworld.net

Expatica
Resource for English-speaking expatriates in the Netherlands and Belgium but expanding to Germany, France, and the UK.
www.expatica.com

Global Network
Run by a British journal, *The Weekly Telegraph,* so geared to Brits, but nonetheless it provides useful info for English-speaking expats.
www.globalnetwork.co.uk

International Living Magazine
www.escapeartist.com/international/living2.htm

Overseas Digest
www.overseasdigest.com

People Going Global
Packed with information via
country-specific links.
www.peoplegoingglobal.com

Planet Expat
Comprehensive site on a wide range of
issues for living and enjoying life overseas.
www.planetexpat.com

Transitions Abroad
www.transabroad.com

Woman Abroad
From the editors of *Woman Abroad* magazine, this site is for British expatriate
women but useful for
others as well.
www.womanabroad.com

COUNTRY INFORMATION

Country Net
Information specifically designed for
business people and others relocating to
countries around the globe; it's fee-
based, but offers a free trial.
www.countrynet.com

Live Abroad
Personal tales about living in many
countries around the world.
www.liveabroad.com

ESPECIALLY FOR RETIREES

**American Association of
Retired Persons**
601 E Street, NW
Washington, DC 20049
Phone: (800) 424-3410
Email: member@aarp.org

Elderhostel
www.elderhostel.org

Senior News Network: Travel
www.seniornews.com/travel

Third Age Living
www.thirdage.com

LANGUAGE PRACTICE

Parlo Language Courses
Classes and practice on your computer.
www.parlo.com

**Travlang's Foreign
Language for Travelers**
Tips and translations for various languages
around the world.
www.travlang.com/languages/

HEALTH CARE

**Centers for Disease
Control (CDC)**
Health advisories for locations abroad.
www.cdc.gov/travel/travel.html

EXPATRIATE INSURANCE PROVIDERS

MediBroker
This is not an insurer but a broker, often using some of the companies below but works to find the right combination of insurance.
www.medibroker.com

Blue Cross and Blue Shield of Western Europe
59, rue de Chateaudun
75009, Paris, France
Phone: (33) (01) 42 81 98 76
Fax: (33) (01) 42 81 99 03

BUPA International
Russell Mews
Brighton, Great Britain BN7 2NR
United Kingdom
Phone: (44) 1273 208 181
Fax: (44) 1273 866 583

ExpaCare Insurance Services
Dukes Court, Duke Street
Woking, Surrey GU21 5XB
United Kingdom
Phone: (44) 1483 717 800
Fax: (44) 1483 776 620

International Health Insurance Danmark a/s
64a Athol Street, Douglas
Isle of Man, British Isles IM1 1JE
United Kingdom
Phone: (44) 1624 677 412

Lloyds Expatriate Protection Plans
U.S. toll-free: (800) 399-3904

PPP International Health Plan
Phillips House, Crescent Road
Tunbridge Wells, Kent TN1 2PL
United Kingdom
Phone: (44) 1892 512 345
Fax: (44) 1892 515 143

SHORT-TERM INSURANCE AND TRAVEL ASSISTANCE

Access America
U.S. toll-free: (800) 955-4002

AARP Health Care Options
U.S. toll-free: (800) 245-1212, operator 36

American Express Travel Protection Plan
U.S. toll-free: (800) 234-0375

International SOS Assistance
P.O. Box 11568
Philadelphia, PA 19116
U.S. toll-free: (800) 523-8662

Medex
Timonium Corporate Center
9515 Deereco Road, Fourth Floor
Timonium, MD 21093
U.S. toll-free: (800) 537-2029

**Travel Assistance
International**
1133 15th Street, NW, Suite 400
Washington, DC 20005-2710
U.S. toll-free: (800) 821-2828

Wallach & Company
107 West Federal Street
P.O. Box 480
Middleburg, VA 20118
U.S. toll-free: (800) 237-6615

**TravMed International Traveler's
Assistance Association**
1765 Business Center Drive, Suite 100
Reston, VA 20190
U.S. toll-free: (800) 732-5309

ACCOMMODATIONS

Home Exchange
www.gti-home-exchange.com

Note: For rentals abroad, search the Internet under the name of the location and look for furnished (or unfurnished) rentals, apartments for rent, homes for rent, or any combination that fits your needs. Also search the classifieds of any online newspaper for your chosen location.

GLOBAL FINANCES

Currency Converters
www.xe.net/ucc
www.Oanda.com

Online Payment Services
www.paymybills.com

The Expat's Guide to U.S. Taxes
by Jane A. Bruno
Bruno Expat Tax Services, 2000

*Personal Finance for
Overseas Americans*
by Barbara Frew
GIL Financial Press, 2000.

MasterCard ATM locator
www.mastercard.com/atm

Visa ATM locator
www.visa.com/pd/atm

GENERALLY USEFUL PUBLICATIONS

Culture Shock! series
(Country-specific titles)
Graphics Arts Center Publishing Company

*The Grown-Up's Guide To
Running Away from Home*
by Rosanne Knorr
Ten Speed Press, 1998

Index